CHIEF
THE FEARLESS VISION OF BILLY DIAMOND

by
Roy MacGregor

*For Steve,
I hope you enjoy reading
Billy's story. Best wishes,
Roy MacGregor*

VIKING

VIKING
Published by the Penguin Group
Penguin Books Canada Ltd, 2801 John Street, Markham, Ontario, Canada
L3R 1B4
Penguin Books Ltd, 27 Wrights Lane, London W8 5TZ, England
Viking Penguin Inc., 40 West 23rd Street, New York, New York 10010, USA
Penguin Books Australia Ltd, Ringwood, Victoria, Australia
Penguin Books (NZ) Ltd, 182–190 Wairau Road, Auckland 10, New Zealand

Penguin Books Ltd, Registered Offices: Harmondsworth, Middlesex, England

First published 1989

1 3 5 7 9 10 8 6 4 2

Copyright© Roy MacGregor, 1989

The following are used by permission
Muller, Hugo, "The Graves" in *Northland* (Moosonee), Autumn 1973.
Scott, Duncan Campbell, "The Last of the Indian Treaties" in *Tales of the Canadian North* (Secaucus, New Jersey), 1984.
From *The Blasted Pine*, F.R. Scott, ed., used by permission of The Canadian Publishers, McClelland and Stewart, Toronto.

Back cover: The President of Air Creebec, Chief Billy Diamond

Maps prepared by Department of Geography, University of Toronto

All rights reserved. Without limiting the rights under copyright reserved above, no part of this publication may be reproduced, stored in or introduced into a retrieval system, or transmitted in any form or by any means (electronic, mechanical, photocopying, recording or otherwise), without the prior written permission of both the copyright owner and the above publisher of this book.

Printed and bound in the United States of America

Canadian Cataloguing in Publication Data

MacGregor, Roy, 1948-
   Chief: the fearless vision of Billy Diamond

ISBN 0-670-82735-5

1. Diamond, Billy, 1949-   . 2. Indians of North America — Canada — Government relations — 1951-   .* 3. Indians of North America — Quebec (Province). 4. Cree Indians — Government relations. 5. James Bay Hydroelectric Project — Social aspects. 6. Indians of North America — Quebec (Province) — Biography. 7. Cree Indians — Biography. I. Title.

E99.C88D53 1989   971.4'100497   C89-093042-2

For my parents, Duncan and Helen,
who taught us all to love the bush.

CHIEF
THE FEARLESS VISION
OF BILLY DIAMOND

CONTENTS

Cree Lands Map		xiii
Prologue		xv
Part One: Earth		1
Chapter 1	Bileesh Diamin	3
Chapter 2	Indian School Days	13
Chapter 3	Arrow to the Moon	27
Chapter 4	Chief of Rupert House	37
Part Two: Water		51
Chapter 5	The Project of the Century	53
Chapter 6	Joanne: Four months, four days	65
Chapter 7	A Secret Ally	81
Chapter 8	Victory in the Palais de Justice	95
Chapter 9	Enter Jean Chrétien	107
Chapter 10	Agreement	119
Chapter 11	James Bay and Wounded Knee	133
Chapter 12	Birth of a Nation	145
Part Three: Air		157
Chapter 13	Philip	159
Chapter 14	"Practically Millionaires"	173
Chapter 15	Pierre and the Pope	185
Part Four: Fire		205
Chapter 16	Home	207
Chapter 17	The Living Flame	223
Chapter 18	Iacocca of the North	243
Chapter 19	Cree-Yamaha	261
Epilogue		277
Acknowledgments		287
Selected Bibliography		288
Index		292

The term person means an individual other than an Indian.
Canadian Indian Act, 1880

Cree Lands and the James Bay Project

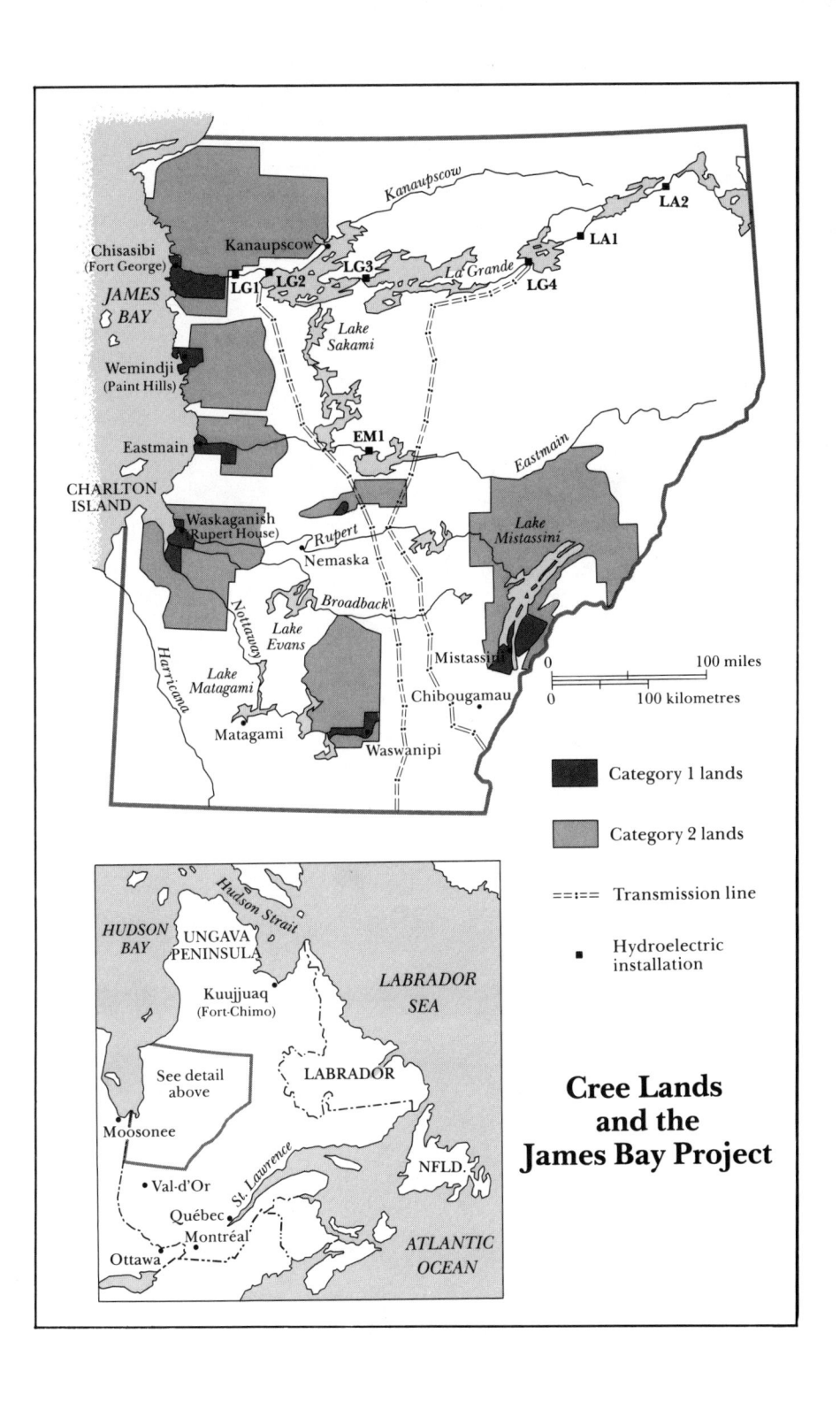

PROLOGUE

Hilda Diamond pulled her heavy woollen sweater tight, twisting in a chair so polished and plush it seemed a shame to hide it with the likes of her. She had no right to be here—an old Indian woman sitting in the Salon Rouge of the Quebec National Assembly, she sitting while the premier of Quebec stood. Robert Bourassa was the most important person in the entire province, the second-most-important leader in all of Canada after the prime minister. And yet this thin, awkward man who kept glancing at her and then quickly away had ordered up a plane especially for Mrs Hilda Diamond, a *special charter* for no other reason than to bring this seventy-three-year-old Cree Indian woman out of the James Bay bush that she had never imagined leaving, brought her out at government expense just so she could sit in the Salon Rouge and watch and—if the premier of Quebec didn't mind—giggle once in a while, very quietly, to herself.

She couldn't help it. She sat in a room where everything from the speeches to the matchbooks was in two official languages, yet she spoke and understood neither. She had just come through a light snow from a hotel room so grand that it was larger by half than the windworn shack on the banks of the Rupert River far to the north, in which she and Malcolm had raised eight children and lost a ninth. She had come in a plane, down in an elevator, over in a black limousine and now she was sitting in a chair that seemed more suitable for a queen than for an old woman who still considered fresh balsam boughs the height of luxury.

Hilda Diamond pulled the heavy blue sweater still tighter, all but covering the simple floral print of her blouse. She ran the palm of her hand hard across her dark skirt, self-consciously ironing, giving up with a giggle. *Why even bother?* The fabrics on the other women sitting beneath the chandeliers shone and sparkled and shimmied in ways she did not even have words for, let alone enough brass to reach out and touch. Hilda Diamond's own fling with being fashionable was still embedded in the fatty portion between the thumb and first finger of her left hand. There, several dozen black dots had been created over long evenings in winter tents, tiny black tattoos formed by kneading a thread in the ash of the fire and then using a needle to pull the sooty cord through her own skin in a pattern she now hid by rubbing her right hand over top of her left.

She glanced up at Premier Robert Bourassa. To her, he looked like someone who'd just stepped out of a picture, but in fact, he was just stepping in, with the official government photographer in steady chase as the premier moved from one enchanted group to the next. The premier of Quebec was now shaking the hand of her own son, the same son she used to tuck up under one arm, his brother under the other and a baby on her back, for the portages. The premier was talking to the child Malcolm had pushed onto the floatplane while she stood weeping on the shore of the Rupert, not believing her husband when he said the boy had to go away so that when he came back he would know how to deal with men like this flitting premier who kept peeking back at her.

Her husband had been right. Malcolm couldn't watch this surprising encounter—he had died three years earlier, in 1984—but he had lived long enough to know that he had done the right thing by forcing the fighting youngster aboard the big black floatplane that each fall came north along the James Bay coastline, swooping down like a hungry gull wherever the Cree villagers pushed another ripe and howling youngster out onto the Hudson's Bay docks. Hilda Diamond's sixth baby was now a man. He had not only learned the ways and language and tricks of the whites, he now had more than a few of his own to offer back. The patched pants he had worn onto the floatplane had been replaced by a three-piece suit as dark and formal and sharply-pressed as the premier's own. And now Bourassa was straightening a silver medal over the chest of her child, making Billy Diamond a Knight of the Order of Quebec. Hilda giggled again. Malcolm, the one they sometimes called "The Shouting Chief," would have laughed out loud, long and without the slightest care of who noticed or wondered why.

The idea of Robert Bourassa honouring Billy Diamond would have struck Malcolm as oddly as it had one of Bourassa's own Cabinet ministers when the premier first read off his Ordre National du Québec list in the Cabinet room of this very same building. *"What for?"* the minister had demanded, "for all the trouble he's caused us?" But Bourassa had insisted, had placed the call himself

PROLOGUE

and had okayed the copy that was being distributed: "Billy Diamond: politician, educator and businessman born at Rupert House (Waskaganish), Quebec, May 17, 1949. Mr. Diamond has been a leading figure in Native politics in Canada and within Quebec for over fifteen years . . . Grand Chief from 1974 to 1984 . . . participating in sub-committees of the United Nations dealing with aboriginal groups and meeting international figures such as the Pope . . . President of Air Creebec Inc. . . . Chairman of the Cree School Board . . . Vice-President of Cree Co. and the Cree Construction Company (Quebec) Limited . . . President of the Cree Housing Corporation . . . ."

Malcolm Diamond would not have been able to restrain himself. Not a single word about *power*, which is what this was all about, whether they were talking about the production of power or the struggle for power. The government writers had taken Billy Diamond and produced a man being honoured for his public service to the province. A curious interpretation of this man's life—especially so, considering that *Newsweek* was researching an international feature on Billy Diamond that would back up his rather brazen claim that, in making war on his own country and province, he had, in effect, "created a nation."

It is a remarkable boast, and yet no one, not even the government officials who wish they had never heard of Billy Diamond, will argue the point. Nearly a decade after a confidential federal government memorandum warned that the cost of the land deal won by Grand Chief Billy Diamond against the province of Quebec and the government of Canada could be "astronomical and beyond the means [of both governments]," this same federal government estimates that more than $1 billion has gone to the ten thousand or so Cree Indians who are now known as "the Arabs of the North".

A Knight of the Order of Quebec—such a peculiar honour for the man who forced that province to accept the first self-government arrangement in all of Canada. The premier of Quebec honours him, while in Ottawa, the assistant deputy-minister of Indian Affairs, Richard Van Loon, concedes that: "Our relations with the Crees are like relations with other governments." In Van Loon's opinion, the Crees of James Bay are "certainly cleverer than a lot of the Atlantic provinces." On another day, Robert Bourassa might concede that dealing with his Atlantic peers is like sleepwalking compared to his nightmarish experiences with this man he now honours. It has been a long, often ugly, battle over power, the power to control one's destiny and the power that runs in the massive, thundering freshwater rivers that empty into James Bay—both of which Robert Bourassa sought to block.

On April 30, 1971, Robert Bourassa was the newly elected thirty-seven-year-old premier of Canada's largest province and Billy Diamond was the newly elected twenty-one-year-old chief of Rupert House, one of Canada's most isolated Indian villages. On that night, Robert Bourassa announced that his province would undertake to build the "Project of the Century." It would be history's largest and most expensive hydroelectric scheme, an engineering feat that would be compared to the construction of the pyramids.

What Bourassa was proposing was to turn the James Bay Quebec watershed—an area two-thirds the size of France—into a convenient wall plug for the New England states. His province, he was convinced, was "a vast hydroelectric plant-in-the-bud." The freshwater that had been flowing into the shallow northern basin of James Bay since the retreat of the last ice sheet ten thousand years ago added up to three million gallons per second—*double* what moves through the entire Great Lakes system. "Every day," Robert Bourassa would later write, "millions of potential kilowatt-hours flow downhill and out to sea. What a waste!"

In the first phase of the project Bourassa outlined that night, four of the massive James Bay rivers were to be rerouted. Six lakes would be created, including the province's largest, and the five reservoirs would form a surface area half as large as the entire expanse of Lake Ontario. There would be 8 massive dams, 203 dikes, 1,500 kilometres of roads built, the largest underground powerhouse in North America. Phase I would cost at least $16 billion and be completed in 1984.

Bourassa's dream would be constructed in a location so incredibly isolated that when early truckers completed the twenty-day, 736-kilometre run from the last northern Quebec town to the main construction site on La Grande River, some of them broke down in tears and begged to be flown out by helicopter rather than face the twenty-day haul back to civilization. Still, Bourassa's "Project of the Century" was completed, though hardly in the fashion he envisioned that night in 1971, and for nearly two decades it has passed by almost entirely unnoticed in North America, a puzzlement that led James Schlesinger—former secretary of defense

PROLOGUE

in the Nixon administration and principal energy adviser to the Carter administration—to speculate that somewhere along the line "we have lost a feeling of awe." Not Schlesinger, though: he believes James Bay to be "an even more ambitious and awesome enterprise" than the Alaska pipeline—an engineering feat that ranks with the digging of the Panama Canal.

"The world begins tomorrow," Bourassa said on the night he announced the massive project. And for the Crees, it did indeed, for it was not until the following day, May 1, 1971, that the Cree Indians who had lived for more than five thousand years on the land the premier was about to flood were told, by radio news reports, what was about to happen to them.

Many months after he first heard the news over his father's old battery radio, the young chief of Rupert House finally got to hear the news in person from Robert Bourassa. Billy Diamond and other James Bay Crees were taken through this same Salon Rouge on a dull October day in 1972 and admitted to the Cabinet room where the young premier was meeting with his ministers. The Crees had finally been granted an audience, and they had decided to use it to ask the premier if he would suspend the project only until they could get organized and make their feelings known.

The younger Crees—led by Billy Diamond, the newly elected chief of Rupert House—spoke in English, with simultaneous French translation, and the premier listened, his impatience apparent to the Indians, as they spoke of land claims and historical precedent and environmental concerns. When the young Cree leader finished speaking, he turned to an old man in a windbreaker and nodded a signal. The old man took to his feet without notes, for the very good reason that he could not write, and speaking loudly in that riveting music that is formal Cree, Malcolm Diamond proceeded to tell Robert Bourassa what it was to have loved land as one might love a wife, to have lived off the land, to have cared for it when it was not well, to have harvested it when it was healthy, to have raised a family and to have lived in an uncomplicated, unobtrusive way that had gone on longer than any Cree or white man could remember.

But the young Quebec premier did not have time. Malcolm Diamond paused for translation, and Robert Bourassa, his patience run out, stood, quickly gathering up his papers. He mumbled something about his being expected at another meeting, and walked out of the room while the old man in the windbreaker stood awkwardly by, staring with shattered eyes.

Though Robert Bourassa would never be told—and certainly

CHIEF: THE FEARLESS VISION OF BILLY DIAMOND

would never ask—it was at this precise moment that began what would one day result in a Cree Nation. It would rise from eight pitifully poor villages that, until Robert Bourassa insulted them, barely knew one another existed. For it was in Robert Bourassa's own Cabinet room that the chiefs of these forgotten villages sat alone after he and his ministers had walked out on Malcolm Diamond, and here they had decided on a course of action that would eventually produce a self-governing tribe that would run its own airline, gain special status at the United Nations, force its own charter into the new Canadian constitution, strike business deals with Japanese conglomerates, and, when necessary, know how to whisper in the ear of Pope John Paul II whenever it wanted to embarrass the prime minister of Canada.

But on that October day in 1972, Malcolm Diamond had been looking for nothing quite so grand. All he wanted the premier of Quebec to agree to was the preservation of the traditional Cree way of life for those who might want it. He and the other elders who had gone with the young English-speaking leaders to Quebec City wanted only to ensure that after they were gone there would still be Cree in this stunted northern forest who would be able to gauge how far a moose was ahead if the frozen droppings had turned light brown, how to look for the rime that gives away the air vent in a bear's winter den, how to place the carcass of the first goose high in the branches of the nearest tree so it might call in others passing over. That was what Malcolm had spoken of, but the premier had snubbed the old man. And his son had watched it happen and had seen a cut reflected in the old man's eyes that made the son vow he would someday repair the damage Bourassa had caused.

And that was why, when Billy Diamond had shown his aging mother to the plush seat in the front row of the Salon Rouge, he had whispered to her in the same language that had gone unheard fifteen years before in front of this same premier. "This is where he shamed my father."

The medal of the Knight of the Order of Quebec felt solid on his chest. Billy Diamond, his hand outstretched, stared straight past the smiling premier of Quebec at his mother smiling back, still tugging on her sweater. He then looked back, staring straight into the eyes of the man who had cut off the old chief and who had set in motion forces that had threatened to destroy his people, nearly wrecked his marriage, all but killed his son .... Robert Bourassa smiled on, shifting so that the photographer could capture the moment. The premier of Quebec, honouring his old enemy, his new friend.

PROLOGUE

But for Billy Diamond it was nothing of the sort. This was not a medal he was receiving. He knew, and the Indian woman in the front row understood, even if not a single word that was spoken during the elaborate ceremony made the slightest bit of sense to her.

What Hilda Diamond saw was her son doing something important for her, for himself and for little Philip Diamond, who had spent 121 days in hospital because of government neglect, and little Tommy Wapachee, who had died before they could even get him to the hospital . . . .

Billy Diamond did not receive a medal when he reached out to take the hand of Premier Robert Bourassa.

He took back his father's honour.

PART ONE

EARTH
ᐊᵸᵢ

At Fort Hope, Chief Moonias was perplexed by the fact that he seemed to be getting something for nothing; he had his suspicions maybe that there was something concealed in a bargain where all the benefits seemed to be on one side. "Ever since I was a little boy," he said, "I have had to pay well for everything, even if it was only a few pins or a bit of braid, and now you come with money and I have to give you nothing in return."

> Duncan Campbell Scott,
> Indian Treaty Commissioner,
> *The Last of the Indian Treaties*,
> an account of the Canadian
> government's negotiations leading up
> to the signing of James Bay Treaty
> No. 9, 1905.

CHAPTER ONE

BILEESH DIAMIN

The Shouting Chief now lies silent under a simple white cross on the banks of the Rupert River, the only information offered to those who pass, that this is the grave of "Malcolm Diamond." No dates, no scripture, nothing to tell what it was like when he was young and the beaver vanished and the people died of starvation, nothing to tell what it was like to be a chief forced to answer to officials who spoke not a word of your language, nothing to tell about that fall of 1984 when an old Malcolm Diamond split wood for two solid weeks until he had filled his basement, gave a local sharpshooter enough shells to go out and down enough geese to fill the freezer, and then went to bed quietly to die.

On a winter's day more than three years after Malcolm Diamond's death, his son, Billy, and grandson, Philip, come in a truck to park between the grave and the river, staring out at a sunset that has turned the sky over the saltwater bay orange and tinted the village pink. The angled light plays on the thick face of the man behind the steering wheel, his skin taking on the colour of flickering coals. Only thirty-eight, the highest hair on Billy Diamond's massive head is already whitening, frosting over the way Malcolm's went only in his seventies. But then thirty-eight is only the simplest measure of all that has passed along this shoreline since Billy Diamond was born.

Much of the river is still open, pink ice floes gliding past the graveyard and out toward the orange fire where they will melt. The mouth is late freezing over this year, but then it has been late every winter since the huge inland lakes were created by the James Bay Project. The government experts had said there would be no such effect in places like Rupert House, but then officials have always come to places like Rupert House and used words that are as filled with illusion and impermanent as the pink light that already weakens on the lower crosses.

"My father taught me one thing," Billy Diamond says. "And that was to never, never agree with the government—no matter what. And I never have. Never."

It was a lesson the Cree Indians of James Bay learned the hard way. Though they now have first say in their own affairs, it took centuries to regain even a portion of the control they had when the European explorers first set out to "discover" them.

Henry Hudson had come to the banks of the Rupert River in 1611, his ship, *Discovery*, sailing in search of the "Western Sea" Hudson was convinced lay just beyond the lands found 120 years earlier by Christopher Columbus. But Hudson could find no passageway to the Orient, and the magnificent furs of the Indians he encountered in this barren land were poor compensation for what he had expected to find. Even so, Hudson did establish the trading pattern for James Bay, as recorded by crew member Abacuk Pricket, who witnessed his captain in trade with an Indian: ". . . the master shewed him an hatchet, for which he would have given the master one of his deere skinnes, but our master would have them both, and so hee had, although not willingly."

Hudson did not, however, have the opportunity to report back to London how easily the "savages" along this northern coast could be fleeced, for six days out of the Rupert shelter the crew of the *Discovery* mutinied, packed the unpredictable Hudson and his young son, John, into a lifeboat with a few faithful rowers and set them adrift, never to be heard from again.

Hudson was followed by an endless flotilla of like-minded explorers, all convinced of finding a secret passage to Cathay: Sir Thomas Button, at the helm of Hudson's ship, *Discovery*; Danish explorer Jens Munk, who lost sixty-one of his sixty-three sailors to starvation and scurvy during the winter he spent near the mouth of the Churchill River; the English captain, Thomas James, who wintered on Charlton Island in James Bay and left behind only his name without sighting a single Cree; and eight other British expeditions, none of them victorious in their search. It would not be until the late 1980s that a northern trade connection would be established to the Orient, and it would be done by a Cree adventurer by the name of Billy Diamond.

The first two explorers to make contact with the Cree were the French-speaking traders Pierre-Esprit Radisson and Médard Chouart, Sieur Des Groseilliers, who came seeking fur, rather than a magical opening to the West. In the winter of 1659–60, while paddling far inland from New France to trade with the Huron, the two *coureurs de bois* had made contact with Crees from the James Bay area, who carried with them the finest quality furs the traders had ever seen. They were quick to trade for these exquisite beaver pelts, convinced they had struck the motherlode of the fur trade. Yet when they returned to Quebec they were far from cheered. Groseilliers was jailed for trading without a licence and, once released, was refused permission to return to the waters where he and his partner had come across the travelling Crees.

Eight years later, having switched loyalties and spent months in England convincing a cash-strapped Charles II to finance an expedition by sea to find the luxurious northern pelts of the Crees, Radisson and Groseilliers set sail in two small ships, the *Eaglet* and *Nonsuch*. They had obtained the financial backing of a curious group of investors including the king's cousin, Prince Rupert of the Rhine, an eccentric bounder far better qualified as an artist or inventor than a businessman. Yet this singular investment would prove to be the opportunity of the age. But at this point it was still a gamble, no matter how out of proportion the return, and indeed, the younger Radisson did not even make it halfway, as the *Eaglet* was forced back by a storm off the coast of Ireland. The *Nonsuch*, however, made it to the coast of Labrador. From there it turned north, rounding the Ungava Peninsula and sailing into Hudson Bay, heading south into James Bay and anchoring on the gravel banks of a river the explorers elected to name after their benefactor: Rupert.

Groseilliers and his men built a stockade and dug in for the winter, waiting for the trappers to come. By the following June, with the bounty from some three hundred Crees who had come to trade, they set sail for home, having proven that the English could engage in profitable commerce with these savages as well as the French. Their approach was entirely different though: they wouldn't even have to bother establishing a colony.

On May 2, 1670, Prince Rupert's gamble began to pay off: by the Royal Proclamation of his delighted cousin, Charles II, Rupert and his fellow adventurers received a royal charter to serve as "true and absolute Lordes and Proprietors" of Hudson Bay, including all the land around the waters that drained into this northern basin. No one realized the extent of the deed then—roughly 40 percent of Canada, a quarter of the world's freshwater surface—nor did anyone care. Only savages were there, and according to Groseilliers, he and the captain of the *Nonsuch* had taken care to purchase the land from the local chief when he came to trade at the new Fort George post on the mouth of the Rupert.

The beaver pelts that came out of James Bay were precisely as Radisson and Groseilliers had promised: finer, glossier and handsomer than anything that had been found before in the New World. The fine hair was shaved off, then beaten and shellacked to become luxurious, waterproof felt for the hats that indicated, more perfectly than anything else, the social and economic standing of the European gentry.

The trading post at the mouth of the Rupert proved to be one of the busiest in the massive domain of what gradually became known as the Hudson's Bay Company. The Crees came willingly, and the English decided to stop swapping useless trinkets and mirrors for the goods and began to trade utensils and tools, muskets and powder, flannel and wool. It was a happy arrangement, confirmed when two of the Rupert River Crees accepted an invitation from the Crown to spend a winter in London.

The Cree "exchange explorers" left a land where the people believed the dead flew off into the night skies to form the stars and stepped ashore in a country where Christopher Wren was already at work on St Paul's Cathedral. They left a people whose existence was nomadic, who trapped in winter, hunted goose in spring, fished in summer, and they joined a people who had come together in the most advanced city of the civilized world. They came from a structure where leadership was unknown, where the height of control was an elder male dividing up trapping areas, and arrived to find a constitutional monarchy and an elected Parliament in a city where the police were expected to make certain the recorded rules were followed by all. They came from a flat, swampy land where the spruce trees rose to the shoulder and where they learned to bounce with the taiga as they moved across it and entered a world where bricks made the ground as hard as stone and the buildings were as high as the stubborn James Bay clouds. They left a land where the blackflies could drive caribou or man insane and came to a place where conversation and shouting and machinery distracted as maddeningly—yet there was no escape. Only one of the two Crees survived the gentle winter in London.

When the ambitious Sun King, Louis XIV, declared war on England in 1689, battles were also played out in Hudson and James Bays. The British fort at the mouth of the Rupert River was burned to the ground at one point, and though the war lasted twenty-four years and the French forces won every decisive battle in the waters of Hudson Bay, in 1713 the Treaty of Utrecht placed all those northern territories back in the firm control of the "true and absolute Lordes and Proprietors" of the Hudson's Bay Company. The French interlude in James Bay was precisely that: a brief circumstance soon forgotten.

And though the shoreline of James Bay would eventually be split between two Canadian provinces—anglophone Ontario to the west and francophone Quebec to the east, the French influence would remain minimal. In a decision of convenience, competing missionaries who arrived in the eighteenth and nineteenth centuries simply divided up the "spoils" of heathen Crees, the Roman Catholics undertaking to spread the word along the Ontario coast of the bay, the Anglicans taking the gospel to the Quebec-area Crees, including the Diamond ancestors. English would be the language of instruction for both, with French a foreign tongue belonging mostly to the western coast priests long after Quebec had been ceded the eastern coast.

For the Hudson's Bay Company, James Bay was run under a simple feudal system that served the company extraordinarily well, with annual returns on investment soon running to 200 percent. Nothing gave the company any inclination to change. The Bay had its loyal employees running its posts at the mouths of the main rivers, but it also enjoyed, at next to no cost, a symbiotic relation with the Crees, in which the company was the main benefactor. The company set the price of barter. The Crees were advanced meagre supplies, and paid for them with the pelts demanded by the Bay, pelts the company then shipped to Europe for processing and sale. The only time actual money ever changed hands was in London, and the suppliers knew neither how much was paid out nor what the paper meant that was transferred from one pocket to another in exchange for their pelts. The Crees did not complain, did not dispute; perfect partners, they simply accepted.

Groseilliers's brag that he had purchased the land would have struck them as totally baffling, for the Crees had no concept of ownership. They simply used the Hudson's Bay Company as a place to swap their furs for objects that made life easier in the bush—guns, kettles, flour—and then quickly disappeared again into the spruce cover. The Crees who traded at Fort Rupert had even designated a special spot where they would meet before heading in to barter. It was at the bend of a creek—a quiet, relaxing spot close to the fort—and here they would wash up, and dress in a style they thought would be pleasing to the Europeans before they gathered up their furs for the actual transaction. For decades "Dress-Up Creek" served as the transition point where the Crees changed into what they believed the traders wished to see. And their role, obviously, was to please their benefactors.

The first to dare question this relationship of convenience was George Atkinson, Jr., the son of an English man and a Cree woman. Atkinson was hired to work "in the service" of the Company but preferred to spend his winters tenting in the bush away from the post, hunting and trapping with the Crees. For eighteen years he served the company faithfully, but on retirement turned into the first angry activist of James Bay.

Atkinson told the Crees that they were fools to hunt geese for the depot whenever the English ordered them to do so, and then not even ask to be paid. Worse, he then tried to convince disbelieving Crees that they were being cheated by the English traders, not the other way around, as so many of them believed. Atkinson argued that their furs had tremendous value when the British resold them, and for that reason the Crees deserved to be far better paid for their troubles. The company response was swift: they dispatched Atkinson off to a better retirement in the Company's distant Red River Colony of the western prairies—well out of earshot of the ignorant Crees.

Even so, there were Crees in the area who had come to their own conclusion that the company was there to use them, not to help. Three years after Atkinson departed the Bay, during the bitter winter of 1832, a dozen starving Rupert River Crees journeyed to the small Hudson's Bay Company outpost of Hannah Bay. There they murdered the master and his wife, killed seven other Crees who worked around the post and then plundered Hannah Bay of the company's trade articles and food. It was an incident so out of keeping with the quiet acceptance of the James Bay Cree that what became known as "The Hannah Bay Massacre" dominates both the written history of the area traders and the oral history of the

Indians—a single, inexplicable explosion in more than three centuries of peaceful coexistence. By the time the manhunt for the murderers was over—with males as young as fifteen being executed on the spot as they were apprehended—sixteen people were dead.

According to the oral tradition of Fort Rupert—soon known as Rupert House—the starving Indians killed the manager because they were outraged over the puny offering of food he held out to them. But others are not so sure. One of the Indians, Shaintoquaish, who turned himself in to the postmaster before being executed, is said to have told the company official that his family had been ordered by the "Spirit above" to do the deed. He claimed the Crees had a divine plan to destroy all the Hudson's Bay posts along the coast and inland and to murder the crews of English ships as they arrived, thereby bringing an end to white dominance in James Bay.

But the overthrow of the English never came about. The sense that England controlled their destinies remained long past Canadian Confederation in 1867. In 1914, when the Reverend Harry Cartlidge first went up into the James Bay country as an Anglican catechist, the people said to him with some amusement, "You come from Canada." Their own country was that foreign to them. The lines of trade and communication still went up through the northern straits to London, and political control was entirely in the hands of the Hudson's Bay Company, not Ottawa, and certainly not Quebec City.

Somehow, when the push was on in the late 1800s to sign formal treaties with the Indians of Canada, the Crees along the eastern shore of James Bay were forgotten. Not so on the Ontario side, where in 1905 and 1906 Indian Treaty Commissioner Duncan Campbell Scott—an Ottawa civil servant with a reputation as a writer and a published conviction that "in the early days the Indians were a real menace to the colonization of Canada"—concluded Treaty No. 9 with the Ontario Cree along the western coastline of James Bay. In return for giving up "forever, all their rights, titles and privileges whatsoever" they were to receive eight dollars per year each "so long as the grass grows and the water runs," reserves, conditional hunting and fishing rights and a "suitable" Canadian flag to do with as they wished.

Fifty miles up the eastern coastline from the main Ontario Hudson's Bay Company post at Moose Factory, there was no thought of treating Crees as generously as Scott believed he was doing along the western shore. Jean-Lomer Gouin, who became premier of Quebec the year Treaty No. 9 was signed and remained in that position during the 1912 expansion of Quebec that placed the area under the provincial domain, thought an annuity of four dollars per capita was overly "burdensome"—even though the federal government had formally instructed Quebec that these Indians must be dealt with as Scott had dealt with the Ontario Cree. Gouin and his predecessors—all the way to Robert Bourassa, who became premier in 1970—simply ignored the command.

No treaty was ever discussed, no treaty ever signed, and along the Quebec shore of James Bay, life merely continued on as long as anyone could remember, with the Hudson's Bay Company in total control. The Bay tried, unsuccessfully, to turn the Indians who were not trapping into farmers—they even sent them haying in the marshes around Rupert House—but there could be no meeting of minds between what the Cree saw as a suitable way of life and what the paternalistic Bay thought was best for its charges. At the end of the First World War, when James Watt arrived at Rupert House to take over as the post's new factor, the outgoing manager, Alan Nicholson, immediately dismissed Watt's concern over the sad state of the locals. "They're always this way," said Nicholson, "a poor, lazy lot, good only for taking fur."

A few years later the unsympathetic Nicholson would not have been able to claim even this, for just before the Depression struck the rest of Canada, the beaver suddenly vanished along the rivers of the eastern coast. Only four pelts came in to the Rupert post in the winter of 1928–29, and the situation soon grew worse. It was not so much the lost fur as the lost food value, and though James Watt continually approached his superiors to show a bit of compassion and offer the Indians help when they most needed it, the Hudson's Bay Company turned a cold shoulder on the victims of this isolated famine.

The Hudson's Bay Company refused to give the Cree further advances, told Watt by letter that it would be the Indians' own fault if he failed to keep up his accounts and threatened to close down the post if the furs were depleted. When Watt persisted, his company demoted him, slashed his salary and allowed him to resign. Only when he appeared to have mended his soft-hearted ways would they take him back. It made no impression on the head office traders in Montreal and Winnipeg that the Blackneds lost ten of their twelve children to starvation or that the thirteen children of Simon and Mary Katapatuk were all dead from lack of food.

It was James Watt, on his return to Rupert House in the midst of the Depression, who convinced the Crees that the beaver could come back. He had determined, correctly, that the beaver had vanished because of over-harvesting brought on when white trappers began travelling north by rail and working the southern limits of the Cree territory. He began paying the Crees for locating lodges, marking them, and waiting, and he and his wife, Maud, convinced the government to set up a beaver conservation area, which gradually expanded into several along the coast. And with time, the luxurious beaver that had so enchanted Radisson and Groseilliers came back.

When James Watt died, the Cree of Rupert House gave his wife, Maud Watt, a money order for $343 and a short note of appreciation: "We will never forget the kindness and guidance of Mr. Watt." It was signed by eighty-five members of the band, among them a young trapper who was identified as "Malc. Diamin."

Malcolm Diamond was not yet chief of the Rupert House band. At the time of James Watt's death, he was just another seldom-seen trapper, a young man with a wife, Hilda, two daughters, Annie and Agnes, and a young son he doted on named Charlie. Soon there were also Gerti and Joey. Then, in the spring of 1949, a sixth child arrived. The Diamonds had been coming off the trapline and were headed into the village with their cache of beaver, otter and muskrat pelts. Another fine season on a dependable trapline. It was May 17 and they had come to the Last Creek camp, a bit behind schedule because the ice had been late going out that spring. But the next day they were intending to make the final leg of the journey.

Around noon, Gerti—carrying her play pail down to the creek—lost her footing and fell in, unable to swim. Her cries were heard by Charlie, then only seven, who went running from the camp to the water. He waded in and pulled her out, then led her back up the bank toward the tent, where a fire was going that could dry them both off. But Charlie would have no time to get dry himself.

Hilda was lying on a blanket, already in labour, Annie and the toddler, Joey, by her side. Malcolm had gone off hunting, certain that by the time he returned the backup in the river would be over and he would be able to prepare the canoe for the final run. He had told Charlie where he would be, and when another Cree hunter came into the camp calling out in search of Malcolm, Hilda found the strength to go out and meet the man, concealing her labour, and asked the hunter if he would take Charlie and together see if they could find her husband. She needed him, she said, but would not explain. And the visitor had the sense not to press.

Malcolm arrived back in time to receive the child and, with Hilda's calm instructions, he was able to use his hunting knife to cut the child's umbilical cord. Annie washed and cleaned and Hilda wrapped the screaming baby in a warm blanket, moving closer to the fire. The new baby was not only the biggest, but obviously the loudest child she had borne.

The kids said he should have a name.

"*Bileesh*," Malcolm decided. "*Bileesh Diamin.*"

When he went away to school, he would be given a number and an anglicized version of his name: Billy Diamond.

CHAPTER TWO

INDIAN SCHOOL DAYS

"I beg of you," the Plains Cree chief, Poundmaker, told the Canadian government representatives who held out the treaty he signed in 1876, "assist me in every way possible. When I am at a loss how to proceed, I want the advice and assistance of the government. The children yet unborn, I wish you to treat them in like manner as they advance in civilization like the White man."

Poundmaker's approach was to embrace all that he encountered. When Governor General Lord Lorne made his tour of the new territories in the West, Poundmaker stood on the podium while Lorne draped a medal about the chief's neck. Poundmaker called the British peer his "brother-in-law" and travelled throughout the tour with the vice-regal party in order to tell other Indians that they needed to have faith in the "Great Mother." Poundmaker did not deny that his people were starving and their children naked and cold, but he said that from now on it would be different for the Crees who roamed the open prairie. "I have never been angry about it," he said of the Indian situation at one stop, "for I knew the Indian Agent was a good friend to us."

A few years later, when the Riel Rebellion of 1885 shook the Canadian West, Poundmaker would be rewarded for his continued loyalty to the Canadian government by being thrown into Stoney Mountain Prison for three years and condemned by this same government for failing to keep the burning anger of his younger warriors under safe wraps and away from the devious hand of Louis Riel, the messianic halfbreed who fought to establish his own independent government. Poundmaker's final address to the Regina jury that convicted him was simply a defeatist, "You may do as you like with me."

In the early 1950s, when Malcolm Diamond became chief of the Rupert House Cree, or Swampy Cree as they are known, he had a rather different opinion of Poundmaker's "good friends," the Indian agents. He even coined a complicated Cree phrase as a title of honour for these government officials who flew in unannounced on the floatplanes. Roughly translated, he referred to them as "the men who get off the plane, take a piss, and get back on." The James Bay Indian agents never knew what the rest of the Crees were laughing about. But Malcolm Diamond knew one thing for certain, and that was that he, unlike Poundmaker, did not want his children to grow up to become whites.

In September of every year, Malcolm Diamond would go to the Hudson's Bay Company store to cash in the vouchers his spring furs had brought, and he would carry lard, flour, tea and ammunition and whatever new traps he could afford down to the long green canoe that Hilda was already packing with utensils and blankets and, from the mid-1930s on, babies and children of various sizes. After Bileesh, who became known as "Billy," there came Albert, then George, and finally Stanley.

Out into the bay they would head, Malcolm steering from the stern and Hilda in the bow, with eventually nine scrapping, singing or sleeping children in between. They travelled at first by paddle and later with the help of a sputtering, smoking two-horsepower outboard, out around the first point in calm weather, across a well-tramped portage in rough, and down the wide Nottaway River toward the family traplines. They would not return to Rupert House for nine months, and for nine months Malcolm and Hilda Diamond would be at their happiest, even as Malcolm poled through the endless rapids while young Charlie pulled from shore with a rope and Hilda, entirely on her own, would portage the year's supplies and the growing family up a safe path to the first point where the water was smooth enough to board again. "There was one year," she says in Cree while her eldest daughter Annie translates, "when I had to carry Albert under one arm, George under the other and the baby Stanley on my back."

They would paddle upstream, back into spruce and bog nearly a hundred miles, stopping along the way to hunt and fish as they wished, required by time only to trap when the ice formed thick enough and to come back out of the bush when the ice itself went out. The only date they observed was Christmas. The children would be allowed to hang a small pot on a string tied from tent pole to tent pole over the child's head, and in the morning there would always be a few cookies and perhaps a candy inside. "The only question we ever asked," Billy Diamond would say on a later Christmas when his own son was counting on a real airplane landing under the tree, "was how did that little old man find his way around the bush so easily."

Up the wide Nottaway they would go, the children lying on the floorboards of the big canoe, sweeping the sky for circling osprey. What they hoped to see was the big white-bellied bird tucking into its screaming dive and falling like a thrown knife, cutting quickly into the waters and quickly out, then circling as slowly as an overloaded floatplane as it rose with a flashing trout in its talons. If they saw a hawk circling instead, they would hound their father until he pulled out his rifle and attempted a single shot, the hawk more often than not folding suddenly and tumbling dead from its hold in the sky while the children cheered. There were more fish in the river than they could even imagine; the osprey was welcome to dine. But hawks took rabbits, and there were never enough rabbits to fill the children's snares.

To say that life in the bush was simple would be to do it an injustice, for though there were no timetables, distractions, school, traffic, stores, newspapers or even neighbours, heading into the bush for the winter was hardly without complication. There were beaver lodges to hunt out, air holes to find and calculations to be made as to precisely where the chute came out and where the trap should be set. There was tracking to be taught, water to be drawn, wood to cut, camps to establish, trails to blaze and brush to clear. And when all the survival chores were done there was still the fur to prepare. Each pelt had to be carefully cut away from the flesh and delicately laid out for drying so the fur would be best presented: strung to a hoop if beaver, turned inside out if muskrat, delicately stretched and dried if fox or marten or, if luck was with them, lynx.

And all this, of course, was done outside the protective flaps of the winter lodge, often in thirty-below-zero weather and usually in the dark, as the northern sun rises late in winter and is gone by mid-afternoon. Inside the tent, where there was always a fire to be kept for heat and light, there was more work to do: food to prepare, sewing to complete and a chance to learn fine Cree embroidery techniques from Hilda. Malcolm would show the children how to sharpen a spruce branch and shove it through the nose of a beaver so a rope could be attached and the smooth, heavy animal dragged home with as little effort as it took to snowshoe. Hilda would show them how to work a smaller sharpened stick through the anus of a goose, how to truss the limbs and fold over the neck and how to use rope and hooks to hang the bird over the fire so it cooked slowly, spinning, the fat dripping into a bowl placed below. Later, with luck, this fat would sweeten the bannock the kids would twist about a longer sharpened stick and cook slowly over the coals.

Sometimes there were no geese to drip or beaver to clean. And if the trapping had not been good the winter before, supplies would be low when they left Rupert and could not be replenished as the winter went on, no matter how bountiful the trapline might prove to be this time out.

"There were some years," says Hilda Diamond, "when I would not even have a single tea bag. I would take some wild meat and boil it, and then scoop out the broth from the pot and sit back and pretend it was tea. One year I had not been able to take any sugar back with us. The babies used to say they wanted candy and I would hurry out with a spoon, fill it with fresh snow and hurry back in, telling them it was sugar but they had to eat it fast. They never knew the difference."

Her sixth child, Bileesh, was a trial, so curious about fire that he had to be lashed to the side of the tent whenever she went outside for more wood. He was a healthy, rambunctious child who refused to believe he was not already grown enough to do the things his father and Charlie did. His grandfather gave him a small axe and he used it to set up his own trapline within safe sight of the camp. He cleared brush, established trails, moved his equipment around and set deadfall traps for creatures that, apart from the odd unlucky squirrel and a weasel, never came near the smell of the smoke from the camp.

He was only four years old when he insisted he was ready to go out to the big trapline with Malcolm. And once he started, no one could keep him back at the camp. Once, when Malcolm and Charlie set off with their rifles in search of caribou, Billy and Gerti and Agnes were left in charge of the beaver traps, and Hilda still weeps with laughter to remember how she sat doing embroidery by the fire and heard something outside, breathing with extreme difficulty. The flap opened and in walked her five-year-old son in snowshoes, a harness on his shoulders and his face soaked with sweat. As he grunted his way deeper into the tent, eventually she saw that the cord leading back from the harness was attached to a male beaver, trussed by the girls as well as Malcolm himself could have done it. "He started talking to me like he was some great hunter," remembers his mother, "some big man who had just done the impossible, and bragging about how he had caught this beaver and now I should cook it for him to eat."

Malcolm and Charlie came back with caribou. The father cut it up and they prepared a feast, but first Malcolm drained off the blood into a sac, which he then tied high along the walls. It would make good flavouring in the meals to come. Billy, however, had other ideas, first talking his younger brother, Albert, into standing directly below the sac, then using one of the roasting sticks to jab up as quickly as possible, drenching Albert completely in a burst of fresh caribou blood.

"When he finally left for school," Hilda Diamond says, "it suddenly got very quiet in our home."

But he did not leave until he was eight years old, a good three to four years after other North American children begin their formal education. Until that time, it was the trapline in winter, goose camps in May and October, fishing in late summer and, at most, a few weeks of each year in the village of Rupert House. The sole contact they had with the outside world was a radio so fascinating to Charlie that as he grew stronger, he would even carry with him on the trapline the huge "Nine Lives" dry cell battery that was as heavy as two extra beaver. Charlie liked the country music, even though he understood nothing of what was said between the songs.

Even so, this radio was the family's first fleeting contact with a world where the Toronto Maple Leafs were kings and Louis St Laurent was a few steps below as prime minister. Later, when the younger Diamond children would learn English and return periodically for the goose hunts, they would tune in to the Timmins radio station, CKGB, on Saturday mornings at 10:00 A.M. for "The District Hour" and listen for the birthday announcements to find out if any were from Rupert House.

Billy, becoming increasingly entranced by the power of the spoken word, would fall under the radio spell of a huge, brusque southern preacher by the name of R.W. Schambach, whose revivals would be carried late at night on the far-reaching WWVA station out of Wheeling, West Virginia. While Schambach would roar down into the James Bay woods pontificating about the evils of greed and the need to send money fast to help him put an end to this greed, Billy would lie with his face to the wall listening, repeating each sentence as he practised the cadence of the "Voice of Power."

At the birth of Stanley, the ninth and youngest child, tragedy very nearly struck the young family for a second time. Only two summers before, eight-year-old Joey had died after suffering a seizure while swimming, and now, over Christmas and New Year's of 1955, another unexpected crisis arose. The family had been in their winter lodge for several weeks, knowing that Hilda was due to give birth to her ninth child around Christmas. Everyone was well prepared for the event. Annie and Agnes were both young adults by this time, and as anxious for the child to present itself as Hilda herself was.

The baby came early in the morning of the 23rd. The birth went well and no complications appeared until Hilda attempted to nurse her new child shortly after he had been washed and placed in a new blanket, with soft, dried reindeer moss tucked in for a diaper. Her milk would not come. Not only that, but her swollen breasts hurt so badly that merely by bringing the baby close she felt as if she was bringing a burning log to her skin. She told the family not to worry, that it would pass, and while she slept Annie and Agnes tried to quiet the baby with a teaspoon and sugar water, but he would not take it. A day passed and still Hilda's breasts ached, particularly on the left side, where her skin was also discoloured. The baby was getting weaker, though the girls were trying their best to get him to take something, and Hilda knew she was simply getting worse, not improving as she had told them. She tried nursing again, but this time only pus came. She was hot, sweating and feverish.

"Charlie—get ready," Malcolm said softly when he found out about the infection. He saw the quandary perfectly: move his wife and the child would die; do nothing and both would die. "You'll go with me back to Rupert."

Annie was put in charge of the baby. They searched through the supplies and found a single, eight-ounce can of condensed milk. Billy and the girls would have to check the traps and look after the two little ones, Albert and George, and Annie would have to keep up the fires and do the cooking as well as care for the infant. Malcolm and Charlie, then thirteen years old, cut extra wood, set some snares within easy walking distance of the lodge and then set off with snowshoes, a sled and a few of the dogs, travelling more than a hundred miles from this campsite near the Harricana, north over the Nottaway and on until they reached the Rupert and the village at its mouth. Here, they would try to summon an emergency plane and direct it to the isolated trapline on the Nottaway.

For a week the weather steadily worsened, as did Hilda's fever. The children drew closer to the fire, becoming increasingly convinced that at the edge of the spruce lurked the hideous Windigo of Cree mythology, waiting and laughing while they starved and then feeding on them when they had grown too weak to fight back. But finally, on the eighth day, barking sled dogs spooked off the imagined terrors and Malcolm and Charlie came shouting through the same spruce that the children had been afraid to look at. Father and son had gone nearly 220 miles, barely sleeping, and had come racing back with canned milk and emergency food supplies, fully expecting the airplane to land there on their arrival, just as they had arranged. But there was no plane, and no one had heard the distant growl of one searching for the camp. Malcolm went over to his wife, wiped her brow dry and, with the children listening, told her, "Everything is going to be all right."

But everything was not all right. When the plane didn't arrive on the arranged day, it became impossible for it to come on the next. The howling north wind the Crees call *chuentenshu* blew furiously out of the north, bringing blowing snow and drifting. And when the snow stopped, freezing rain came in from the south, turning the snow to a crust too dangerous for landing even if a plane could locate the camp through such a low ceiling.

It was now to the point of desperation. The baby was getting weaker all the time despite the new supplies of milk, and Hilda was in extreme pain. They waited ten days for the bad weather to pass, making it more than three weeks since the baby had been born and Hilda had fallen so ill. The kids began to believe that their mother would die, and probably the baby, too.

During that night the abscess on Hilda's left breast broke, and though the fever stayed, much of the pain left. She could move again, if barely, and Malcolm decided they would have to break camp and chance carrying her. He reconfigured the sled so that it would hold her, and they carried Hilda out and wrapped her warmly. Annie, who had already been away to residential school at Moose Factory and who could read and write, scribbled a note for the pilot, if he ever showed up, and pinned it on the flap of the tent. It told him that they had waited and now had gone ahead. Malcolm had described the swamps they would be going through, and Annie had written it all down in English.

They spent that first night at another camp and then moved again, following the crude trail Malcolm and Charlie had fashioned nearly two weeks earlier. They began walking at dawn, the sled bogging them down considerably, and sometime shortly after they should have stopped for lunch, the kids thought they heard a plane far in the distance.

"Make a fire, *quick!*" Malcolm shouted to the girls. It was raining lightly again and they had trouble getting the fire to catch with the iced-over wood, but eventually it took, and Billy and his brothers ran about ripping off green spruce boughs that would throw up a smoke. While the kids worked on the fire, Malcolm and Charlie tried to slash a runway for the plane through the sparse spruce in the swamp. The plane came closer, dipping a wing when the pilot spied the smoke and passing over once while the kids screamed and jumped, waving. It was BSC, the big black Norseman of Austin Airways that came in so often to the Rupert House dock. The plane circled again, coming in low over the makeshift runway and then rose and turned again, deciding to chance it. He came down softly, a perfect ski landing in the middle of the James Bay forest.

"I'm taking her straight in to the hospital," the pilot said the moment he saw the hollow, ghostly cheeks of the woman on the sled.

They put Hilda on and then Malcolm insisted that the children be taken on, too. All but Charlie. He and his eldest son would stay and check the traplines, and come in later. Hilda would be taken eventually to Moose Factory in Ontario, where they would treat her with antibiotics, and she would fully recover by the time her husband and son made it back to Rupert with the season's take of fur.

Up the plane rose, the youngest children on their very first flight, the sensation they had always dreamed about as they stood at the Rupert House docks and watched the black Norseman howl out over the chop, skip and then rise off magically over the open bay. But now they were crying as loudly as the dehydrated baby. Billy pressed his face to the window, staring down as his father and brother stared up, waving, still staring as Malcolm turned around and went back to his work.

Most years the Diamonds spent only a few weeks away from the bush, in a tiny grey shack high on the south bank of the Rupert

River, on the bay side of the Anglican mission and the government docks where, in the summer of 1954, Joey Diamond had suffered the seizure while swimming. He and another eight-year-old boy had been poking through the garbage of the Catholic mission and eaten some potatoes that had been thrown out—local potatoes that had been grown in Rupert since Maud Watt introduced the idea at the height of the starvation years. The potatoes had apparently been sprayed with some toxic substance, but the youngsters, thinking only that they had scrounged a free and favoured snack, ate them raw and immediately went off swimming. Joey's reaction was by far the worse; he floundered while swimming off the shore and went into seizure when the other children dragged him onto the beach. By the time the chief could be summoned, it was too late. With Malcolm Diamond holding the rambunctious second son of whom so much had been expected, Joey twitched violently, shuddered and died.

"I always thought that he had a plan," Billy Diamond says of his father. "He was going to take his eldest son off trapping with him. He would know the tracking skills and he would receive the land and train his own children to receive the land from him. The others he would send to school where they would earn another set of skills and come back to help. I've always wondered what dreams he had for Joey."

Malcolm first wanted a child to pass the trapline on to, and so Charlie was never permited to go to school but was always kept in the bush with his parents, a fact he resented bitterly during his teenage years when his siblings would speak English whenever they wanted to keep anything from him. Malcolm needed a child to translate for him when he dealt with the whites as chief, and so, in 1946, he sent his eldest girl, Annie, off on the doctor's boat to the Indian residential school at Moose Factory, eighty miles down the coast and just across the Ontario border.

The Hudson's Bay Company had strongly resisted the original drive to establish a school in the James Bay area, as Governor George Simpson considered any attempt to permanently settle the Crees to be "very prejudicial to the Hon. Company's interests." Eventually, however, the missionaries prevailed, and the idea first proposed by the Reverend George Barnley back in the 1840s—to establish a residential school where the Indian children might be trained to become farmers—became a reality.

But Malcolm Diamond had other plans for his educated children. When Annie returned from school, it was not to dig a garden back of the Diamond shack, but to go everywhere the

Rupert House chief went and weed the tricks out of the language. With Annie along, Malcolm was no longer forced to rely on the translations offered by the Bay manager or one of the village missionaries, interpretations he had long since learned to distrust.

In late August of 1957, Chief Malcolm Diamond walked into the Hudson's Bay store on the south bank of the river, placed his order for winter supplies and asked the manager if he would make the necessary arrangements to send eight-year-old Billy to this same school. A day later the manager informed the village chief that he had been in contact by radio phone, but unfortunately there was no space available. There might, however, be room if one of the expected children failed to show. Malcolm elected to finish packing, load his supplies and the rest of the family, and leave his son behind with Annie, who had married that summer and would be living in the village.

"I went into total shock," remembers Billy. "I went down to the dock and helped him load in the dogs and I realized that I was being separated from my parents. My mother was crying, my brothers were crying, I was crying and he calmly weighed his packs, threw them in and headed out into the bay." A floatplane came into the docks and took away the children who had already been accepted, including Billy's older sister, Gerti, but there was still no word of whether or not Billy would be able to go that year. September came and he passed his days hunting snipe with a slingshot down along the Rupert beach, and he began to like the idea of spending the winter with Annie and her new husband. But then word came through the clerk of the store that Indian Affairs had issued the eight-year-old a food voucher, and more news would be coming shortly on what would become of him. He picked up his voucher, cashed it in on as many cans of Klik processed meat and sardines as the clerk would permit and went back to Annie's shack, where by morning the food was all gone. But with morning also came word that room had been found for three more students, and Billy Diamond was one of them.

The black Norseman BSC came into the docks on the last run before freeze-up. Annie walked the crying child down, handed him a paper bag half-filled with candy and gum, tucked a toy helicopter into his jacket and forced him aboard. He did not even have a second pair of socks to pack for the year-long trip. Still crying when the Norseman taxied in to the Moose Factory dock, the eight-year-old was met by a foreboding white man, who told him to get into the truck that was parked at the edge of the dock. He did not understand the language, had never seen a truck, could not believe it when it began moving. Nor could he comprehend the size of the three-storey brick building that loomed in the distance. All the shacks of Rupert House stacked and nailed together would not match such a house. And now they were telling him to hurry up and get inside it.

The one other boy he knew, Clifford Hester from Rupert, was older and so they were separated, as were the boys from the girls, so there was no chance of being comforted by Gerti. The supervisor took him to the dining room and walked him through the line, filling a plate with food he had never seen before. Not delicious beaver paws or moose nostrils, but hard pork chops; not bannock but vegetables. He could not eat.

After dinner they ushered him up to a shower. He had never before heard of such a thing, and when they turned on the water and told him to take off his clothes, he began to sob uncontrollably. "I thought they were going to boil me," he remembers. "I was terrified." The staff, however, were well accustomed to such shows of despair. No Cree child ever reacted differently, for it was always precisely the same culture shock. What the school officials had determined over the decades was that a system was necessary to break the child from the bush. No Cree was to be spoken; numbers were to be issued to each child; three sets of clothes would be issued to cover school, play and Sunday; children would line up for the morning dab of toothpaste, the daily vitamin, the cod liver oil, the meals, the showers, the morning chapel service and church twice on Sunday. They would live from September to July on the island of Moose Factory, not allowed to go for so much as a walk without an escort. In the school they would march single file, and even if passing by a sister or brother be forbidden to speak. Any children caught speaking Cree in the huge dormitories stood a chance of having their mouths washed out with soap.

But the supervisors were not entirely without compassion. They did not take away Billy's toy helicopter, and he was permitted to carry it with him to his very first class—only to have Georgie Visitor order his grade one gang to remove the toy from the newcomer and turn it over to the class leader. "I learned very quickly the political system," Billy says. "There was one leader—Georgie Visitor—and he used certain other boys to get what he wanted. Others had taken it, but I knew he had the helicopter, and a few days later we had a confrontation. I said I'd make him a deal: If I could steal bread from the dining room and give it to him, how long would it take me to get the helicopter back?

"I didn't pay any attention to his sidekicks. I dealt straight with him, not his men. I think he was a bit surprised. But we struck a deal. I kept up my end of the bargain and I got back my helicopter. I got what was mine—and I never let it go again.

"What I learned right away was that if I wanted to survive I was going to have to set up my own system. I got some men of my own—grade one kids from Paint Hills—and we grew fast."

The winter of that first year away, the youngster nearly died. He came down with a difficult combination of measles and mumps that failed to clear. When his continuing illness was mistaken for homesickness, the school nurse began carrying him over to the girls' side and putting him into bed with his sister, Gerti, but nothing seemed to help. He lapsed into an unconscious state for more than a week, and, according to Gerti, there was great concern that he might not survive. But as easily as he had slipped into the coma state he emerged, quickly recovered and returned to class.

It was in class that Billy Diamond began to find some advantages to the school. He learned to speak English quickly and to read almost as fast, and from the earliest moments was bewitched by the books in the school's library, moving quickly through the early readers and into the popular Hardy Boys series. By grade four, however, he was no longer able to see words clearly, and an eye test revealed a shortsighted condition that was deteriorating at such a rapid rate the optician who gave the youngster his first glasses thought Billy would probably be legally blind by the age of sixteen. He did not, however, cut down on his voracious reading. And when the library books ran out, he turned, gratefully, to the personal collection of one of the more encouraging instructors in the school.

Other relationships with teachers and supervisors were not so beneficial, however. One teacher seemed to take uncommon delight in spanking the bare bottoms of young Crees while the rest of the class stared and puzzled over why the teacher became as flushed as the student's bottom. Certain male supervisors showed an abiding interest in the young Cree boys, enticing them to their rooms with sugar cubes while older boys awkwardly tried to explain why they should not go. And one woman who worked in the school would take her showers with the younger Cree boys, ordering them to scrub her breasts and pubic area while she moaned and the boys laughed hysterically at the peculiar mannerisms of the whites.

More important than any contact with white teachers was the

contact with other Crees from up and down the James Bay coast. Two years after Billy Diamond arrived on the black Norseman from Rupert House, a nine-year-old named Ted Moses came in on the same floatplane from Eastmain, the next village up the Quebec side of the coast from Rupert. He had also come from a bush family, but, unlike Billy Diamond, had come against his father's wishes because he himself felt a need for something different than a hunter's education. Ted Moses' father, Eastmain trapper Willie Moses, had finally given in to his son's pleading. And when the boy boarded the plane for the school, Willie had emptied out his entire wallet, pressing sixty-five cents into Ted's hand as he shook it in farewell. But when the youngster arrived, the supervisors immediately took away the money, and he did not even have the words to ask them why.

Within two weeks, however, Ted Moses—who would one day be the chief to gain the James Bay Cree a status at the United Nations much like that enjoyed by Amnesty International—was aware of the political structure surrounding him. The whites had all but total control. Soon, Ted Moses of Eastmain was part of the growing gang that included Billy Diamond from Rupert House—winner of the Honour Student Award in the grade six graduation class—Walter Hughboy from Paint Hills, Steven Bearskin from Fort George, and a handful of other young Crees who were then interested only in sticking together and getting away with whatever they could under the watchful eyes of the supervisors. Little did this miniature gang know that, one day, they would be known collectively along the coast of James Bay as "The Leadership".

And already, first among equals in that special group was a swaggering little Cree by the name of Billy Diamond. "He was," remembers Moses, "a bossy little kid." But he had something that made the others defer to him, a blend of stubbornness and determination and pride that created a formidable force even when he was in the primary grades and dealing with grown adults. What established his leadership firmly began as a simple refusal one evening to eat his vegetables.

Billy Diamond, not yet ten years of age, sat with his arms folded defiantly while the meal supervisor ordered him to finish his meal. With the rest of the school staring on in fascination, the supervisor recognized that an important point needed to be established, and so he announced that Billy would sit there until he ate his vegetables, and only then would be allowed to return to the dormitory. It had worked before, on other kids foolish enough to test the system.

Billy Diamond sat without eating for eight hours, the plate in front of him and the supervisor pacing behind until finally, at two o'clock in the morning, with the vegetables cold and still untouched, the supervisor caved in and sent the boy up to the darkened dormitory, where dozens of boys still lay with their eyes closed, feigning sleep while they awaited the outcome of the vegetable standoff.

From that point on, his leadership went unchallenged. Georgie Visitor, who had taken the helicopter, now became one of Billy Diamond's gang. And Billy Diamond—even after he had become grand chief and dined with heads of state—never ate another vegetable, ever.

CHAPTER THREE

ARROW TO THE MOON

Hilda Diamond still recalls the first letters her son wrote home from residential school and how one of the girls would translate them aloud to her while she fought back tears. "I'm coming home," he would tell them. "I'm coming home and I want you to keep me at home. I want to go back in the bush. I don't ever want to go back to school again."

But by the time he had graduated from the Moose Factory Residential School as the top student and seen his name etched on a small trophy, he no longer signed his name to such pleas. Now school was everything, and when the floatplane arrived to pick him up for the flight to Moosonee and the connecting train to Sault Ste Marie for grade seven, he was first aboard. Leaving Rupert House now meant adventure and learning and new friends, even if it still meant anguish for Hilda Diamond. Each year when the plane arrived she would weep at its sight, and she would weep again on its departure, never convinced by her husband that the children would all be coming home one day, and that when they got home, they would know how to deal with the changes that were coming. Sitting in her new home so many years later with a new colour television in front of her and, beside her, a brand-new ghetto blaster given to her by the same son she always thought she would never see again, Hilda Diamond now laughs at her old tears. "He was right," she says. "They did come home."

At the end of a very long train ride through the barrens of northern Ontario, Billy Diamond was taken to the Shingwauk Indian Residential School where he was assigned to another dormitory. From here, he was bussed into the city where he went through grades seven and eight at Campbell Public School and then moved on to the Bowating High School for the remainder of the six years he spent in "the Soo". He would spend his most formative years there, passing through puberty and caring far more about the messages passed on through the pounding drums of the Rolling Stones than about anything his father might want to tell him about the power of a Cree hunter's drum.

The summer he was fifteen, however, his Uncle Philip Diamond reintroduced Billy to the bush, taking the teenager and another area hunter, Mark Blackned, up the eastern coast to the mouth of the Pontax River and then inland up the rapids. It was late summer, the flies down, the berries almost done, the first geese arriving, the black bear gorging himself for the winter's hibernation, and the three Cree men—apart from the luxury of a small outboard, two rifles and a shotgun—returned to a way of life that the James Bay Cree were practising when Henry Hudson first came down the coast in 1611.

Philip, a man crippled from a childhood accident yet a recognized master of the bush, taught his nephew how to read the eddies and white water of a rapids, how to pole and how to work an outboard backwards through a swirl. They built a wigwam. They caught sturgeon and smoked it, set nets for whitefish and stored it in the natural summer refrigerator that hides beneath the soft reindeer moss at the foot of the black spruce. They shot geese and put out bait for a black bear that decided not to bother. But more than anything else, they talked. Not of the Rolling Stones or the prime minister of Canada, but of hunting and trapping.

At night they took the canoe out along the tributaries of the Pontax, paddled upstream and drifted back, Philip's stern paddle a bare whisper in the water, the other two men sitting on the bottom of the canoe, watching for beaver, muskrat and otter as they floated silently under the moonlight. Twice they saw bear and simply sucked in their breath and admired the animals, Philip letting the current take the canoe quietly out of sight and back toward the camp for a long, warm night of talk.

When the teenager got back to Bowating High, he fell under the spell of an inspirational English teacher named James Whitehead, who encouraged Billy to write. And thanks in large part to the stories his Uncle Philip and Mark Blackned had passed around the campfire that summer, Billy began researching Indian legends. From the legends he moved quickly into the history, and the history soon brought him up to date with the Indian situation in Canada.

Soon, he was less interested in the Beatles than in stories about loyal Poundmaker and the Plains Cree renegade, Almighty Voice, and tales about Joseph Brant, the Mohawk chief who fought with the British during the Seven Years' War and the American Revolution, then voluntarily brought his people to the Six Nations reserve in southwestern Ontario, living out his life in the luxury of a nearby town, Burlington. In the white history books, Brant was always portrayed as a great hero and inspired leader. But this interpretation struck the young student as flawed, and he began to sense a widening gap between what he was taught and what he believed. He took to eating his lunch alone in the woods, then with some of the other Indian students who were at the school, particularly Philip Awashish and Henry Mianscum of Mistassini, another James Bay village inland from Rupert House.

When Ted Moses, who had been attending grades seven and eight in Brantford, Ontario, transferred up to the Soo for high school, it took him a couple of weeks to figure out that Billy and several of the other Crees were skipping out of the cafeteria at lunch. He followed their tracks until he found them, sitting in a circle at the bottom of a small ravine, smoking cigarettes and speaking Cree. "Everybody had a special spot where they sat," remembers Moses, who immediately staked out his own.

It was a time of a great awakening for these young Cree students. They dreamed about girls, tried smoking and drinking and worried about complexions. Typical teenagers, with one crucial exception: unlike their white peers, who were busy trying to imitate the styles, manners and codes of other teenagers hanging around the local Dairy Queen, the Crees were growing increasingly interested in the innate differences.

Billy Diamond had studied the past and the traditions of Canadian Indians, and was beginning to question what had become of these people who had accepted the guidance of the Joseph Brants and the Poundmakers and the promises of a government that spoke constantly of a "trustee" relationship with the country's original peoples. Back home for the summer in Rupert House, he was to witness first-hand the difficulties that his generation faced.

Chief Malcolm Diamond intended to change dramatically the James Bay concept of what a chief was and what a chief was able to do. It was a formidable task, for a chief among the James Bay Cree was quite unlike the leaders of bands in other parts of the country. Before the arrival of the fur traders, in fact, there had been no such thing as a chief in Malcolm Diamond's world. The Jesuits had introduced the notion of a designated leader to the area when they began referring to the leading Indian in any particular group as the "captain," and the Hudson's Bay Company had readily adapted this title, embellishing it considerably with a uniform that included a bright red coat with regimental cuffs, a waistcoat, breeches and a coarse hat topped with dyed ostrich feathers.

The Crees of the eighteenth and nineteenth centuries were much amused by the white obsession with designating a leader. More often than not, the fancy clothes of the "captain" and his "lieutenants" would be ditched the moment the Indians were out of sight of the post and stashed in a safe cache like the one at Dress-Up Creek until they were needed for the next trip back to the fort. The traders were never aware that their "captains" were anything but deeply honoured by the titles the post had bestowed on them, yet proof that the Crees did not take such designations seriously can be found in the language itself. The head of a trapline was called *ocimaw*, the chief of the settlements became *ocimakan*—the suffix *kan* translating roughly into *made*. In other words, phoney chief.

It was Chief Malcolm Diamond's intention to change that perception of powerlessness. He began by refusing to follow the custom of using the local Bay manager or the missionaries as interpreters, turning instead to his daughter, Annie.

Malcolm argued with the government officials and fought with his summer employer, wealthy Kentuckian Charles Stewart MacLean, who held a ninety-nine-year lease on a nearby island that he had turned into a private hunting and fishing preserve. When MacLean sought to prevent the Rupert House Crees from hunting within a wide sweep of the territory around his island, the fight against him was led, and won, by his chief guide, Malcolm Diamond, who summarily told MacLean—through an interpreter—what he could do with his six-dollar-a-day job.

The summer Billy came back home, the battle was over education, a simmering conflict that lasted for several years during the mid-sixties. The issue was whether instruction in the small schools being established in the village would be in French, as the provincial bureaucrats and local priest wanted, or in English, as the parents desired. The provincial educational authorities maintained that the Rupert House Crees specifically requested French instruction; the Indians claimed they had only asked that French be one of the courses, not the language of instruction itself.

What most offended the parents, though, was that the battle over language had become a battle for the stomach. The French-language school run by the local priest began offering snacks of oranges and apples and Dare marshmallow cookies, an enticement the small English-language school could not hope to compete with by offering only powdered milk and a vitamin biscuit the Crees jokingly called their morning "dog biscuit." The kids were eager for the marshmallow cookies; the parents were furious that, to get it, they had to ask for the treat in French.

The first time the issue came to a head, Chief Malcolm Diamond used the radio phone to contact Robert Kanatewat, a young Cree leader in Fort George, who had gained a reputation similar to Malcolm's as a defier of authority, but who had the distinct advantage of being fluent in English. Kanatewat flew south along the coast and arrived at Rupert House, where he explained the misunderstanding to the officials. He informed them that the Rupert House parents would not consent to having the government school instruct in a language that was even more alien to the Crees than the English that had been introduced by the Hudson's Bay Company traders. Strong words were exchanged, but Chief Malcolm Diamond—with the help of the determined young man from Fort George—won the day. The bureaucrats agreed that instruction would be in English, as the parents requested. Malcolm Diamond thanked Robert Kanatewat and Kanatewat left immediately for the docks, where another floatplane was to be waiting for him.

A crowd had already gathered to see off the militant young leader from Fort George, and among the onlookers was a skinny seventeen-year-old student with a high, wavy pompadour. Billy Diamond had been fascinated by what he had heard: Kanatewat, it was said, had simply told the white government people that English would be the language of instruction and there would be no more discussion. No Cree had ever spoken this way to government officials before.

The pilot of the Austin Airways Norseman was getting edgy, staring out into the bay and shaking his head at the dark clouds rolling in from the north. "It's closing in!" he shouted to the people on the dock. "I can't wait!" The pilot slammed the door and pulled back on the throttle. He taxied out, turned and took off into the wind without granting the young man from Fort George another minute's grace. "Then we saw him," Billy Diamond remembers. "Robert Kanatewat was coming down toward the dock, walking as calmly as you could imagine. He was wearing a blue suit, a white shirt and a tie, dressed like we never saw Indians dressed, and he was carrying a *briefcase*—a *briefcase* in *Rupert House*!

"Every eye was on him, not because of the way he was dressed or anything, but because of the way he carried himself. He had a unique stature. So calm, so sure of himself. Someone in the crowd yelled out, 'The plane's left,' and he just says, 'I can see that.' You could tell he was mad. 'Where's the radio?' he asks, and someone took him up to the store where he made a call down to the Austin headquarters. Fifteen minutes later there's this buzz out of the clouds and no one could believe what was happening—the plane was coming back! 'Wow,' we said, 'this guy's got *power*. He called an airplane back!'

"I got in as close to him as I could, just looking him up and down from the shiny shoes to the briefcase, and he just stared back and smiled. The pilot taxied up, hurried down and *apologized* to him. No one had ever seen anything like that before. *Never*. This was the kind of authority a real chief should have. And from that moment onward, I had a hero."

The incident could not have happened at a more opportune time, as back at the Sault Ste Marie high school Indian pride and political awareness were beginning to blossom in Diamond and his colleagues. Sitting in the bush one lunch hour, they began to wonder how many Indian kids were attending schools in the Soo, and after a few inquiries had determined there were nearly 250 Cree and Ojibway students in the city. They made contact with the others and together formed an Indian Students' Council. By its second year, with Billy Diamond on the executive, it had become a significant force in the city.

A sympathetic Anglican minister, the Reverend Frank Coyle, arranged that a church hall be open to the group every Friday evening. They held dances, set up an arts club and a drama club, put together a band and, during the city's annual winter carnival, ran Jean Lontitt, a Cree from Moose Factory, for Snow Princess—and she won. Mistassini's Morley Loon, who became a Cree recording star before he died tragically of cancer, was in the band. Buckley Petawabano, also from Mistassini, was in the drama club and went on to become a star of the CBC television series

Rainbow Country. Billy Diamond was also involved with the Indian drama club, and soon landed a role with a local amateur production, playing the general in *The Emperor's New Clothes*.

It was the stage that cured Billy Diamond of his acute shyness. Scarred by a vicious hockey crosscheck across the forehead that had required sixteen stitches to close, sick through much of grade eleven with pleurisy, he had become a self-conscious teenager who preferred dealing with the printed word to speaking out, and treasured the bush lunches, not class discussions. He had become editor of the group's Indian student newspaper, and using the editorial page, had campaigned successfully against the curfews Indian students were given. But it was only when he went on stage that the consummate performer in him was unleashed.

In Canada's Centennial Year, 1967, the Reverend Frank Coyle suggested that the young actors put on a special play to bring their own heritage to the attention of other Canadians. The Indian students went to work eagerly. A script was written, with numerous playwrights contributing, including the students themselves and some well-meaning advisors. In four acts, it would be called, they decided, *Arrow to the Moon*. Act I showed an ancient hunting scene, done entirely in mime and ending with a scene depicting the coming of the white man. Act II, the story of Father Jean de Brébeuf and the Jesuit martyrs at Fort Ste Marie, was written by the Reverend Frank Coyle. Act III, in which traditional ways were contrasted with new ways as the youths saw them, was the creation of a local lawyer—now judge—Ray Stortini, whose wife, Helen, produced the play. The final act was to be set in a modern high school corridor, showing how Indian students had graduated into the mainstream of Canadian society. It was written by a local counsellor working for Indian Affairs.

Some of the apparently more serious scenes were most humorous to the Native students. During the act featuring Father Brébeuf, Maggie Bearskin played Mary in a Native nativity scene. Buckley Petawabano and Philip Awashish were to chat quietly in Cree during the scene while Brébeuf wrote his letter back to France telling his brothers of the joy in hearing their voices—voices that, to the few who understood Cree, were asking each other, "Who farted?" and describing their sexual parts with extraordinary adjectives.

But it was the third act of *Arrow to the Moon* that made the sprawling play worthy of serious note. Starring Alan Neacappo as the old chief, Beothuk, and Billy Diamond as the impatient young brave, Nootka, it was staged on an entirely black set with pencil-point lighting and the chilling cry of a loon in the background. The act was riveting enough that the Canadian Broadcasting Corporation elected to film and televise the production and the play was taken to Toronto and staged at the Ontario Pavilion of the Canadian National Exhibition.

The act begins with a narrator describing all that has passed since the white man arrived. The *voyageurs* are mentioned, the missionaries, the settlers, the battles between the European arrivals and the aboriginal tenants. Old Beothuk is a Plains chief, complete with headdress, buckskins, moccasins, and peace pipe. Nootka wears buckskin chaps and a single feather headdress and carries a bow.

> NOOTKA: The new ones brought steel axes, ploughs and saws, when our people were using stone tools which barely bit into hard trees and dry ground. The new ones showed us how to use the wheel.
>
> BEOTHUK: The son of a chief can go alone into the forest with only a stone-bladed knife, and survive.
>
> NOOTKA: The *tribe* must survive. Not only the son of the chief.
>
> BEOTHUK: The curlew and the pigeon are no more since the new ones settled in our land.

But Nootka will not be swayed from his conviction that the old ways must be abandoned for the new. "The guns and the horses brought by the new ones have made it possible for us to run faster than the buffalo and to kill him faster," he says. "If we do not change our ways and even our paths, our villages will be as empty as our stomachs.... The books of the new ones show the paths of change."

"I am too old to change," the old man says. "I die as a hunter, even as I lived as one. A chief is a chief of his people forever. My son, you must go the way of your heart. If you be wrong, and your path be wrong, our people will be no more in the time to come."

But the young brave played by Billy Diamond is not listening. Moving to centre stage, the pencil light playing on his hands as he raises them upward, he offers a prayer to Manitou which ends with: "The new ways show a way to work and live but the old ways have shown us how to die."

The light fades, a loon echoes madly in the distance and the scene goes completely black.

Twenty years later, the Reverend Frank Coyle, now retired, still shivers at the memory of this moment. "Billy came across as so poetic and sensitive," he says. "It was a heart-breaking moment. He held his hands up and he had the entire audience in his hands. It was a majestic moment, truly majestic."

When the Cree chiefs of James Bay saw the film of this same moment, they had no comment to make at all. They said later that they were embarrassed, shocked at how thoroughly white society had brainwashed the children they had sent off to the southern schools.

CHAPTER FOUR

CHIEF OF RUPERT HOUSE

The "old ways" were certainly in disfavour back in Rupert House when Billy Diamond graduated from Bowating High School with his grade twelve certificate and headed home for the summer. He was hoping to convince his father that the next logical step was university, wherever "the paths of change" would take him. He was returning to a village where the inhabitants lived in poverty, but at least no longer starved. It was a village where, to Billy Diamond's mind, the last vestiges of the old ways would soon fade into history, where they belonged.

The last shaking tent ceremony—during which a Cree shaman summons up the spirits who can foretell the future—had been performed on the banks of the Rupert River in 1962, and then only for the benefit of Richard Preston, a trusted anthropologist from McMaster University. The younger hunters no longer hurried to put out their campfires when the northern lights began to crackle across the skies. A sneeze did not now mean that your enemies were talking about you. It was even said that the younger women had eaten from the front paws and head of the bear, something that short years ago would have been sacrilege in the land of the James Bay Cree. Nor did they often speak of *Wisagatcak*, The Trickster, the Cree god of campfire tales who had the wisdom to construct a raft and take on the animals when the flood came and the waters grew higher and higher, and who had used his great magic to call upon the wolf to run about the raft with a ball of moss in his mouth until a new world was formed for the Cree, a world where they could hunt again in peace.

Little did they think that, in the summer of 1968, a modern Trickster—nineteen years old, his hair still Brylcreemed and nursed into deliberate folds, his mind on university—might be stepping off the pontoons of the old black Norseman BSC and onto the Rupert House docks. With a suitcase filled with worn jeans and books, Billy Diamond moved quickly up through the cord moss and blooming fireweed toward the old chief's house, where Malcolm Diamond was waiting to speak to his son.

The chief needed help. He was beginning to attend meetings with other provincial Indian leaders, and he wanted a second who had control of one of the other languages spoken, French or English. Together they soon went off to a meeting of the Indians of Quebec Association in Quebec City. The IQA—a political organization controlled by two key southern Indians, Max Gros-Louis of Huron Village near Quebec City and Andrew Delisle of the Mohawk reserve, near Montreal—was holding consultation meetings on the Indian Act, which the new federal minister, Jean Chrétien, a scrappy young lawyer and Liberal from Shawinigan, Quebec, was reconsidering in a government White Paper. Chrétien's policy proposals would be released for discussion the following year, but were to stir up so much controversy that they would never become government policy.

At this Native political meeting, the young student's eyes were opened. He and his father arrived in Quebec City without money, without knowing even where to go. The IQA arranged to billet them in a private home, and for three days the father and son from Rupert House sat and listened while the southern Indians kept them spellbound with oratory.

"They were more articulate than anyone I had ever known," remembers Billy. "They weren't frightened of anyone. They were aggressive when they went after the government officials who came in, and never backed down. Their style of dress was impeccable and they had opinions on everything. We went out with Max Gros-Louis for dinner and he ordered wine—I had never tasted wine before—and he talked about all that Indians could do for themselves."

The meetings also influenced Malcolm. Not that he wanted to change his dress, but he wanted to change the style of the Rupert

House Crees. He had already decided to step down as chief in favour of a younger man, Isaiah Salt, who could speak English, but he hoped his son Billy might develop into a leader in the mould of Robert Kanatewat in Fort George or the dynamic IQA leaders they were meeting in Quebec City. He suggested to his son that he forget about university and accept that he now had all the formal education he would need. He would be far more useful to his people at home than away at school, and the son reluctantly agreed. They returned to Rupert House and Billy went to work, operating a bulldozer part-time when there was construction work, and handling the band welfare payments when there was no work to be had by anyone.

His job with the band had little structure. An idle day might be followed by a day translating documents aloud for the men who could not understand English. Basically, he was to be on hand when needed. When Malcolm's successor, Isaiah Salt, came to the Diamonds' house one day to say that two of the village girls had run away from their boarding homes in Rouyn, Billy knew that it would be his job to find them.

He had no information to go on. Sitting down with a map of northern Quebec and northern Ontario, he stared at an area larger than France and, in the end, could only ask himself where he would go if he was running away himself. Obviously, to some place where your own people were, and since Rouyn was on the western edge of Quebec, that would have to be Moosonee, the nearest James Bay port on the Ontario side. He flew out in the morning.

A Cree working at the Hudson's Bay post in Moosonee had seen one of the girls with an aunt, and soon Billy was sitting in that aunt's home telling one of the runaways how essential schooling was and how they must not be so foolish as to squander such an opportunity. The conversation bothered him more than it seemed to bother the girl, but in the morning, when he carried his own pack down to the old floatplane that was about to head up the coast toward Rupert House, both girls were there, waiting. The one he had spoken with in the aunt's home had found her friend, and it seemed his arguments had swayed them both.

It was a melancholy flight back to the village. The two girls sat tucked into adjoining seats, their heads down, whispering about what would happen when their parents got hold of them. The young band worker sat off to the other side, staring down over the harsh coastline as the single-engine canso bore into gusting headwind. The girls had not said a single word to him, and as the old floatplane sighed and dropped into its approach, he turned and stared at the one sitting closest to him, a young Cree like himself who had, unlike himself, come to the conclusion that school was one of the great curses of life. She was a remarkable looking young woman—slim, graceful, with straight black hair long down her back, a clear, healthy complexion, dark eyes and a seductive overbite—and he wondered why, in all the past summers at home, he had failed to notice such a blossoming beauty. But he also wondered what they could possibly have in common apart from the fact that they both came from Rupert House and were thinking of running away. Only with him, it was *to* school.

Billy could not deny his father, however. And when old teachers back in the Soo tried to contact Billy over the radio phone to talk to him about going on to further education, he did not return their calls. "I couldn't call them back," he says. "It would have been too painful for me. I knew they would never understand what my Dad was asking of me. A few wrote later, but I never wrote back."

After years of student employment in Sault Ste Marie—packing groceries at Safeway, once even working as an "Indian" at a local tourist attraction—he could not adjust to what passed for an economy in the backward village. Convinced they had found just the employee to take over the meagre Rupert House books, the band passed a resolution whereby it would assume responsibility for the administration of its own welfare program. The total budget was $34,500. Ten percent of that—$3,450—would go towards office overhead and a suitable salary for the young high school graduate, an offer they presented to him complete with a series of "X" marks to indicate where Malcolm Diamond and the other councillors had signed their approval. But it wasn't enough. Billy signed on with Fecteau Air Transport as their dispatcher for the supply planes that came into Rupert House and landed on skis each winter on a flat field above the village, and he even applied for work with the Department of Indian Affairs in Val d'Or. He had heard in Quebec City that Chrétien was much in favour of bringing in Natives to work on Native projects. And if that was going to be the new path, he meant to follow it.

Shortly after the New Year, he received a call from Jean Bourassa, the Indian Affairs representative in Val d'Or (no relation to the new premier of the province, Robert Bourassa), and Billy was invited down for an interview. Bourassa was much impressed with the younger Diamond and hired him on the spot. Billy's job would be to go around to the various bands and hand out welfare cheques.

It was a simple job, and he was treated royally whenever he appeared with the treasured cheques. Yet this same experience, more than anything else, convinced him there had to be an alternative. Welfare was not only demeaning, it offered no potential for escape: the poverty-stricken Cree remained poverty-stricken on welfare, and welfare also meant that they would not risk alternatives for fear of losing the only support they had. When the final negotiations were underway for the James Bay Agreement, the elimination of the welfare system would become a central aim of the Crees.

From Val d'Or, Indian Affairs sent Billy Diamond to Notre-Dame-du-Nord in southern Quebec. Here, he was told, he would board with an Algonquin family and learn all about Indian Affairs. Whatever it was he was supposed to learn didn't take long to sink in. He began work Tuesday morning and quit on Friday morning. "I couldn't take it any more," he says. "There was nothing happening. I decided on my own to go back to Val d'Or."

But he was hardly welcomed back. "What the hell are *you* doing here?" Jean Bourassa shouted when he saw his young charge walking into the regional offices. Billy Diamond said nothing. He followed Bourassa into his office, closed the door, and said, very quietly: "Don't ever yell at me again." He told Bourassa he was bitterly disappointed by what he had seen in Indian Affairs, that the effort was going toward the bureaucracy, not the people. Bourassa countered that the decisions that matter were made in offices like this, and if he wanted to do something worthwhile he would have to accept the fact. But the young man could not. "I'm going home," Diamond told his superior, "and I'll get more done for my people there than you ever will here." The last thing that Billy Diamond heard before the door slammed shut was Jean Bourassa bellowing, "*You'll never make anything of yourself, young man!*"

Back at Rupert House, Billy Diamond set about to prove Jean Bourassa wrong. The local Oblate priest, Father Maurice Provencher, had been showing old movies in the village for a small admission price every Saturday night for years. It was hardly a booming business, but Billy Diamond decided the priest should have some competition. He had the band apply for a government grant and they were given $866.95—the first recreational grant ever awarded in Rupert—toward the purchase of a projector. While Father Provencher continued to bring in old black-and-white Gene

Autry pictures, the new movie theatre began with *Cat Ballou*. Soon the priest closed down his Saturday evening enterprise, and the band had full control of a profitable small business.

Diamond then set up a proper band office in the rambling J. S. C. Watt Memorial Hall down by the Roman Catholic mission. The hall had been built in the late 1940s as a "Longhouse Memorial" to the sympathetic Depression-era factor of the Hudson's Bay Company store, James Watt. Although the local Indians did not care much that the building had no traditional connection to the Crees, they did resent the official history of the structure. According to the accepted story, Maud Watt had returned to Rupert House after her husband's death and established a small bakery, putting up $12,000 of her own money toward the project and the Natives lovingly donating $20,000 of their own. Undoubtedly, some did freely contribute, but many Rupert House Cree hunters now claim they were forced to hand over a "tithe" of beaver pelts each time they came into the village to trade while the building was being constructed. Some of the younger Crees, Billy Diamond first among them, had long held up to ridicule the legendary "Angel of Hudson Bay" for this perceived historical inaccuracy. For these more political Crees, it was a particular delight when Billy Diamond managed to usurp a portion of the hall for the band office. Soon the memorial building that Maud Watt had hoped would be the setting of banquets had become a wildly successful bingo hall, with Kung Fu movies slated for the weekend.

Week by week, Billy Diamond began to emerge as a major player in the small village. He took the money that Indian Affairs still owed him in back salary and purchased one of the new snowmobiles that were just beginning to show up along the bay. Still eager for learning, he enrolled in an evening French course that was being offered at the local government school, and was delighted to discover that a couple of rows over sat Elizabeth Hester, the lovely young runaway with the overbite. When they finally spoke she said she could not remember him coming to bring her home from Moosonee, but that first disappointment was quickly overcome when she readily agreed to go for a ride on the shiny new skidoo parked outside the school.

It was a clear, sharply cold night, with the stars three-dimensional and thick in the sky, the spruce casting shadows on the clear trail that headed up past the landing strip and into the bush beyond. Long into the night the new machine purred, stopping frequently, and when it returned to town it brought back a young man with a dilemma: two girlfriends. There was Nellie, the young woman everyone expected him to be with, and now Elizabeth, the sixteen-year-old beauty who lived with more brothers and sisters than seemed possible in a dismal little structure down by the Anglican church.

He was twenty years old, an age when the young men of the village were far more interested in partying for days than in settling down forever. While Billy tried to see Elizabeth—and for a while Nellie, as well—during the days, most evenings and all weekends were reserved for getting together in large gangs and going until everyone dropped. Using washtubs they would ferment yeast and currants into a very cheap, very potent drink known in the village as "Quickie," and a party was seldom complete without a fistfight to bring it to a surly conclusion.

It was during one of these "Quickie" weekends that Billy Diamond found himself in a fight with a white man who did not feel the situation had been resolved with a few inept blows and a Monday hangover. He radioed the police in Great Whale, a Cree and Inuit village farther up the coast, and the police soon arrived by floatplane, took down the details and arrested Diamond on a charge of common assault. He was put onto the plane and transferred to Montreal, where he went before a judge and, not knowing what else he might do, pleaded guilty and threw himself on the mercy of the court. Mercy turned out to be three weeks in Montreal's Bordeaux prison, one of the toughest jails in all of Canada.

"It was just like going to residential school," he says. "The bell rang. The door opened. You lined up for breakfast. You lined up for lunch. You traded for smokes and matches. You went for a walk in the yard. You lined up for supper. You went to your room. The lights went out." The difference was that when he left residential school, he carried with him a certificate for being top student in the graduating class; when he left Bordeaux, he had a criminal record, and he was deeply concerned about what that might mean for his future. Here he was, about to become a responsible father, and he had just been let out of jail for acting so irresponsibly he was frightened to think of what he might do next.

"I went home and I was a *hero*," Diamond recalls. "A bunch of my friends and a few of the elders wanted to have a meeting with me. What they wanted was to ask me to run for chief. 'We need somebody aggressive,' they said. 'Somebody who's going to knock down doors.' They thought I was special because I had survived the white man's system—and all I'd been thinking was that my mouth was getting me in too much trouble."

On election day, July 7, 1970, the Crees of Rupert House gathered to elect a new chief. Nominations were open to anyone who cared to make one, and the nominees moved—some quickly, some reluctantly—to the front of the hall and stood, waiting. When nominations were over, the electors went and stood behind their choice for leader, and the candidate with the largest pack behind him became the new chief. Billy Diamond captured fifty-six percent of the vote. The immediate runner-up had only thirteen percent—Malcolm Diamond. The two men walked home together, laughing.

"Don't make the mistake of looking on this as a status symbol," his father told him when they were inside. "This is your work." It took no more than a single day for the gloss to fade. On July 8, eight bedraggled Cree elders walked into Rupert House and asked to meet with the new chief. They had come from the inland trading post at Nemaska, nearly a hundred miles up the river, and they were in desperate straits. They said the Hudson's Bay post had been closed and their chief had abandoned them. Coming through the bush, they said, they had run into land surveyors who told them that one day their magnificent lake was going to be flooded. So they had come on to Rupert, frightened for the lives of their people. They could not understand what was going on.

It did not register with the young Rupert House chief what had happened. He dismissed the surveyors' story as little more than panicking fantasy, but he also felt that these people—abandoned by both their chief and their trading post—were helpless and needed some place to go. He had no choice: he told them to bring their people to set up their own village within Rupert. "I told them I would try and arrange for them to get welfare," Diamond remembers. "I said I'd contact the government. But they kept saying to me that the government had closed their store at Nemaska and that the government was no longer willing to provide for them. I realized then that they thought the Hudson's Bay Company *was* the government."

A month after word had gone down the coast that Rupert had a new young chief and that he had taken in several families from Nemaska, the Indian Affairs Otter came swooping down from the southern skies, settled on the bay, and taxied in slowly to the village docks. The Crees came running from shacks all along the shoreline, hurrying down to see Chief Billy Diamond's first meeting with the ones who controlled their lives. The floatplane door swung open and out popped the head of Jean Bourassa.

"Well," said Bourassa as the young chief made his way through the crowd, "I see you've got yourself elected chief, Billy."

Bourassa bounded out onto the dock and stuck out his hand. "I can only spend twenty minutes with you," he told the new chief. "Tell me what your problems are."

"Jean," the new chief said, smiling widely, his arms still folded, "you can fuck your twenty minutes."

And with that Chief Billy Diamond turned, cut again through the gasping crowd and walked back up the hill to his father's shack, where Malcolm Diamond was laughing so hard he could not even ask his son what the English words meant that had so upset "the man who gets off the plane, takes a piss, and gets back on."

The cocky attitude of the new chief and the furious red face of Jean Bourassa marked a turning point in the relations of the Rupert House Crees with government bureaucrats. The village now had a leader as powerful and fearless as the renowned chief of Fort George, Robert Kanatewat. The idea that his own people were comparing him to his idol struck Chief Billy Diamond as both a great compliment and enormous good luck. Right from the start, his authority would go unchallenged.

"The thing I am most proud of in all my years of being chief of Rupert House," Billy Diamond would say many years later, "was that I never got beat up. I can remember my Dad coming home many times when he was chief, cut, beaten, kicked from trying to break up a fight. But he had to do it. He was the only authority in town."

He had not only taken on responsibility for the village, he was about to take on the added responsibility of a family. In the spring Elizabeth had announced she was pregnant. As for Nellie, she had left the village rather abruptly, with no explanation. And it was only years later, when she returned with a young boy called Christopher that Billy Diamond discovered he had a son he had never known. Nellie had said nothing when she left, and said nothing when she returned so much later with the child, who was eventually told that he was the son of the young chief who had gone on to become grand chief of the James Bay Crees.

In August, Elizabeth gave birth to a healthy baby girl the parents decided to name Lorraine. And on October 23, 1970, Billy Diamond and Elizabeth Hester were married in the Anglican church down by the riverbank. Billy, his thin frame wrapped in a densely striped suit, wore a store-bought and hastily shipped rose in his lapel, the signature of the politician he most admired at the time: Pierre Trudeau. Elizabeth, her long black hair sparking in the sun that broke through, clutched her tapered wedding gown in the breeze coming in off the water. They posed for pictures on the bank of the Rupert, the black water swirling out toward James Bay, Malcolm and Hilda Diamond standing at the end of the line as if their romance was just underway itself. Billy was twenty-one years old, Elizabeth seventeen, Lorraine into her third month.

Billy Diamond now had a family, and being chief, he was one of the few men in the village who had a job apart from what could be made through trapping. Still, it was in its own way a job with as much unpredictability as would be found by those who hunted and trapped every day in the bush. The paperwork was the easy part, for being chief also meant being the one who would be called first to break up fights, deal with the drunks and mediate domestic disputes. As chief of Rupert House, Billy Diamond would be the one to dive off the end of the docks into the icy Rupert to save a young girl whose brakes had failed on her bicycle. He would be called upon when Solomon, down along the river, stopped taking his medication and began sitting on his steps, loading and polishing his rifles while his family cringed behind. The new chief would talk to Solomon until the nurse could get there with a hypodermic and enough tranquillizer to knock him out so they could lay him out on the floor, nail his clothes to the boards and wait for a southbound plane that would begin the long haul to the Montreal psychiatric hospital. Being chief also meant being the one who would meet the planes bringing back the dead from the southern hospitals. This was the hardest task, as it too often involved a young child on whom a hasty autopsy had been done, the body then simply stuffed in a plastic body bag, tagged and sent to the family—a traumatic shock to parents who would have received no word that matters had taken a turn for the worse in the hospital and had come down to the dock only because a parcel had come in tagged with their name.

For a young man so anxious for change, it was often a time of frustration. The actor who had called for an end to "the old ways" was now the chief who had to deal face-to-face with past beliefs that defied his own reasoning.

The arrival of the Nemaska families had resulted in resentment that often led to fistfights between the Nemaska Crees and the Rupert House locals who did not feel the young chief's sense of obligation to take them in. The fighting he could deal with, but the effects of a curse laid on a young Rupert House woman by a Nemaska elder was another matter. The elder had denounced the young woman for the debauched carrying-on of his sons and had publicly announced that she would pay for her crime against his family. A few days later, the woman went missing and was later found dead in the woods by a search party led by Malcolm Diamond. Chief Billy Diamond called in the police, who brought a coroner, and it was determined that the young Rupert House woman had merely wandered away, become disoriented, ill, and then had choked on her own vomit. The death was officially listed as "accidental," but accepted locally as the work of the spirits—a chilling reminder to a young chief who then laughed openly at the absurdity of the "old ways."

But he would discover that the new ways, the ways of the whites, also had their biting edge. As the new chief, he and Elizabeth found themselves on the guest list to have Christmas dinner at the priest's home, joining in with the educators, missionaries, nurses and whatever other whites happened to be in the village at that time of warmth and sharing. For Billy and Elizabeth Diamond, however, the experience was no celebration. "When they came to serve the meal," says Elizabeth, "we all went into the dining room where it was being set out. But everyone looked at us. 'Not here,' the priest said. 'Out there.' And he showed us out into another room where they had TV tables set up for the two Indians."

Revenge was sweet and prompt. When the Catholic mission began setting up a high fence to mark out its territory—the main line running right across centre field of the village's only ball diamond—the young chief used his earlier training as a bulldozer operator to fire up the band's old machine and knock down the new line of fenceposts.

On April 28, 1971, the alarm clock went off at three in the morning in the small room in Malcolm Diamond's shack shared by Billy, Elizabeth and their eight-month-old baby, Lorraine. The spring goose hunt was beginning. Malcolm and Hilda had already gone ahead to the camp, and Billy was planning to head out now to join the hunters. Elizabeth got up, leaving the baby asleep in their bed, made her husband breakfast and packed a lunch as he got out the shotgun, enough shells, a white polyp jacket for camouflage, hipwaders and a few extra decoys for the open water on the edge of the blind. They talked about the ice conditions—it had been slushy the day before, but during the night the temperature dropped well below freezing—and Elizabeth said how nice it would be to eat some fresh goose. "It looks like it's going to be a perfect day," she said as she saw him out the door.

And indeed it was. He headed out on the skidoo, onto the frozen bay in the dark and turned south to head down along the leeward side of MacLean Island, where the others had already set up the goose camp. He stopped periodically on the way, checking for the black flashes that indicated open water, listening for shifts in the ice. A warm wind was blowing from the south—perfect for the returning geese—and dawn was just now singeing red through the far edge of the dark cloud cover.

Malcolm Diamond was already at the blind. He had the decoys set out in a pattern that the blue goose would find far too inviting to pass, and he was full of hope. "*It's Annie's birthday!*" he shouted, and the geese were always plentiful on Billy's older sister's birthday. Philip, the crippled uncle, was also there, just as certain that this would be a particularly blessed hunt, and the three men sat and talked, waiting for the first distant *ka-ronk* that would tell them the geese were calling ahead, wondering.

Malcolm teased Billy about his first winter as chief, but the son could see that the father was proud, and Malcolm lectured yet again on the importance of helping these people who had no idea whatsoever as to how to deal with the whites from the south and went on to talk about whatever it was the whites would bring next to the Cree. It was an old lecture, and Billy only half-listened, thinking not of whites but of the blue geese that would come out of the south.

The sun rose large and orange, cutting through the dawn shadows and making the men wince as they stared into the wind that would bring the game. The first geese drew in cautiously from the southeast, almost directly out of the sun, and the men could not see well enough to shoot. Philip, however, lay on his back, calling back up through the cup of his hand—"*Ka-ronk! Ka-ronk! Kaaaa-ronkkk!*"—and the lead goose banked right, his big wings sighing as he came low over the blind, fluttered in mid-air and settled among the decoys, the entire chevron following close behind. The men rose and blasted as one, and the wings, still sighing, now pounded, but five pair less than the moment before. It was going to be a wonderful day.

When the sun finally set, Billy decided he would take Elizabeth a few of the fresh geese. They would celebrate tonight. Malcolm warned him to stick to the shore, that the ice could not be trusted when the sun had shone so brightly all day. Billy laughed and said goodbye to his father and uncle and started back toward the village. He passed another hunter and the two men stopped their machines to talk. The other man had not seen any geese.

"Maybe there will be a circle around my name this year," the hunter said, using the Cree style of describing an unsuccessful hunt.

"Well, there'll be no circle around mine," Billy laughed, pointing back to the pile of geese in the sled. "This may be my best year ever!"

Carrying the bounty, he hurried from the shore up to the shack, backing in the door still laughing, spilling the kill in front of Elizabeth so she could cheer.

But Elizabeth did not even look at the geese.

"You'd better turn on the radio," she said. "There's something about James Bay."

PART TWO

WATER

ᓂᐱ

Before the feast began, the flag was presented to Missabay, the newly elected chief, with words of advice suitable for the occasion. Missabay received it and made an eloquent speech, in which he extolled the manner in which the Indians had been treated by the government; advised the young men to listen well to what the white men had to say, and to follow their advice and not to exalt their own opinions above those of men who knew the world and had brought them such benefits. Missabay, who is blind, has great control over his band, and he is disposed to use his influence in the best interests of the Indians.

> Report of Duncan Campbell Scott,
> Indian Treaty Commissioner,
> to the Superintendent General of
> Indian Affairs,
> November 6, 1905

CHAPTER FIVE

THE PROJECT OF THE CENTURY

On April 30, 1971, Robert Bourassa bounded up onto the stage of the Quebec Colisée, the arena still chilled from a long but never boring hockey season in which Guy Lafleur, the darling of the hometown Remparts, had scored an astonishing 130 goals and then led his team on a brawl-filled but ultimately successful journey to the Memorial Cup, the prize reserved for the best junior team in the country.

Bourassa's winter, however, did not compare to Lafleur's. Elected just over a year earlier on the promise of a hundred thousand jobs, the thirty-seven-year-old premier had failed to deliver much more than a few patronage appointments to friends who already had work. Worse, he had come out of the 1970 October Crisis, with a crippling image as "ineffectual messenger boy" for Prime Minister Pierre Trudeau. During the Crisis a handful of Quebec *indépendantistes* had kidnapped a British diplomat, James Cross, murdered Pierre Laporte, Bourassa's labour minister and caused the federal government to invoke its highly controversial War Measures Act. With both the prime minister and Bourassa being Liberals, this October embrace—with Trudeau clearly assuming the superior position—was perceived as a potential kiss of death in a province that so often prides itself on its ability to dangle two jealous, and contradictory, suitors—the party running the province being the direct opposite of the party sent to Ottawa."

If Bourassa needed proof of how much his political stock had fallen, he had only to cast his eyes over an arena that could pack ten thousand screaming fans in for every game. There were only three thousand faces quietly looking back at the young premier, all loyal Liberals who had paid out five dollars apiece for the privilege of being the first to hear what the young premier intended to do to turn party fortunes around. Clearly, their expectations were not high: in the moments before the young premier had bounded up onto the stage, organizers had tried to whip the crowd into a "Bou-raa-sssaa!" chant, but the people had remained in their seats, silently waiting to judge.

"The world," Robert Bourassa began, his rising voice bouncing like a puck around the boards, "begins tomorrow!"

He had a plan, a plan so grand he believed it would be looked upon by the world as the "Project of the Century." Three huge linked video screens told the story of the untapped electrical resources of James Bay, dams forming magically to music that thundered about the arena and drowned out the commentator's sonorous voice. But Robert Bourassa, his confidence rising as he followed through, spelled out the only point that truly mattered: this $6 billion project would create 125,000 jobs.

"James Bay is the key to the economic and social progress of Quebec," he told the now-stirring faithful, "the key to the political stability of Quebec, the key to the future of Quebec."

That Hydro-Québec would be tied to the national aspirations of Quebec was entirely natural, for the public utility had symbolized the *"maître chez nous"* ("masters in our own house") ethic since 1962, when Premier Jean Lesage's ambitious young natural resources minister, René Lévesque, had led the provincial takeover of the then privately owned electrical companies. Under Lévesque's direction, the Quebec government had formed a Crown corporation that instantly became the largest Quebec company managed by French Canadians, with French the language of everyday operation.

Bourassa was not the first Quebec politician to dream of harnessing the power of James Bay. Four years earlier, in 1967, Premier Daniel Johnson had castigated Hydro-Québec officials for their lack of interest in James Bay, an interest he himself had nurtured since the 1950s when he was minister for hydraulic resources in the Union Nationale government of Maurice Duplessis. The basic plan that Bourassa had announced—apart from the dramatic promise of 125,000 jobs—had actually been put together in 1964 by the Liberal ministry of Lévesque in the days when he was still a closet *indépendantiste*. And the original idea that hydroelectric projects might one day be established so far north went back to the 1930s, when a private company had gone so far as to do some quiet preliminary survey work in the area.

But the Crees who hunted and trapped along the very rivers the three giant screens said would be blocked off and flooded had neither seen the early surveyors nor heard of the later plans. They didn't even know about electricity—let alone Hydro-Québec. In fact, they had barely managed to coin a word for this creature called "electricity," using a phrase—"*nimischiiuskutaau*"—which, translated literally, means "the fire of thunder."

They had no idea, on that late April night when Robert Bourassa finally moved the three thousand loyalists to their feet, just how soon the early claps of this *nimischiiuskutaau* would pull them directly into the gathering storm itself.

But the Crees had more to discover than the plans that danced in the mind of the young premier. They had also been ignorant, for the most part, of the changes that were taking place among other Indians in the province. Only two months before the premier's announcement, a provincial commission that had been set up five years earlier to examine land disputes between Quebec and Newfoundland released a report castigating the province for failing to come to terms with its aboriginal peoples. Quebec was urged to take over responsibilities that had previously fallen to Ottawa. It was recommended that the reserve system be abolished and that Indians and Inuit be given proper political representation in Quebec's National Assembly.

The report of the Dorion Commission was basically a repeat of the argument made more than a year earlier in Jean Chrétien's controversial White Paper on Indian Affairs, a paper that had thrown Native organizations throughout the country into such a panic that Chrétien was forced to shelve the policy suggestions and rethink his approach. Indians across Canada agreed that the system was severely flawed and that it did nothing but harm, yet they clearly preferred the despised system of Ottawa having total control to being thrown to the mercy of provincial governments that had historically shown Indians little but animosity.

The Indians of Quebec Association had been the most vocal about any shift toward provincial control of Native affairs. A 1969 land claim by the IQA that Indians owned 85 percent of the territory of Quebec and might be willing to settle for $5 billion had been met in Quebec City first by laughter and then by a blunt "No." Quebec's attitude toward Natives had, in fact, never progressed much beyond that of Captain Joseph-Elzéar Bernier, who in the early part of this century explored several of the Arctic islands and laid claim to them for England. "I first took possession of Baffin Island in the presence of several Eskimos," Bernier told the Empire Club in 1926. "After firing 19 shots, I instructed an Eskimo to fire the 20th, telling him he was now a Canadian."

Quebec had expanded northward twice since Confederation, in 1898 and 1912, taking over tracts of land each time that were far larger than other complete provinces. The government, however, had done nothing whatsoever to come to terms with the Native populations living there, despite urgings and indeed specific demands by the federal government that had engineered the expansions. In 1939 the province had even unsuccessfully petitioned the Supreme Court of Canada to have Inuit declared "Indians" within the meaning of the Canadian constitution. This would mean they would become Ottawa's responsibility rather than Quebec City's.

When Robert Bourassa came to power, Quebec's Indians did not even have the right to vote in provincial elections, unlike Indians in other provinces. Quebec's approach had not progressed much beyond that of a country which, less than a century earlier, had held a parliamentary debate over what was the minimum amount of food an Indian might be fed to ward off starvation. "They are simply living on the benevolence and charity of the Canadian Parliament," Prime Minister John A. Macdonald had told the House of Commons, "and, as the old adage says, beggars should not be choosers."

The Canadian response to its aboriginal people has roots so strong that Macdonald's attitude can be viewed as neither curious nor vindictive. Perhaps it could even be termed enlightened compared to that of his governing predecessors. In 1763, the commander-in-chief of British North America, Jeffrey Amherst, advised his successor "to infect the Indians with sheets upon which smallpox patients have been lying, or by any other means which may serve to exterminate this accursed race." By 1830, Sir George Murray, secretary of state in the British government, had come to the conclusion that Indians were "an irreclaimable race ... inconvenient neighbors whom it was desirable ultimately wholly to remove." Lord Sydenham, the governor of the colony that would become Canada, wrote in the 1840s that the Indian "does not become a good settler, he does not become an agriculturalist or a mechanic. He does become a drunkard and a debauchee, and his females and family follow the same course. He occupies valuable land, unprofitably to himself and injuriously to the country. He gives infinite trouble to the government, and adds nothing either to the wealth, the industry, or the defence of the province."

After Sydenham's tenure was over, legislation was passed permitting certain Indians to "fly up" or be promoted to the position of whites. In order to do so, they would, of course, have to renounce their own people. They would also need to be over twenty-one, "sufficiently advanced in the elementary branches of education, of good moral character, free of debt," and able to speak either English or French well. And if they met all these requirements and if a government official and a missionary were to examine them and determine no trickery was at work, they would be allotted fifty acres somewhere and be "no longer deemed an Indian." The idea that Indians were somehow less than human was even formally voted on and passed into law, section 12 of the Indian Act of 1880 cautioning that "the term person means an individual other than an Indian."

Throughout Canada's brief history, Indians were seen to be but awkward footnotes. They were forbidden by law to drink, gamble, dance or play pool. They had no vote in a Parliament that, only forty years before Bourassa's announcement, had seen fit to pass a law making it an offence for anyone, Indian or non-Indian, to raise money for the purpose of arguing Native rights. So there was little wonder that when the young premier had put the final touches to the speech he would deliver that night, no one in his entire government had even considered for a moment that there was an obligation—even if only out of politeness—to let the Crees know what the government had in mind for their land and rivers.

The Crees of James Bay were simply forgotten people. Though anthropologists believed they had hunted and trapped along the coastal rivers for more than five thousand years, not once in those five thousand years had they ever held so much as a meeting. There was no organization apart from the hunting groups, no concept at all of an overall Cree leader.

Though they spoke much the same Algonkian language as the Plains Cree of the western Prairies, the James Bay Cree had no contact, no awareness even of other histories. There had been no Almighty Voice in the history of the Swampy Cree of James Bay as there was in the past of their Prairie cousins. Almighty Voice, born in 1874 at an Indian settlement near Duck Lake in what would become the province of Saskatchewan, had arrived during a time of frightening change to the Plains Cree, a time when the buffalo had vanished and the railways were coming, when his people were being rounded up and placed on reserves. As a two-year-old toddler, Almighty Voice, son of Sounding Sky and Spotted Calf was herded into the One Arrow reserve, along with all the other Plains Crees of Duck Lake. The story of Almighty Voice is well known, if often inaccurately told. The toughest and probably most accurate portrayal appears in Pierre Berton's *The Wild Frontier*, and describes an angry young man who floundered from one small error—the stealing of a settler's cow—to grave disaster: the murder of Sergeant Colin Campbell Colebrook of the Mounted Police.

The killing had occurred in the aftermath of the Riel uprisings, and it was immediately noted by government officials in the West that, since the murder, "a different manner [was] to be noticed in many of the Indians, one of independence and defiance, which was not noticeable formerly." With such a threat in the wind, the Mounties moved dramatically. Almighty Voice and his two teenaged pals were hunted down and surrounded by one hundred armed men and two cannon while settlers and other Crees came to watch, among them Spotted Calf, who sang for her son. When the shooting was done and the last of fifty shells had landed in the bluff where the Indian youths made their last stand, three Mounties, a white civilian and three Indians—one of them thirteen years old—were dead. It was perhaps the most destructive confrontation between Natives and governmental authority in Canadian history.

When Almighty Voice committed his first murder and flashed briefly into the history of the Plains Cree, he was twenty-one years old, the same age as Billy Diamond when he was elected chief of the Rupert House Crees of James Bay. The difference was that when Billy Diamond was first confronted with an authority with which he could not possibly agree, he chose not to shoot and run. When the short news item about James Bay came on the radio that spring day in 1971, Chief Billy Diamond knew he would have to do something, but he wasn't sure what. All he could think about was what would happen to his village once they dammed the river.

"You're awfully quiet," Elizabeth called from the kitchen, where she was beginning to clean the geese. He said nothing.

"What does it mean?" she asked as he came into the kitchen, the taste for the first goose of spring suddenly gone. He didn't know.

"Won't it mean jobs?" she asked.

"Not for our people," he said.

"Maybe we'll get a road," she said, smiling.

"Do we need a road?" he asked, not smiling.

The first call Chief Billy Diamond of Rupert House made was to Chief Robert Kanatewat of Fort George. It was a short call, complicated as always by the necessary "rogers" and "overs" that slowed up all conversations by radio telephone, but very little needed to be said. Chief Robert Kanatewat had also heard, and Chief Robert Kanatewat was even less taken with the idea of plugged up rivers than was Chief Billy Diamond.

Robert Kanatewat was then thirty-six years old. Over the years he had changed from a child who believed that whites were "naturally and rightfully dominant" into a man who believed Indians deserved the same respect as all other human beings. Kanatewat had been born in the James Bay bush to simple, extremely poor trappers who had never married. His mother had been a partially crippled woman from the village of Eastmain and his father an independent loner of a man from Fort George. When he was six, his father had died mysteriously—cursed, it was said, by an enemy from Eastmain. And when Robert was eleven, he lost his mother as well when she died at a sanitarium in Hamilton, Ontario, where she had been sent two years earlier.

"I don't think I would be what I am today if I had not lost my parents like that," he said many years later when he had himself become a grandparent. "I was on my own from such an early age, passed around from family to family, whoever could support me. It made me aggressive and it made me want to fight for the rights of others when I had a chance."

Powerfully built and strikingly handsome, Kanatewat had been elected chief of the Fort George Crees in 1967, and had forged the James Bay Crees' initial contacts with the southern-based Indians of

Quebec Association. Because of this, he had formed a deep friendship with Malcolm Diamond, the old chief of Rupert House, who passed on to the younger Fort George chief a vision of the future that would involve a fight far rougher than anything they had so far imagined. "You cannot describe the way this man saw," Kanatewat says of the old Rupert House chief. "How did he understand? I just don't know, but he saw it coming."

When the call came from the new chief of Rupert House—the son Malcolm Diamond had sent away so he might come back and help when the fight began—Robert Kanatewat was ready.

The second call Billy Diamond made was to his old school friend, Ted Moses. Moses could not believe the story Diamond was passing on about the rivers. It sounded like a practical joke. "I didn't think it was possible to do something like that," he says. "It would take a miracle to do such a thing." But far more than the magnitude of it all, Ted Moses was struck by the insensitivity. His own father, Willie, had buried a child one late fall on the banks of one of the rivers the premier was now saying would be flooded over, never to be travelled again. And Bourassa hadn't even shown the decency to let them know.

All across the northern brow of Quebec there were similar shocks. Philip Awashish—who had gone briefly to Montreal's McGill University after starring in *Arrow to the Moon* and then dropped out to return to his home in Mistassini—had just come down forty miles of mud and ruts to the mining town of Chibougamau the week of the Bourassa announcement, and only learned about it when he picked up a day-old Montreal *Star*, wondering if Guy Lafleur or his arch rival, Marcel Dionne of the St Catharines team, was going to be the first pick in the National Hockey League draft. Bourassa's scheme was all over the front page and disturbingly detailed inside. The Awashish family had hunted and fished and trapped along the headwaters of the Rupert River forever, he had always believed, and now it seemed forever was coming to an end: seven power stations would be built along the Rupert alone.

Awashish tore off the front page of the paper and carefully folded it to take it back up the forty miles of muck road to the village. He wondered if his old friends from the Soo—Billy up in Rupert, Ted in Eastmain—had heard, and what they thought could be done, if anything.

Several hundred miles still farther north, beyond the swamps and north of the tree line, Charlie Watt was walking into the post office at George River when he noticed other Inuit gathered about a bulletin board, talking excitedly. He went over, pushed through and read for himself about the colossal scheme to harness the rivers of James Bay. There were also plans for the waters running off the Ungava Peninsula, the home of the Inuit that Quebec had tried to rid itself of in 1929.

At the time of Robert Bourassa's announcement, Charlie Watt was twenty-five, married with three children, an angry young Inuk who had just taken the extraordinary step of walking out of a promising government job to set up a political organization he was calling the Northern Quebec Inuit Association. He read the announcement twice, and then called over the young man who had walked into the post office with him, Zebedee Nungak.

"*This*," Watt told his friend, "this is the opportunity we've been waiting for."

Watt had been looking for a fight since he left home at fourteen, the first Inuk sent off across Hudson Bay and farther west to Yellowknife for schooling. In the territorial schools he had picked up English just as Billy Diamond and Ted Moses and Philip Awashish had learned it in the residential school at Moose Factory and Robert Kanatewat had picked it up around the docks of Fort George. From Yellowknife he had gone on to Kingston, Ontario, for more schooling, and eventually ended up going to military school. Fluent in English and looking more European than Inuit, Charlie Watt could have made a career out of government work. He trained briefly in Ottawa and eventually began working for the Department of Indian and Northern Affairs, where he soon found he had free access to the interdepartmental mailroom and began, out of curiosity at first, reading any and all letters that originated in the Far North.

"I found one letter from the administrator up there," Watt, who is now a Canadian senator, remembers of this time, "and it was to the deputy minister. I couldn't believe what I was reading: 'The best thing for the Government of Canada to do to these Inuit is to establish one big apartment building in southern Ontario and move them all down there.'"

After two frustrating years, Watt left Ottawa and ended up on Baffin Island in the Canadian Arctic, looking after cargo for the United States Air Force, which was involved in work along the Distant Early Warning (DEW) Line. And it was here that he had an experience that would set in motion the anger that would eventually cause him to join forces with the James Bay Cree against the governments of Quebec and Canada.

"I was at the canteen one night with two friends," Watt remembers, "two guys from Nova Scotia, and after a few beer I said I knew of a party in one of the Eskimo homes. This guy I'd been to school with in Yellowknife.

"I'd never told anyone I was an Eskimo. Not because I was ashamed or anything—I just didn't want to have to translate if it got out that I knew the language. So I never said anything. Anyway, we had a few more beer, went to the party, and got caught. You're not supposed to fraternize with the 'Natives,' you see, and there was this argument and the RCMP came and I was reported.

"Next morning I got hell. The super hammered me. He said I was not to mix with the Native people, not under any circumstances. So I asked him, 'Why the fuck do I have to stay away from my *own* people?' "

Soon he was back home in Fort Chimo, frantically working to set up a political association with a single purpose in mind: "To get rid of the outsiders." He had no other work and spent the family savings before he was able to wring a $9,000 grant out of the government. He got the money, but not before an Indian Affairs official in Ottawa warned Watt: "Speaking out is not good. The only one who can speak for the Inuit people is the Bishop of the Arctic." The Bishop, of course, was the prime example of the outsiders he intended to banish from the North.

Night after night Watt would stay up till the personal hours of the morning, just thinking and walking about the living room of his tiny home in Fort Chimo. After some months both he and the rug were worn, and his wife became frazzled. He could not sleep, he now says, he was so "pissed off"—but wasn't sure at what—and then, apparently out of nowhere, came Robert Bourassa's "Project of the Century."

The James Bay Hydro Project was not a threat to Charlie Watt. It was a target. He finally had somewhere to aim his fury. But who, he wondered, could he contact among the Crees? He knew no one.

Back down below the tree line, Philip Awashish had taken the front page of the paper he had picked up in Chibougamau and included it in a short letter to his old school chum, Billy Diamond. *I'm sure you've heard about this thing,* Philip wrote. *Do you think there is any way we could bring together the Cree chiefs and talk about it?*

Awashish's instincts had been right. Something needed to be done and who better than Billy Diamond to help organize? Already, and almost by accident, Diamond was emerging as the spokesman for the James Bay Crees, who had neither an organization nor an obvious leader. The opportunity had simply dropped from the sky when a chartered helicopter came in low over the mouth of the Rupert and settled on a flat surface back of the shacks. Inside the helicopter was James Stewart, a reporter with the Montreal *Star*, and he stepped out to receive the hand of a skinny young man who looked like a teenager but claimed to be chief. It was Billy Diamond's first encounter with the press, and though he was only twenty-one, it seemed he understood both the medium and the message as well as Pierre Trudeau or Marshall McLuhan. The young chief had a rough sense of the political history of his land, and told Stewart of Quebec's failure to follow through with the legal promises of the 1912 territorial extension and the implications of the recent Dorion Commission report. "Hydro-Québec never discussed this with me or with any other Indian," Chief Billy Diamond told the reporter. "They just came in and are taking away land that belongs to us."

While Stewart scribbled notes, Diamond squatted in the yard, smoothed the red dirt with his hand and then laid down three sticks. "This is the Nottaway River," he told Stewart, pointing to one of the sticks. "Here's the Broadback River and this is the Rupert River. Over here twenty families have traplines. What's going to happen when these rivers are diverted? This is Nemaska—250 Indians moved out of there because it's going to be flooded. Here's the Nottaway. The geese follow the Nottaway. What's going to happen to the geese when the Nottaway is diverted?"

Carefully, he jabbed another stick into the ground at the heel of the third lying there. "That's Rupert House," he said, rising, then savagely kicking the jabbed stick away, "No more Rupert House. Just a swamp, *a slum at the end of a booze road*!"

CHAPTER SIX

JOANNE: FOUR MONTHS, FOUR DAYS

When Philip Awashish came back to Mistassini with the newspaper story of Bourassa's announcement, the old people of the village would hear nothing about it, laughing at the very suggestion that their land would disappear forever under the flooding. But Smally Petawabano listened and wanted to know more.

Petawabano had been chief of Mistassini since 1964, and could read the newspaper himself, thanks to the two years he had spent away at school in northern Ontario. The first white man Petawabano ever saw as a child had terrified him—the skin so sickly, the hair falling out—but "Smally" had grown into a hulking Cree who now frightened others, a man renowned for his ability to pull a two-thousand-pound load on a sled and, fortunately, also for his patient gentleness. Petawabano had a good relationship with the anthropologists from Montreal's McGill University and McMaster University of Hamilton, Ontario, scientists who had become entranced with the uniqueness of the Cree hunting society, and his friendships helped him gain some funding from the Arctic Institute of North America for travel. Contact was also made with Max Gros-Louis, one of the dynamic leaders of the Indians of Quebec Association. And so, with institutional funding and IQA organizational skills, the first formal meeting in James Bay Cree history was scheduled for June 28, 1971.

They met in the one-room schoolhouse. Chief Robert Kanatewat came down from Fort George. Chief Billy Diamond came from Rupert House. Chief Fred Blackned was there from Paint Hills, Chief Peter Gull from Waswanipi, Chief Bertie Wapachee from what was left of Nemaska, and Chief Matthew Shanush came from Eastmain, where he was renowned for flying the flag of Quebec upside down in front of his band office. Philip Awashish was already there. Ted Moses remained in Eastmain, wishing he—not two older men from the village—had been invited. Charlie Watt was in Fort Chimo, unaware that the meeting had been called. But Malcolm Diamond was there, pounding his fist and shouting in Cree. Each chief had been asked to bring a second, and while some elected for younger men who could translate for them, Chief Billy Diamond had considered no other but his own father.

"I wanted the best advice I could get," Billy Diamond says. Yet sweet as it was, listening to Malcolm Diamond speak about the treasures of their land, this was not the highlight of the gathering for the young chief: "Finally, I was sitting side by side and working with the chief who had missed his plane and ordered the plane back—Robert Kanatewat."

When they first gathered, Smally Petawabano did the introductions and allowed each chief a few moments to speak. Billy Diamond was the last to stand. A small buzz went through the schoolroom as they noticed his age and the older trappers realized that this was the son of the tough-talking Rupert House trapper Malcolm Diamond. Billy was nervous, and spoke mostly in Cree. "This is our land," he said. "No one has obtained surrender from us. We never lost it in war. We never lost it in battle. We never signed a treaty. No one has taken it, and we're not allowed to let anyone take it from us."

Max Gros-Louis had brought along the lawyer for the Indians of Quebec Association—Jacques Beaudoin, a jolly, flamboyant young lawyer with a love of the good life. And in halting English, Beaudoin had outlined the legal aspects of Indian rights in Quebec, something of which most of the Crees gathered in the schoolhouse had never heard before.

They talked for three days, gradually moving from Cree into English as minor differences in dialect periodically confused them, and also because Max Gros-Louis of the IQA was moving ever nearer the centre, with the Crees' blessing. Gros-Louis, after all, knew the enemy best. He was keen to have the Crees enter into a treaty of solidarity with the rest of the province's Natives, and the lawyer, Beaudoin, argued that since the Crees had never surrendered their land, they should consider it a reserve under federal jurisdiction, which meant they could then ask the minister of Indian affairs in Ottawa to block the provincial project.

The Crees, however, did not even have a word for "reserve," and so it was impossible to explain such a concept to the older men like Malcolm Diamond, who understood not a word of the English exchanges. Besides, Philip Awashish stood in the crowd to point out that both levels of government were Liberal, and given the delicacy of the current Canadian politic, Ottawa was unlikely to take a tough stance against Quebec over an issue that affected only a few thousand Indians. On and on the debate raged while the older Crees shifted restlessly in school desks made for children half their size, understanding little of what was said. The significance, however, was far less in what words were sailing through the air than the fact that the Crees were finally together.

"We were in shock," remembers Billy Diamond. "There had been no consultation, nothing. This was our land. We believed this land had been created for us. We felt we had a responsibility to protect it, to make sure no one harmed it. Did we get riled up! The more we talked, the more we realized that what all Crees had in common was their reliance on the land. And we knew that if the land was destroyed, the animals would be destroyed—and if you killed the animals, you would kill the Crees.

"What this was, was a war council. Never before had there been a Cree meeting. Never before had there been a need for a full Cree council. But this was a war council, and what we declared was that we were totally against the James Bay Project. We demanded that they desist and withdraw."

In the end, the Crees elected to follow a portion of the advice of Jacques Beaudoin, and they drafted a clumsy resolution which all present signed. It was addressed to "The Minister of Indian Affairs" and read:

> "We, the representatives of the Cree bands that will be affected by the James Bay hydro project or any other project, oppose to these projects because we believe that only the beavers had the right to build dams in our territory, and we request the Minister of Indian Affairs Northern Development, to use his legal jurisdiction to stop any attempt of intrusion of our

rightful owned territory by the government of province of Quebec, or any other authority. And we have signed this document on the first day of July, 1971."

Max Gros-Louis returned to Quebec City with the resolution. He handed it to a secretary saying it should be sent immediately to Indian Affairs Minister Chrétien in Ottawa. For some reason, however, the resolution was filed away and never sent. Jean Chrétien never received it.

Thirteen days after the Mistassini meeting broke up, Premier Robert Bourassa used his Liberal majority in the National Assembly to pass Bill 50, thereby creating the James Bay Development Corporation. Under the terms of the bill, the Crown corporation would have absolute responsibility for the creation of the enormous hydroelectric project the premier had announced nearly three months earlier.

It was a controversial move. The opposition could hardly argue that development was wrong and jobs unnecessary, but they did react with outrage against Bourassa's scheme to place a fifth of the surface area of this huge Canadian province under the board of a five-man government. Furthermore, they argued that Hydro-Québec itself was certainly capable of managing such a project. What Bourassa was doing, they claimed, was setting up "a parallel government" for the North which he could control through patronage.

The parliamentary summer break had already been delayed by two weeks over this legislation. And lack of air conditioning in the National Assembly meant that already-short fuses burned even faster. Two members locked hands in a scuffle at one point, one yelling to the other that he intended to "smash [him] in the mouth." A Liberal backbencher made threatening gestures toward Parti Québécois House Leader Robert Burns. But in the end, the government majority prevailed, and on July 14, 1971, Bill 50 passed third reading and became law. A delighted Robert Bourassa declared it a perfect "present" for his thirty-eighth birthday.

Most curious was the silence in Ottawa. Though Jean Chrétien had never received the Mistassini resolution, he was acutely aware of Bourassa's plans. Chrétien and his deputy-minister, John Ciaccia, had discussed the Cree situation at length, and knew precisely what political risks were involved in any battle that might pit the federal Liberals against the provincial Liberals. An open fight was to be avoided at all costs. Ciaccia—an Italian immigrant who had become a wealthy Montreal lawyer before joining Indian Affairs—knew the possibilities. Northern Quebec had not so long ago been federal territory, handed over to Canada by the Hudson's Bay Company in 1871 and then in stages to Quebec, with clear instructions to the province that it must negotiate treaties in the same way that Canada had in other areas, and just as Duncan Campbell Scott had done in 1905 along the west side of the saltwater bay. In Ciaccia's opinion, the aboriginal claims of the Cree Indians of the east coast were still valid, and he could foresee that the Indians might call upon Canada to revoke the Boundaries Extension Acts of 1898 and 1912 and return the land to the Natives. But such an action was unthinkable in 1971, with Pierre Trudeau determined to give Canada its own constitution and the relationship between the two key players, Ottawa and Quebec, delicate at best since the October Crisis.

Consideration also had to be given to the sudden popularity of Bourassa's "Project of the Century." Quebeckers—the James Bay Crees and a few sympathisers excepted—were in full agreement with the sentiments expressed in the first releases of Bourassa's James Bay Development Corporation: "Objectively, unemotionally, one can state that the development of James Bay will set Quebec on a new road to progress. It is an undertaking which once again will furnish tangible proof of Quebec's vitality and spirit of enterprise, for the development of James Bay is the most daring project in Quebec's history. James Bay is the land of tomorrow." But all was not objective, and the situation was certainly not without strong emotion. Early on, ecology groups began protesting in the streets of Montreal, and to appease them a federal-provincial task force on James Bay ecology was set up under McGill anthropologist Richard Salisbury. The task force was asked to report on where the project might best be built: at the north or the south end of the James Bay coast.

At the end of July several of the James Bay chiefs went to Quebec City, where the Indians of Quebec Association called a press conference to denounce the project. Saying that they faced "extermination" if the "Project of the Century" went ahead, the seven thousand Crees of James Bay would be calling upon both Prime Minister Pierre Trudeau and his minister of Indian affairs,

Jean Chrétien, "to meet [their] obligation as protector of Indian rights and do all in [their] power to put an immediate stop to this project."

While the other leaders held fast to the familiar rhetoric that they would be "massacred" and that this amounted to "extermination," the surprise star of the press conference was the funny young chief from Rupert House. Billy Diamond joked about "those damn dams" and, in a sadly serious voice, told the assembled press why he had gone home to a different life. "I went to school for thirteen years," he said, "and I'd had enough. I felt like I'd been processed through a factory. I felt like canned fruit. I didn't want to be that, so I returned home to the life I knew. When this hydro project tears up our land, will our children and our grandchildren be able to go back like I did?"

Gradually, other complainants came forward, often from opposite fields. Eric Kierans and Jacques Parizeau, both economists but the former a fervent nationalist and the latter a provincial separatist, both attacked the scheme as financial madness. The Sierra Club, a leading international ecology group, said it was sending a team to the Rupert River and began hinting that such massive flooding might cause winters in eastern Canada to become considerably longer. Other ecologists were warning that the breeding grounds of the blue, snow and Canada geese would be severely threatened. In the early stages, no one spoke for the Crees but the Crees themselves, though the Crees also bred in this distant territory and were well accustomed to long, miserable winters.

Billy Diamond used the opportunity of being in Quebec City to meet with another of the IQA lawyers, James O'Reilly. O'Reilly, a wiry little man with fiercely independent hair and the distracted, obsessive air of a theologian wrestling with the meaning of life, had just come under fire in the IQA for his links with the exclusive Montreal law firm that had drafted Bill 50. O'Reilly himself had been involved—inserting the only protective clause the Indians enjoyed, he argued—and there had been calls for his head. Get out of your conflict-of-interest situation, Diamond told O'Reilly, and come and help the Crees. O'Reilly, fascinated by the legal case the Crees offered, agreed that he should and said that he would.

The young Rupert House chief was quickly moving out in front of the other Cree leaders. He arranged with the IQA to be taken on as a researcher working exclusively on the Crees' problem with the James Bay Project, and the association obtained a grant from Indian Affairs that led to the hiring of Philip Awashish, as well.

The two friends went to work fighting the project full time in January 1972.

Nearly nine months after the initial announcement, the James Bay Development Corporation finally agreed to meet with the Crees and show them the detailed plans they had for the project. Finally aware of the true scope of Bourassa's dream and equipped with maps, Billy Diamond and Philip Awashish set out to visit the eight Cree villages and explain in detail. But they did not go alone. Increasingly media wise, they decided to approach certain journalists to accompany them, writers like the Montreal *Star*'s feature writer Boyce Richardson, a transplanted New Zealander with a great empathy for Canadian Indians, and a young cartoonist by the name of Terry Mosher, whose caricatures under the "Aislin" signature were beginning to set the standard in Canadian political satire. To finance the journey they turned, ironically, to the James Bay Development Corporation itself, and the corporation, anxious to establish itself as a good corporate citizen, agreed to fund a journey north.

"Our plan was to generate the fighting instinct," remembers Diamond. "Some of the trappers would be coming off the lines when we got there and we planned to show them exactly what the white man was planning to do with their land. Trappers can't read or write, but they do know a map, and we blew up maps so we could show them where their land would be flooded. This was destroying a way of life—and right away the issue caught the imagination of the people." It was a remarkable tour, complete with daily reports in the Montreal *Star*, the Montreal *Gazette*, *Le Soleil* and on CBC and Radio-Canada. The Paris newspaper, *Le Monde*, interviewed Max Gros-Louis and ran a story tying the Quebec Indians to the Ibos in Nigeria and the Bengalese of Bangladesh, chastising the government for holding to the attitude that *"le problème Indien est un mythe."* Ralph Nader, then at the height of his fame as a fighter for the American underdog, also spoke out in support of the Crees.

The most dramatic moment came, appropriately enough, at Rupert House, where Chief Billy Diamond was the first to address his people. "Throughout the country the Indian people have been the social casualties of development projects," the young chief said. "I have seen it out in the West, towns booming, but the Indians poor, gone in prostitution and booze." The fact that he had not yet travelled out West did not faze him.

Next to speak was old Malcolm Diamond. He rose and began nearly to shout in Cree, using the long, dramatic, evocative structure Crees favour for speeches. During the pauses for translation, he would stare hard at the reporters to make sure they understood the intensity as well as the meaning. He told of the situation in Ontario, and how Ontario Hydro had continually ignored the Indians there. He reminded them of the sorry conditions of the Crees on the other side of the Bay who had signed those pitiful treaties back in his grandfather's day when the writer-bureaucrat, Duncan Campbell Scott, came paddling up with his security guards and cache of one- and two-dollar bills. Soon the trappers were punching the air with their fists, furious that such a thing could happen without anyone coming to them to find out why it should not.

They turned then to the task force report on the ecology of the area. A 300-page draft had concluded that less damage would be done if the project was moved farther north than if it remained in the area of the Nottaway, Broadback and Rupert rivers. That version had been squeezed to 55 pages and a portion of this had in turn been translated into Cree. The Cree version had arrived in the village just before the meeting. It was 17 pages long. Annie Diamond took one of the orange brochures and began to read it. But the translation was so poor that Annie, a professional interpreter, could barely work through the first paragraph.

"She doesn't understand it!" Billy Diamond called out. "Does anybody understand it?"

"No!" they called out as one.

"What shall we do with this report?" their young chief asked, egging them on. "It's translated into Cree and we cannot even understand it."

"Burn it!" shouted Malcolm Whiskeychan, sitting in the front row.

"*Yes! Burn it!*" they shouted. The air was filled with orange brochures flying toward the laughing young chief at the front, who was busy gathering them up in his arms.

Out to the front of the J. S. C. Watt Memorial Longhouse they ran with the brochures. A man who had a lighter sprinkled some fluid over the brochures, then put the flame to them while all the Crees in the village stood around cheering and all the reporters in the village stood scribbling in their notebooks.

"The government had underestimated the resistance of the Cree," Diamond says. "With those daily reports coming back from the North, it was obvious that the Crees were beating the war drums.

We had to beat them loud, and we used the media to make certain they were heard."

Chief Billy Diamond had become so wrapped up in the fight that it barely registered with him that Elizabeth was now showing heavily, pregnant for the second time. She said the baby would come before summer and begged that he come back. She was having trouble caring for Lorraine on her own, and the pregnancy was difficult at times. Billy told her not to worry, that he would be back long before the birth, back to stay. He promised—but it was the first of many he would fail to keep.

On April 18, 1972, the Cree chiefs gathered at Fort George to discuss the progress of the fight. The tour had been a complete success. The Cree people had given the chiefs an absolute mandate to do what they wished. There was talk of a court case, though much of the talk was cautious. The Nishgas of British Columbia were currently having their huge land claim judged by the Supreme Court of Canada, and Native leaders everywhere were worried that this landmark case, *Calder* vs. *The Queen*, would go against the Nishgas and, potentially, spell an end to all talk of aboriginal land claims in Canada.

Chief Matthew Shanush of Eastmain proposed the strategy of taking the James Bay Development Corporation to court, but not for a lands claim. Instead, he thought, if they threw some weak ammunition at the corporation, the Crees would then get some sense of how the government was going to react, and they could progress from there. James O'Reilly, who was still considering leaving his legal firm and striking out on his own, was on hand and immediately came up with a number of ways in which the Crees might go after the corporation using federal legislation. The best bet, he believed, would be to try to have the provincial corporation judged under laws relating to navigable federal waters and migratory birds. Before they could carry the meeting much further, however, there was a disruption at the door. Two Inuit men had arrived and were asking if they might come in.

Charlie Watt had heard about the Fort George meeting while visiting Great Whale, a coastal settlement more to the north that was part Inuit, part Cree and might be affected by the Quebec government's flooding plans. With Zebedee Nungak, Watt had come ahead, uninvited, only to be met by an immediate motion put forward by Max Gros-Louis of the Indians of Quebec Association that they be kicked out of the meeting. The two visitors, after all, were neither Indian nor members of the provincial association. "But Billy Diamond fought for us," says Watt. "We waited outside while they had a meeting and then Billy came out and brought us back."

"I knew that bringing the Inuit in with the Cree would only strengthen the case of both," says Diamond, "particularly in light of the 1912 act to extend the Quebec boundaries." Diamond was far more advanced in the legal arguments than Watt. While James O'Reilly discussed the options before them—using environmental laws for a court case or, more risky, going before a judge to ask for an interlocutory injunction that would force the James Bay Development Corporation to stop work on the project until the Native claims had been properly heard—Charlie Watt and Zebedee Nungak sat in a far corner and listened with fascination. "I didn't even know the meaning of 'interlocutory injunction,'" Watt says. "I had to ask the lawyers what it meant."

The decision made at the meeting was to initiate some sort of court action, even if nothing came of it. In the opinion of the lawyers, O'Reilly and Jacques Beaudoin, the legal action would serve as a sort of Damocles' Sword to be hung over the head of the provincial government, prodding Bourassa to negotiate in good faith.

And so, in early May, the Crees filed an action in Quebec Superior Court through the Indians of Quebec Association, contending that the legislation establishing the James Bay Development Corporation was unconstitutional. No one had any illusions that such a case would ever be won, but it kept their cause in the press and it maybe gave them a bit more time while they considered the far more serious step of seeking the interlocutory injunction.

Two weeks later the James Bay Development Corporation announced that its plans were changing. All along, it had never been specific as to which project would begin first, the massive flooding along the Nottaway, Broadback and Rupert, the damming of the huge La Grande River beginning at Fort George, or the blocking of the Eastmain River in between the two areas. Engineering reports had argued every possible version, but finally it was decided—undoubtedly for political reasons as well as physical—that the Nottaway, Broadback and Rupert would be the most difficult. The corporation opted for the La Grande scheme farther to the north, which would affect only one river and one main village, Fort George. This would be "Phase I" of the James Bay Project.

But just as the government now had a clear focus, so too did the Crees, and a task force was immediately set up to assess the damage that might result from the construction of this massive complex. Billy Diamond threw himself full tilt into the project, and when Elizabeth was taken to Moose Factory to await the birth of their child, he managed to visit only once, staying briefly before racing away for yet another meeting in Montreal.

Elizabeth could see what others were also observing. Chief Billy Diamond was changing. He was putting on weight with his new southern diet and, at times, putting on airs with his new southern knowledge. Having chosen the path of the "new ways," he was himself becoming more modern with every step. He carried a briefcase and was becoming something of an expert in ordering the restaurant wine he had so marvelled at only a few short years before. Elizabeth had no concept of this alien world, apart from the fact that it seemed in danger of turning her husband into a stranger himself, but all she could do about it was tell him again and again over the phone that she was eagerly awaiting his return, and then return to the waiting.

Certainly, he was not exaggerating when he complained to Elizabeth about how busy they were. When Diamond and Philip Awashish had taken over the research for the IQA they had asked for the file on the James Bay Project and been astonished to find it contained no more than one letter: a quick note from Josie Sam Atkinson of Fort George asking the IQA for a copy of all the information they had on hand concerning Bourassa's James Bay scheme. The IQA had sent him nothing, which was, of course, everything they had on hand.

Soon, however, the files were bulging. The lawyers had done the legal work. Philip Awashish had concentrated on the hunting and trapping, which everyone believed would be the issue at the core of this fight. Then there were the vast reports and statistical evidence arriving weekly from the academic experts who had rushed to the aid of the Crees and Inuit: sympathetic Canadian anthropologists like Ignatius LaRusic, Harvey Feit, Adrian Tanner, Richard Preston and Brian Craik, and engineers like Einar Skinnarland. "These scientists played a very valuable role," says Billy Diamond. "Our people knew where the data was—the animals, what they did—but we needed the scientists to write it down so it would become scientific evidence."

Diamond himself had taken on the historical data and the media, and was so busy that there was only time for a telephone call when Elizabeth gave birth on May 30 to a second girl, a small baby that she would be taking home to Rupert House. They decided to call her Joanne, and the new parents kissed over the phone, father promising mother yet again that he would be back as soon as possible.

Away from home, everything seemed to be falling into place. O'Reilly was setting up his own small law firm. Indian Affairs in Ottawa was arranging a loan so that the Crees could do the required research and organize properly. Boyce Richardson had left the *Star* and was setting out to make the first of several films about the Cree way of life. And, in a moment that passed unnoticed by almost everyone, biologist John Spence of McGill discovered the major whitefish spawning ground of the La Grande River.

When word was first received that the damming would take place on the La Grande River, the hunters of Fort George had claimed it would affect the summer whitefish harvest—they would no longer be able to smoke the sweet meat of this catch and store it as a winter delicacy. The scientists hired by the James Bay Development Corporation had countered that this would be no problem, because the round, silver fish simply did not exist on the river. Spence was convinced the hunters were right, and all summer long he had searched for the fish along the river. Finally, one August day when he was standing on a rock below the part of the river that the Crees call First Rapids and where the engineers were calling for a dam, Spence stared into the clear water of a pool and counted more than one hundred large females, all mature, all spawning. Just as the hunters had claimed.

In September, the chief of Rupert House finally came home. Billy Diamond was exhausted, looking forward to seeing his new daughter, and then taking his young family out to the goose camp for a well-deserved escape from the radio phones that had been tracking him north. But on his return, he found a distraught wife with a sick baby.

The illness—diarrhea and an inability to keep down foods—settled down enough for them to move out to the camp, but as soon as they arrived the four-month-old baby became sick again with a vengeance. The parents hurried back to the village, where Elizabeth, with medicine from the nursing post, tried to stop the baby from vomiting and attempted to get her to take fluids to replace what she was losing.

The father felt guilty for not arriving sooner; the mother was too exhausted to forgive and offer comfort to yet another; the toddler, Lorraine, cried constantly, sensing the tension. And the baby, Joanne, continued to grow more and more ill. Tiny, drawn, her eyes not focussing properly, the child took another turn on the evening of October 3. There was blood in her diarrhea. She was feverish, her temperature higher each time they were able to take it. The young parents panicked. Lorraine was given over to the care of Hilda and, with the baby bundled against the cold, they raced past the church and up the gravel hill to the small medical clinic, where the nurse tried to bring down the fever with new medicine.

But it was too late. With Elizabeth and Billy holding each other tight and sobbing as they stood by, helplessly watching the nurse fuss, Joanne Diamond, aged four months and four days, took a final shallow breath and died.

"He scared me," says anthropologist Brian Craik, who was doing land-use research in Rupert House at the time. "He seemed so angry and was gruff and threatening to anyone who was white. We steered clear of him as much as we could." The young chief took his fury with him to Quebec City shortly after Joanne's funeral and her burial in Rupert's tiny Anglican mission cemetery. Bourassa had finally relented, agreeing to meet the James Bay Crees face to face. Malcolm Diamond was part of the contingent, and while his son dressed in a suit and carried a briefcase of notes down to meet the plane that would begin their journey south, the aging father came down from his shack wearing bush clothes and a windbreaker, holding a small suitcase containing a clean shirt and a change of underwear.

They gathered in Quebec City with the other Cree chiefs, the leaders of the Indians of Quebec Association and the lawyers, and they went in force to "The Bunker," the bizarre concrete fort that Bourassa had constructed in the aftermath of the October Crisis. Their strategy was simple: to make one final plea to the premier to stop the work until the overall question of Cree rights was settled. It would be a plea on a man-to-man basis. They had even taken the precaution of bringing along their best spokesman.

But all did not go as planned. The IQA representatives spoke and the young chiefs spoke and the premier shifted in his Cabinet chair, appearing both bored and impatient. His ministers seemed even less interested. The Crees decided to play what they expected would be their trump card—the old man in the windbreaker who could speak with such force and eloquence that, once he was finished, even the man who had dreamed up the James Bay Project would be convinced it would have to be stopped.

Malcolm Diamond, the old Rupert House chief, stood and, staring directly into the premier's shifting glances, he began to speak in Cree about the magnificent land—the Cree garden—that this man, in his ignorance, was about to destroy.

But the premier would not even wait for the first translation. He rustled his papers and took the floor himself. "There are expropriations in all parts of the province," he said impatiently. "You will see that the damages are not as great as you expected."

While the old man waited to begin speaking again, the premier looked around and informed the Crees that they were hardly a case alone in this province, that expropriations are continually done when building highways and roads, and besides, he had a meeting he was already late for. "I cancelled my lunch to be with you," the premier let them know, perhaps expecting them to apologize, and then he was gone, his Cabinet scurrying behind him.

The Crees were left alone in the Cabinet room of the Quebec government. The old man, realizing that his speech was over before it had even begun, stood motionless while the glint washed in his eyes. The Cree they had all wanted to speak was now speechless, shaking with rage and humiliation. But then he spoke, talking to them all but staring directly at his son, Billy Diamond.

"It's in your hands," he said in Cree. "It's up to you to fight the white man. We cannot even talk to him. We raised you for this moment and you must now make the decision to stop this white man who has destroyed our land and brought us shame." And then Malcolm Diamond—convinced in his own mind that this ignorant premier had stolen his honour—sat down and waited.

Within five minutes the Crees had made a major decision. They would go ahead with the court case they had been holding in reserve. Malcolm Diamond had said at one point that they should use the white man's own laws against him, and in the end that is what they determined to do. They would take the enormous risk of seeking the interlocutory injunction that would put a stop to the damming of the James Bay rivers.

It was a gamble. Even if they won, it would probably mean only a temporary halt. And if they lost in court, they would lose forever.

They were convinced, however, that Robert Bourassa had left them no other option.

And so, on November 7, 1972, James O'Reilly filed the Cree action: *Chief Robert Kanatewat et al.* vs. *The James Bay Development Corporation et al. and The Attorney General of Canada.*

CHAPTER SEVEN

A SECRET ALLY

The Crees of James Bay were duly informed that the Superior Court of the Province of Quebec would be expecting them at 9:30 A.M. in Courtroom 515 of Montreal's brand-new Palais de Justice, December 3, 1972. There, under strategically placed fluorescent lights and on a grey carpet that still smelled of the factory, they would be given a short hearing. And at the end of the proceedings, Superior Court Judge Albert Malouf would determine whether or not these Natives had the right to proceed with their case.

The court would weigh only the value of the legal arguments. No consideration would be given to the fact that the vast majority of the Crees and Inuit who were coming down did not speak French, did not speak English, and had never before been in a city. No one was there to appreciate what it meant when later the first load of Cree witnesses refused to board an Air Canada jet in Timmins because they believed the propellers had fallen off. And only the stewardess was surprised when she began her rounds, asking each of the old trappers in turn if there was anything she could get for him and one finally summoned up enough courage to ask for a single slice of bread.

Once they arrived in Quebec City, Charlie Watt took to hanging a box on a rope out the window of his hotel room, keeping it filled with raw caribou meat for the Inuit hunters who could stand no more of the overcooked food of the South. It was certainly better to hang the box out the window than to have to deal again with the outraged manager who had demanded to know what the pulpy carcass of a seal was doing in one of the bathtubs.

But the old people were determined not to miss the hearing. "I have told their lawyers that it is hardly necessary for their clients to appear in court at this stage," Justice Malouf said before the proceedings began, "but he has said they are so eager that he cannot stop them."

They came in windbreakers with checkered shirts hanging out, with unlaced work boots and crude haircuts. They misinterpreted the function of the policemen standing about the building waiting to testify, thinking that they had been sent to this remarkable new building to make sure the Indians and Inuit caused no trouble. They thought Malouf—resplendent in a flowing black robe trimmed with red—was a minister who would shortly begin preaching to them, as had all the white men who wore such magnificent garments.

But they misread Malouf. Like the Crees, the fifty-five-year-old judge was a minority within a minority, a member of the Montreal Lebanese community who had never been to James Bay and whose knowledge of the bush consisted almost entirely of what he had encountered on the longer par fives of his private golf club. It hardly mattered, for what he did not know he simply learned, by listening so intently and expressionlessly that soon even the Crees were using his court nickname—"the Sphinx"—when they spoke of Malouf. The only hint that Justice Malouf would one day say that case 05-04841-72 "was without a doubt the most important case I've ever handled" came from the fact that his right hand moved incessantly while others spoke, a pen on a simple pad taking down almost verbatim the arguments why the project should be blocked and the reasons why it should not.

The arguments against proceeding with the case were delivered by C. Antoine Geoffrion, a man who appeared each morning not as if he had just shaved and dressed himself for court but as if he had drawn himself for an editorial page: a rich Montreal lawyer with impeccable government connections, eloquently bilingual, wide of girth and full of chuckle and harrumph. Standing in his favourite position for addressing the court, his left thumb was hooked in his waistcoast and his right hand ran through his curly white hair, still holding the glasses that he used less for sight, perhaps, than for blurring the opposition's points. Geoffrion had, however, only two points of his own to make. His first was that since the James Bay Development Corporation is a Crown corporation, it enjoys Crown immunity. His second, even simpler, was that Indians have no rights in the province of Quebec. Never have had, never will.

But if C. Antoine Geoffrion appeared to be the caricature of a lawyer, James O'Reilly, who led the Cree argument, seemed an understatement. Half the size of Geoffrion and cursed with hair that distracted rather than flattered, O'Reilly was more comfortable with quiet, difficult, tangential argument than loud and quick humour. While Geoffrion had commanding presence, O'Reilly had difficulty getting served during the lunchbreaks. But he did have more than two arguments.

O'Reilly's task was to convince Malouf that the Natives had a genuine claim to these lands, enough of a claim, anyway, to permit them to bring their evidence to court. If he lost the preliminary argument, there would be no case and the battle would end, effectively, right there under the track lights of Courtroom 515. O'Reilly spoke for nearly five hours. While Malouf scribbled on his pad and Geoffrion shook his big head in good-natured astonishment, O'Reilly argued that the Crees and Inuit sitting behind him and leaning against the walls at the back represented all the people of Mistassini and Waswanipi and Rupert House, Eastmain, Paint Hills, Fort George, Great Whale River and Fort Chimo. He argued on the grounds of "collective territorial rights" and made brief reference to a fresh phrase which was then beginning to come into use in Canada—"aboriginal rights."

He quoted from the Royal Proclamation of 1763, twisting his tongue around the language of the Court of St James while the lawyers for the government laughed and elbowed each other:

> We do therefore, with the Advice of our Privy Council, declare it to be our Royal Will and Pleasure, that no Governor or Commander in Chief of any of our Colonies of Quebec, East Florida, or West Florida, do presume, upon any Pretence whatever, to grant Warrants of Survey, or pass any Patents for Lands beyond the Bounds of their respective Governments, as described in their Commissions; as also that no Governor, or Commander in Chief in any of our other Colonies or Plantations in America do presume for the present, and until our further Pleasure be known, to grant Warrants of Survey, or pass Patents for any Lands beyond the Heads or Sources of any of the Rivers which fall into the Atlantic Ocean from the

West and North West, or upon any Lands whatever, which, not having been ceded to or purchased by Us as aforesaid, are reserved to the said Indians, or any of them . . . .

He quoted directly from the instructions the British monarch of the time, George III, had issued to Governor Murray in the new colony:

. . . whereas our Province of Quebec is Inhabited and Possessed by several Nations and Tribes of Indians with whom it is both necessary and expedient to Cultivate and Maintain a strict friendship and good Correspondence . . . You are on no Account to molest or disturb them in the Possession of such Parts of the said province as they at present occupy or possess; but to use the best means you can for conciliating their Affections, and uniting them to our Government.

"It's absolutely clear," O'Reilly argued, "that they were meant to continue their same way of life. Why? Because in those same instructions they set out specific regulations for the fur trade. Who did they depend upon for the fur trade but the Indians? No hunting and fishing by the Indians, no fur trade."

O'Reilly then went on to produce the order-in-council that admitted Rupert's Land into Confederation in 1870, quoting directly from section 14: "Any claims of Indians to compensation for Lands required for purposes of settlement." He referred to the order-in-council of January 17, 1910, that specifically commanded the province of Quebec to deal with the question of land title through clearly established treaty practices—a federal order Quebec ignored again during the further expansion of 1912.

But O'Reilly most relished the moment when he produced the controversial Bill 50 itself, the very legislation that Geoffrion argued gave the corporation Crown immunity. O'Reilly read from section 43 of the act—"This Act shall in no way affect rights of Indian Communities living in the territory"—and smiled to himself. One of his last acts before leaving his former law firm, Montreal's large Martineau, Walker, had been to insert this very clause into the bill the firm was hired by the province to prepare.

So masterly was O'Reilly's command of constitutional law that others in the room puzzled over how he had, in such a short time, managed to cull it from the meagre library in his fledgling firm. But O'Reilly was actually playing a remarkable trump card that would be kept secret for a decade and a half, right up until the death of the young lawyer's crucial mentor: F. R. Scott.

It was the long evenings spent with Scott at his McGill office that laid the strategic groundwork for the case. The famous Canadian poet, philosopher and constitutional lawyer was then seventy-three years old and had retired from his longtime post as dean of the Faculty of Law. Even so, he was renowned as *the* expert in Canadian constitutional law and was still a leading advocate of civil liberties and minority rights. But it was as a poet that Scott—no relation to Duncan Campbell Scott—had spoken most eloquently for the Natives. Using only six lines of rhyming couplets, he had many years earlier stated his case clearly and unequivocally in "Brébeuf and His Brethren":

When Lalemant and de Brébeuf, brave souls,
Were dying by the slow and dreadful coals
Their brother Jesuits in France and Spain
Were burning heretics with equal pain.
For both the human torture made a feast:
Then is priest savage, or Red Indian priest?

It had been Scott who had successfully defended D. H. Lawrence's *Lady Chatterley's Lover* in the Canadian courts, and Scott who had fought successfully in the Supreme Court to overturn the province's Padlock Law, which gave the attorney general authority to charge and convict, without trial, anyone suspected of publishing Communist propaganda and close down their operations permanently. And it was Scott who had spoken out against the War Measures Act only two years earlier and who would serve secretly as the legal strategist behind *Kanatewat et al.* vs. *The James Bay Development Corporation et al. and The Attorney General of Canada.*

"Jacques Beaudoin and I would go up to his office and just talk about what might be done," O'Reilly remembers. "It was Frank Scott who confirmed the essential legal strategy, and that was to go for the interlocutory injunction on environmental rights but make sure you have your constitutional arguments down as well."

It was old Malcolm Diamond, sitting toward the back of the courtroom in his windbreaker, who gave O'Reilly the nickname *machimanituu*—"devil"—that the Crees adopted as his permanent label. "Don't ever let him go," Malcolm told his son, Billy, at the end of one of O'Reilly's attacks on Geoffrion. "He's a real terror. If you ever need help, just unleash him."

Two days into the proceedings, O'Reilly received a telephone call from John Ciaccia, Jean Chrétien's deputy minister in charge of land claims in Ottawa. Ciaccia, who had known O'Reilly ever since they were both rising young Montreal lawyers, asked O'Reilly if he might take him out for lunch, just a little something to celebrate the birthday that, until Ciaccia called, had entirely slipped O'Reilly's distracted mind.

It was a long, meandering lunch, complete with toasts and enough wine to make them forget the time and make O'Reilly late for the afternoon session, but there was also a clear message: Ottawa was cheering for the Crees. The trouble was that Ciaccia's minister, Jean Chrétien, could not go public in any way. The situation was too dicey for the federal Liberals to touch. If the federal politicians had to choose between aligning themselves with the Crees against the bulldozers and the Bourassa Liberals against the growing menace of separatism, the choice was unfortunate but obvious. The Crees were on their own. Ciaccia did not use the official phrase of the Ottawa position—"alert neutrality"—but the lunch left little doubt in O'Reilly's mind that Chrétien was monitoring the situation with increasing concern.

Five days after the court session began, Justice Malouf announced that he had come to a decision on whether or not the hearing would continue. Malouf first noted the documentation that O'Reilly and Beaudoin had presented—so much of it approved by Frank Scott—and he said these acts and orders-in-council and proclamations "show, without doubt, that the Government of Canada recognized that Indians were entitled to exercise rights in the territory described. To say less than this would render these words meaningless.

"[The] petitioners have therefore established that they have some apparent rights in the territory, and having succeeded in so doing, are entitled to present before this Court such evidence and proof as may be required . . . ."

Still unsmiling, Malouf turned to O'Reilly and said: "You may call your first witness."

James O'Reilly turned and looked into the crowd and found the one they had agreed would speak first. Not the constitutional experts. Not the anthropologists with their charts. Not the biologists with their data. But a witness who sat waiting near the back, nervously clutching the hand of a pretty young girl in an embroidered jacket—a twenty-three-year-old kid with horn-rimmed glasses and Elvis Presley sideburns. O'Reilly turned back to Malouf. "I call Chief Billy Diamond of Rupert House."

Chief Billy Diamond, "hunter," as he identified himself to the court when he was sworn in, sat in the witness box and stared fixedly at the smiling teenager near the back. He knew that if he looked only at Elizabeth, he would not panic as he had become convinced he would earlier that morning when the Crees and their lawyers gathered at the nearby Laurentian Hotel to discuss precisely this possibility. Billy and the younger Crees had suggested leading with an elder—ideally, Malcolm Diamond, who was there—and some others had leaned toward the titles and long credentials of the experts. Jacques Beaudoin, however, had argued that court cases are often won or lost immediately. What often mattered far more then either research or legal argument, he said, was the *tone*, and he suggested that Billy Diamond would set a tone that would affect the entire proceedings. James O'Reilly had agreed. So had Robert Kanatewat. And when they had turned to the young Rupert House chief, Billy Diamond had confidently nodded his approval.

Inside, however, he was petrified. But once he moved to the witness stand the same calm settled over him that had come when he first walked out onto the high school stage in *Arrow to the Moon*. The performer within simply took over. It began, of course, with the listing of his profession as hunter, though bureaucrat, politician, researcher, band employee and even bulldozer operator were all rather more accurate. He knew that though it was late 1972—after Kent State in the United States and well after the October Crisis in Canada—the media were still easily captivated by romantic notions. Land was sacred, faith admired, simplicity sought—and a hunter made much better copy than a bureaucrat.

"I tried to live in the South," he told the judge, "in Val d'Or and Quebec City—but there is always a need to be next to the wilderness. An Indian can't relax in the city. In the wilderness, the mind and the body can find release."

Much of the testimony might well have been declared irrelevant were it not for the fact that Malouf was himself so captivated with the detail. He not only failed to sustain objections, but actively encouraged the witness when Diamond told of paddling up the Nottaway River with old Malcolm. So lenient was Malouf that, at one point, Billy delivered a short treatise on how to cure impetigo with the oil obtained from boiling down the fat of a black bear. He told the court what it was like to be sent off to residential school at Moose Factory and then to Sault Ste Marie. And he talked of the trouble Crees had with white man's food, speaking eloquently of the taste of bannock and wild meat and he was allowed to describe, for the court records, a quick recipe for the making of pemmican.

"Slow down!" the elders whispered when Malouf called a short break. "Slow down, Billy! He's listening to you. Give him time to write it down."

With O'Reilly leading the testimony, the young chief of Rupert House told how the people of Nemaska had deserted their pitiful village when they began running into surveyors in the bush and hearing tales about how their magnificent lake would be flooded by a huge dam. He told of roads being bulldozed across traplines, and he said that the noise of the machinery was driving away the animals. He even had a film that he and another man had made from a Beaver floatplane flying low over the Fort George River, and presented to the court thirty-four still photos of sand pits, slashings, construction camps, airstrips and thirty-ton trucks moving over taiga where the Cree hunters had always believed they would walk, unmolested, forever. It was a marvellous performance, one that at times had the older Crees giggling into the sleeves of their windbreakers as their sons and daughters beside them whispered quick translations.

Part way through the proceedings, the ebullient Geoffrion was replaced by a stern Jacques Le Bel, the provincial government's own prosecutor. Le Bel had a few points to clear up. Surely when Chief Billy Diamond had spoken so romantically of paddling up the rivers he was fully aware that the outboard motor had long been available throughout the North. And surely the chief of Rupert House who had waxed eloquent about the dog sleds of James Bay was more than familiar with the skidoo that had been rolling off the Bombardier assembly line in Valcourt for the past thirteen years.

"How many skidoos have you got, personally, chief?" Le Bel asked.

"I have two," Billy Diamond conceded.

But he would not back down. Yes, it was true that trappers used outboards now when heading up the Broadback or the Nottaway or the Rupert, but they still also paddled in the rapids; and while there were forty-eight skidoos that winter in Rupert—sixteen more than there were hunters, in fact—the trappers were sticking to their dogs.

Snowmobiles, they had concluded—though it was an opinion they would soon change—simply scared away game that was growing ever scarcer. Le Bel charged that the Indians of James Bay hunted caribou from planes: Billy Diamond said not the people of his village. Le Bel launched a full attack on the young chief's claim that the people of Nemaska had given up on their village not because of the scare of the surveyors' news, but for the very good reason that the Hudson's Bay Company store had been closed up and abandoned. Billy Diamond said yes, that was undoubtedly a factor.

For those sitting in the courtroom during those days, it was a series of riveting exchanges. Le Bel, the intense and provocative lawyer, leading Diamond into certain ambushes; Diamond, the sincere young man with a mind so quick that the ambushes often ricocheted back. What, Le Bel wanted to know after one short adjournment, was he to make of a petition he had come across requesting a road to be built from Lasarre to Rupert and signed by the Rupert House band? Would that not in itself be surrender of the Cree land? The young chief never even blinked: it could indeed be seen that way, he replied, except that the petition Le Bel was referring to had been initiated by the white Quebeckers in the village, had been signed by less than half the band and had been written entirely in French, a language none of those who signed understood.

But Billy Diamond's finest moment came when he was challenged by Le Bel to show the court proof of any effect the project had already had on the Cree. Certainly, the young chief replied, and he proceeded to outline to the court what was happening to the young Cree men who were being lured away for work on the road construction for the highway from Matagami to the main construction site. The worker earns more than $1,000 in two quick months, Diamond said, and the money is directly deposited into a bank account in Matagami. The worker quits or gets laid off, withdraws every cent of it, goes on a two-week drunk in Matagami, charters a plane back to Rupert for $143, fills the plane with beer and lands to be greeted by the Bay manager holding up the bills the worker's wife has run up at the Hudson's Bay store. "He ends up $700 in the hole," said Diamond. "I have seen this quite often since the project has started." With cold fury, Le Bel demanded that this anecdote be declared hearsay, but, of course, it had been heard by all and would instantly paint the running argument for development—money for the Crees, as well—in a hopelessly bad light.

"My people," Diamond said in a rising voice as he turned to face directly the Crees and Inuit in the audience, "are not prepared for the impact of economic development."

Seven months later, when the longest hearing for an interlocutory injunction in Canadian history was finally brought to a close, and when a proper tally had been made—78 days of testimony, 167 witnesses, 312 exhibits, more than 10,000 pages of transcribed evidence—the burden of proof would fall more on the experts than the Cree. The experts, after all, offered quantifiable evidence—statistics, empirical observation, precedent, documentation—all material that could be measured, digested and decided upon in an objective manner.

The expert witnesses were a formidable force on the stand. Toronto engineer Einar Skinnarland—a commando who had gone back to Norway during the war to successfully destroy its heavy-water installations before the Nazis gained possession of them—took his seat and began to speak of the size of the dam the James Bay Development Corporation was proposing. The room went completely silent. "There are rapids in the whole region now," Skinnarland said with his measured words and slight accent. "By the time you build a dam, they will be under the lake . . . there will be no more rapids in the river. The river will disappear."

When the time came for John Spence to testify as to whether or not the whitefish spawned on the proposed site of the first dam along the Fort George River, he argued that spawning had indeed been taking place when he was there, that the fish the Crees were taking in their nets were all sexually mature, with well-developed gonads and ripe ovaries.

"Did you take any samples of the fish?" O'Reilly asked.

"Yes," answered the crew-cut Spence. "One thing I did sample was the status of the ovaries of all the females that we caught, and I've brought one sample to the court—it may be of interest."

Malouf was dubious. *How would one tag ovaries?* Irrelevant, challenged the James Bay Development Corporation lawyers. Absolutely pertinent, argued O'Reilly. If the corporation was going to deny that they were tampering with the natural instincts of the whitefish of the Fort George River, this, surely, was tangible evidence that those same fish came to this very spot to spawn. Malouf conceded the point, and for the first time in the history of Canadian jurisprudence, ovaries were placed on exhibit in a Canadian courtroom.

There seemed to be an expert for every possible circumstance. Dr Garret Clough testified about the effects of the project on the beaver of the river. Dr Frank Banfield spoke of the migration patterns of the Ungava Peninsula caribou and how they might be affected by flooding. Dr Brock Fenton argued that the flooding would seriously affect smaller animals in the territory. Dr Harvey Feit worried about a depletion of game through the increased sports hunting that development and roads would bring to the James Bay area. Dr William McKim of the Department of Indian Affairs and Northern Development in Ottawa verified that the James Bay Cree had never signed a treaty or ceded their land. Research provided by anthropologists like Brian Craik of Rupert House clearly established that the Crees had possession of wide tracts of land in all but actual deed.

The evidence was vital, accurate, quantifiable and, to a Canadian court, familiar. But it was the Cree testimony that unleashed the raw emotion surrounding this political issue, trappers and hunters speaking in their own language of their own lives and lands. There was no way to measure it properly, often no way to verify what was said, but just as Jacques Beaudoin had predicted, it was the Cree testimony that set the tone of the hearing.

When the Cree elders spoke, they looked at Ted Moses, the young man from Eastmain, and then Moses would turn and tell the judge and courtroom what each man had said. The very language barrier that had so tried Premier Robert Bourassa's patience and eventually driven him from his own Cabinet room in October worked very much to the advantage of the Crees with the ever-patient Malouf. And much of what could be described as the tone of the hearing came through entirely by accident. When Job Bearskin of Fort George was asked to give the court his address, he simply sat with a perplexed look on his face and refused to comment. Asked again, he was able to say, in Cree, "I have come from what I have survived on." When pressed further to identify where he lived, he offered: "I have lived in the bush. I come from the bush." When François Mianscum, a Mistassini hunter, was asked to place his hand on the Bible and tell the truth, the whole truth and nothing but the truth, he asked first to consult with the translator. They spoke for a while and the translator turned to the judge, helpless. "He does not know whether he can tell the truth," the translator told Malouf. "He can only tell what he knows."

As the testimony of the older trappers and hunters continued, it became clear that these James Bay Indians—like the first Crees

Henry Hudson encountered in 1611—had no concept of *owning* their land, which would have made it rather difficult to have ever officially handed it over in trade, as Des Groseilliers had claimed three hundred years earlier. "I always refer to it as my land, as long as I am depending on it," said old Sam Blacksmith. "But really, nobody can own or possess it . . . nobody can, because eventually everyone dies."

It was, for so many of these older Crees, the first time they had spoken from their hearts of this barren land that so many of them referred to as "the Cree garden." The organizers began bringing down Cree youngsters with their parents, just so they would be able to see what was so important that it would cause their parents to leave the bush and fly to Montreal. One of those who came down south for a week was seventeen-year-old Dianne Ottereyes of Waswanipi. "All I could do was stare at the judge, Malouf," she remembers. "He just sat there, no expression whatsoever. I wondered if he was listening and I asked my Dad if he thought the judge was paying attention. 'Doesn't look like it,' my Dad said. I was really concerned."

Malouf was indeed listening, and perhaps never so intently as when Matthew Shanush, the old Eastmain chief, spoke for those who could not be there. "My people have relatives buried on their traplines along the Eastmain River," he said in his quiet, slow Cree, waiting for Ted Moses to translate each phrase. "Even myself. I have five children who are buried along the river and on my trapline. My mother is buried there also. These bodies of our relatives are very sacred to us and we do not want to see them buried under water." The lawyer for the James Bay Development Corporation then asked Chief Shanush if he really thought the buried dead would be any worse off, and the sixty-one-year-old hunter, showing admirable manners, refused to debate the point.

The exchange so upset Father Hugo Muller, a Dutch-born Anglican priest who long served in Waswanipi, that he poured his rage into a poem that he titled "The Graves."

> The chief did not answer you directly, Maître,
> he had too much civilization to do that—
> To lash back with the same viciousness
> that you displayed.
>
> It's easy, Maître, with your background, your education

A SECRET ALLY

to attempt to show up an Indian who must use an
interpreter
—you are not only a language apart,—but more:
a thousand tears, a choked cry, a silence of
sorrow.

You did not have to dig your mother's grave
yourself in the dead of winter, in the awesome
silence of the bush did you?
You did not have to sit up that night
when Elizabeth became so ill
and worried all that night and the next day
and into the long night again
when all of a sudden her flushed face became very
white
and very still
and very cold.
It was not your tears that fell on Elizabeth's
face
at that time when the cry of distress seemed
frozen in the still air.
It was not you, Maître, who once again went to dig
a grave
reading portions from the battered prayer book.
It was not you, Maître,
whose voice was heard that day
breaking when the hymn was sung and the prayer
said.

When your mother was buried, Maître,
there was grief, certainly,
measured sorrow restrained by ceremony
and those who know what to do:
—there was also the parish priest to soothe it
with the dispassionate majesty of the Requiem
—there was the funeral director with his cool,
correct efficiency
and just the right touch of everything
and all of that was much comfort
and the laborers came after to fill in the grave
when you had already gone in the black limousine.

—Have you ever carried a dead child, Maître,
the cold, limp body in your arms.
Have you ever dug the grave with your own hands
have you ever knelt in prayer in the cold snow
under a powerless sun in the few hours' daylight
in the silence of the north,
your tears frozen when they touch the ground?

That ground is sacred because of those tears,
those bodies lying there
awaiting the resurrection of the last day.

But you would not understand, Maître,
you think only of progress, and snowmobiles and
outboards
bringing benefits to those people who do not even
speak your language,
whose children you have never seen
whose eyes have never enchanted you
whom you have never kissed or carried or played
with
or prayed for
or buried.
You talk of progress and development to these
people that will never understand.

I pray that you will never have to bury your
children, Maître
or have your mother's grave
flooded by progress.
I do not wish it on you,
I only wish
you would understand.

CHAPTER EIGHT

VICTORY IN THE PALAIS DE JUSTICE

As the court case continued on into 1973, Chief Billy Diamond began to change visibly. It was not just the disappearance of the skinny kid that struck people, but a growth more difficult to measure except to say that he came to dominate whatever room he happened to be in. First the elders gave way, bowing to the young leadership with their command of English, then the young leadership itself bowed to the emerging control of Billy Diamond. Billy was the one the media wanted to interview. Billy was the one the lawyers deferred to. Billy was the one people wanted to be seen with. "It was instant," says Ted Moses. "He was now the leader."

He was twenty-three years old, had a grade twelve education, and suddenly he was being asked by university and college groups to come and address them. They wanted him in British Columbia to talk about land claims, in the Prairies to talk about the Indian situation. At McMaster University in Hamilton he filled a hall, standing at the podium with the lights sparking off his glasses while he held his audience spellbound with outrageous—and perhaps exaggerated—stories of black bears being drugged and loaded onto helicopters, flown to a height of 1,500 feet and then dropped onto the rocks, merely to keep the animals away from the endless garbage pits the James Bay Development Corporation was digging throughout the Crees' beloved garden.

But it was not all applause. The pressures began to take their first toll. The more he emerged as the leader, the more it became apparent to him that what he decided would affect not only himself, but all the Crees of James Bay and all the James Bay Cree to come. Elizabeth had just announced that she was pregnant again, and while the news seemed to be a comfort to her, so soon after the loss of baby Joanne, for Billy it led to more anguish about the kind of world this child would be coming into. For that matter, what kind of world was Malcolm Diamond about to come into? Billy Diamond and Robert Kanatewat had known in their hearts from the moment they sat down opposite Robert Bourassa that they would never be able to stop this massive project, but they knew that hundreds of Crees were expecting them to, and thousands of others were counting on them to get a good deal out of it.

But it was not only the Crees who were putting on the pressure. Other Natives saw the Cree movement as fitting in perfectly with their own plans. For the Indians of Quebec Association, the Crees were the vehicle they had been looking for to gain a settlement of the entire Indian rights question throughout the province. The Crees, however, thought otherwise, and relations between Diamond and Andrew Delisle, the IQA head, grew steadily cooler. Chief Billy Diamond was also becoming the target of the pro-project forces, particularly Quebec labourers who were starving for construction jobs. Newspaper clippings began arriving at the office of the Indians of Quebec Association, pictures of Billy Diamond and Robert Kanatewat and Philip Awashish speaking to the press and a red circle around one of them, along with the crude message: "This one is a dead man."

Far more disturbing for Billy Diamond and Robert Kanatewat at the time, however, was the sudden interest shown in James Bay by the American Indian Movement. AIM had actually been launched in 1968 in Minneapolis, Minnesota, by a group of Indian ex-cons who believed they could translate the consciousness-raising sessions of the prison into their Native languages. But it was during the Malouf hearings on the James Bay that the AIM movement captured international attention with a bitter, tragic seventy-one-day siege of Wounded Knee on the Sioux Pine Ridge reserve in South Dakota. The image of berets, braids and bullets had so shocked the United States of America that spring that the tremors were instantly felt in Canada. Immediately, the RCMP stepped up its surveillance and investigations—Diamond himself was trailed by a policeman he came to know on an awkward but friendly basis—and so seriously was the militant Indian movement taken that within two years (and less than five years after the 1970 October Crisis), the Mounties would report to Solicitor General Warren Allmand that Canadian Indian militants were "the principal threat to national stability."

Naturally, the recruitment of this emerging young leader from James Bay became part of the AIM agenda. Calls were made, and through the Indians of Quebec Association, a message went out to Chief Billy Diamond of Rupert House. "It was put to us that we might learn some tactics," remembers Diamond, "some guerrilla warfare in case it ever became necessary. AIM sent their delegate up and we attended a meeting, and it very quickly became clear to us that those people would never work in our area. We just weren't compatible. Crees are not violent people. Our situation was not a violent situation. We knew that the solution would have to come from within. It would have to be a Cree that did it, not someone from AIM.

"A few months later we were informed that they wished to have another meeting. This time someone was coming direct from Wounded Knee. I said we weren't interested. I said the Crees would never be put in a position where their issue would be used to benefit others. We would use the courts instead. We would turn the white man's laws on himself. That got us into a heated discussion about who was more of an Indian. This AIM guy said, 'You're really not an Indian—Indians have a fighting spirit.' I told him we wouldn't turn people into violent people, into maniacs. I said, 'We don't want to change the people, we want to change the situation.' And I told him that he would not be allowed to go up into our territory, that we would kick him out. There was a lot of swearing and then the young AIM guy left, huffing and puffing."

At such meetings, Diamond was at his very best, sure of his facts, aware of the jugular and possessed of a wicked humour and stinging tongue that soon wilted those who took him on. It was when he was alone that he was least in control. He was eating and drinking far more than he needed, the food making him bulge, the drink first dulling his doubt and then, as the drinking went on, cruelly sharpening it. He would periodically fall into deep despair, imagining himself as a modern-day Joseph Brant being deceived by the government and willingly leading his people into a trap laid out for them by the government bureaucrats. This obsession with Brant had been with him since his high school history days. He knew everything about Joseph Brant—Chief Thayendanegea: his fighting for the British during the American Revolution; his journey to England to ask George II to return to the Iroquois land overrun by the American rebels; the gold watch Brant brought back home; and the King's promise that turned to dust when the land went to New York state. Another broken agreement in the Ohio Valley eventually led to reserves for Brant's Six Nations Indians in southwestern Ontario, while Brant retired royally to a mansion on the shores of Lake Ontario. Where his white classmates had left Brant retired in Burlington and honoured by a huge memorial statue in Brantford as the great noble savage of Canadian history, Diamond had read on, retracing the broken promises and Brant's role in them. He understood why so many younger Indians had felt betrayed by Brant. He saw the symbolism when he learned that Brant's own son had attacked him with a knife, and how in the ensuing struggle Joseph Brant had killed his own offspring.

No matter what happened in the battle over James Bay, Billy Diamond made a vow that he would not go the route of Joseph Brant. Others might hate him, but his own children would never turn on him—not with knives, not even with disappointment. It was a severe burden to place on oneself, and there were times when he caved in under the weight of his own imaginings. He went on periodic drinking binges during which he would go days without sleep, becoming more and more manic about the situation as his friends began dropping off, desperately in need of sleep. At one point, during a crucial part of the Cree testimony, he failed to appear. Robert Kanatewat and James O'Reilly went to the Laurentian Hotel and up to Diamond's room on the fourteenth floor, but they could not convince him to open the door. "He was in a bad, bad state," says Kanatewat.

They pounded on the door and pleaded, but nothing they could say would convince Diamond to open up or even talk to them through the closed door. Eventually another young Cree leader, John Mark, was brought in and persuaded his drinking friend to let them in. The chief of Rupert House was sitting in his pyjamas, surrounded by bottles, crying. He had come to the conclusion that it was patently absurd for seven thousand nearly illiterate Crees to think they could go up against the province of Quebec and huge multinationals like the American engineering firm, Bechtel Corporation, and think even for a moment that they were going to change anything. There was no use going on, he sobbed. He was quitting, finished, beaten.

"We pleaded with him," remembers O'Reilly. "We begged him

to come back. 'Get a hold of yourself,' we told him. 'You're essential.' He was in that room for more than an entire day, but then, suddenly, he just snapped out of it and came back, as good as he'd ever been."

Robert Kanatewat was also buckling under the pressure. Once the James Bay Development Corporation made its announcement that it was going with the more northerly plan, it put his village of Fort George on the mouth of the La Grande—a lovely, wide river called Chesasibi by the Crees, Fort George River by the whites and, more recently, La Grande by the French—at the very heart of the "Project of the Century."

"Everywhere we went," remembers Kanatewat, "it was the same thing: 'We're going to do whatever the Fort George people say.' But even the Fort George people didn't know what to do—and I was their chief. They couldn't visualize it. The old people wouldn't believe it could be done. But I knew they were going to go ahead and dam the river. And every time a decision had to be made, I had to ask myself the same question: Am I doing the right thing?

"During the hearing I suddenly realized that every time I sat down, even if just for a coffee, I *had* to have a drink. I'd wake up and it was automatic—I had to find a drink. I never told anyone, not even my wife. I hid my drinking completely and never even told anyone after it was all over. But I forced myself to stop. I realized that I can't turn history around. I have to deal with what's happening. And I had to believe that whatever I did was on behalf of the people. If I wasn't here, then somebody else would be. But I was there—and so I had to do what I could live with."

The lawyers were drinking too much as well. It was the only way to wind down from such intensity. And each time someone buckled, it was invariably the easy-going, likeable Jacques Beaudoin who went and talked him through the crisis. He was better than O'Reilly with people. A round *bon vivant* and *raconteur*, Beaudoin could be relied upon to hold the private dinner and do the cheerleading: some good food, lots of soothing wine, a few cognacs to pump up the spirits, lots of smoke in the air and bravado in the heart.

On separate occasions he took both Billy Diamond and Robert Kanatewat out for long, wet dinners, and over liqueurs he told them that the case was already won. But the stress was taking its toll on Beaudoin, as well. Only forty-one, he was nevertheless in no shape for such a pace. Three years earlier he had been in a bad car accident and the recovery had been slow and painful. He never exercised. And while he would be the first to charge off to support another, he asked for none himself, disappearing each Friday to return to his young family in rural St-Joseph-de-Beauce and hurrying back each Monday morning to begin again with the hearing. It was on one of these hurried weekends home that Jacques Beaudoin suffered a massive heart attack. It was serious, but not fatal, yet the early prognosis was that he would be out of commission for at least a month. Before the month was out, however, he suffered a second attack and died.

At the funeral held in the St-Joseph-de-Beauce cathedral, there were almost as many Crees as friends and neighbours in the congregation, many of them weeping openly for the big French Canadian who had so openly loved life.

In the spring, the James Bay Development Corporation was finally able to present its counter-evidence. And though the hearing had begun with Antoine Geoffrion appearing to consider the Cree suit little more than a nuisance, by the time the Crees and various experts had finished testifying, the corporation and government lawyers had changed tactics completely. They had a list of forty-five witnesses, and more were expected. They had documentation and precedent and, they firmly believed, a final argument that Justice Malouf would not be able to ignore: the cost of stopping now would simply be too much for the province or the corporation to bear.

The corporation and the various contractors that had also been named in the action argued that the Indian fears of damage were exaggerated. They produced evidence of good fishing where other reservoirs and dams existed. They argued that power was a necessity and would greatly benefit the entire province of Quebec, the Crees of James Bay and the Inuit of the Ungava Peninsula included. They argued that the Crees gained most of their annual incomes from sources other than fur, and they disagreed most vehemently with the hearing's first witness, Chief Billy Diamond of Rupert House, who had maintained that the greater part of the Crees' diet came from what they called "country food": the wild meat of the beaver, moose, caribou, rabbit and bear. The defence even produced eyewitnesses from Chibougamau, who testified that they had often seen Cree Indians visiting the local Kentucky Fried Chicken outlet, but these witnesses could not further confirm that they had actually seen the Indians eating the fast food. Diamond's contention that the

Crees took 90 percent of their food "directly from the bush" simply could not be shaken, and was subsequently backed by further expert witnesses.

The strongest argument the James Bay Development Corporation lawyers could present concerned the "balance of inconvenience." Stopping now, they contended with massive statistical back-up, would cost a fortune. They had figures for every possible contingency: demobilization, lost material, interest and insurance, caretaker costs, non-recoverable purchases, a winter road for withdrawal purposes, the potential cost of having to start up again after a suspension, escalation costs, contracts, preliminary studies costs, money already spent. In one study the cost was estimated at $87,438,000, in another $37,731,000—but just over $58 million seemed like the most likely scenario.

The Natives had only one short answer to all the accountants' charges: *not stopping would cost more.*

On June 21, 1973, Justice Albert Malouf declared that the final witness had been heard. He left the room without offering the slightest hint of which way he was leaning. And with Jacques Beaudoin dead barely a month, there was no one present to wrap a big arm around the Crees who sat there on that last day, to smile and laugh and say not to worry, he could tell, and it was obvious to anyone who knew how to look that the Natives had won over the Sphinx. The Crees and Inuit walked out of Courtroom 515 of the Palais de Justice expecting the worst. And why not? Wasn't that what they always got when they came up against the white man?

While Malouf was deliberating, the fight continued outside the courts. The Quebec government had indicated they would be open to a quick settlement, and meetings took place between the two groups, though they were light years apart. The bureaucrats were talking about a cash sweetener and the setting up of reserves just like the ones where the poverty-stricken Crees on the Ontario side of the bay had lived since 1905.

When word came down from Ottawa in May that John Ciaccia of Indian Affairs wanted to meet the Crees to find out what might be agreeable to them, O'Reilly and Billy Diamond sat down together to list their demands. While the chief of Rupert House took off his glasses, rubbed his eyes and talked, O'Reilly scribbled down the points on a single piece of typing paper. "Reserves" was written at the very top in O'Reilly's tortured scrawl, then were listed hunting and fishing rights, exclusive trapping rights, royalties on resources, a right of first refusal to own and operate hunting and fishing camps, participation in the governing of the territory, Native representation on the board of the James Bay Development Corporation, major modifications to the project, a say in policing, employment opportunities, a guaranteed minimum income for those who wished to hunt and fish as a way of life, and a cash settlement of $1 billion.

O'Reilly puffed his pipe and laughed as point after point began to fill up the page. When O'Reilly finished the last point and placed the cap back on his pen, the chief of Rupert House put his glasses back on and grabbed for the pen and the piece of paper. Writing furiously and giggling, he scribbled straight across the bottom of the sheet: "and etc., etc., etc., etc., etc."

Ciaccia met with O'Reilly and let the Crees' lawyer know that Jean Chrétien intended to be very much involved in any negotiations that might take place. The attorneys might even like to begin talking about the matter now, since they would certainly be involved in the later stages, and perhaps Chrétien could initiate the talks by negotiating directly with the provincial government. First, however, Indian Affairs would need to know what the Crees were seeking in a deal. O'Reilly told Ciaccia what had been discussed with Billy Diamond, and shortly afterwards Ciaccia sent a confidential memo to his boss. Every point that O'Reilly had noted on the paper was raised, including the $1 billion cash settlement. Ciaccia suggested this might be negotiable, but whatever amount was offered, it "must be substantial, in the hundreds of millions of dollars." What would not be negotiable, he further advised, would be the Crees' insistence that major modifications be made to the plan, particularly in the area where the whitefish of the Fort George River came to spawn.

Meanwhile, relations between the Crees of James Bay and the Indians of Quebec Association were becoming deeply troubled. During the trial, Billy Diamond had taken the spotlight from Andrew Delisle, and Delisle's nervous performance on the stand had been one of the weakest. The Crees were not amused by provincial official Jean Prieur's perception that negotiations were best carried on by white lawyers, and the results then delivered back to the Indians, but they were even less pleased by Delisle's indication that he was prepared to begin talks with the province on behalf of the Crees.

VICTORY IN THE PALAIS DE JUSTICE

On July 9, Billy Diamond took the first step in what would eventually amount to a complete severance with the Indians of Quebec Association. Using the association's own letterhead, he wrote to Delisle and bluntly told him that there would be no settlement until they had heard from Malouf. Further, if negotiations were to follow, they would be handled by a four-man negotiating committee, of which two would be from James Bay. Finally, the Rupert House chief told the chief of the provincial organization that he was to stop speaking to the press about the subject. Billy Diamond was moving to take complete control.

In September, with the Malouf judgment now overdue, the province of Quebec submitted a secret offer that, for some reason, never became known to the public, not even in the later histories of the battle. It contained two options, one much like the traditional treaties of the past century, the second claiming to allow the Natives more involvement in their own political and economic development. The cash settlement under the first option would be a lump-sum payment of $427,000 and an annuity of $438,000. Reserves would be established on a basis of 640 acres per family, to a total of 815,360 acres, the usual health and education and welfare services would be provided and all hunting and fishing and trapping outside the reserves would be, of course, subject to provincial regulation. Under the second option, the Crees would be given full ownership of the land presently covered by the villages. Certain other areas would then be set aside for Native hunting and trapping. A cash settlement of $20,000 per family would be offered, and essential services would be provided. The handful of Cree leaders who were told of the offer refused even to discuss it, and the two options were never again put forward by the province.

On November 12, 1973, Elizabeth Diamond gave birth to her third child, her first boy, and he was named Ian. Billy Diamond was about to take them home from the hospital when word came that Justice Malouf had reached a decision, and would be reading it at the Palais de Justice on the morning of November 15.

It was a massive decision—170 pages long—which the ever-serious Malouf insisted on reading in great detail. And nowhere was there the slightest hint of which side he was leaning toward. One by one he addressed the issues raised in the testimony, finding on the side of the corporation in some, on the side of the Natives in others. In page after page he traced the historical documentation and said he was forced to conclude that: "The evidence also shows that the rights of the Cree Indian and Inuit populations have never been extinguished." James O'Reilly smiled. His fundamental point had been won.

This land, Malouf believed, had the status the old trappers had claimed it had: it was their garden, which had provided them with their livelihood for longer than history could record. That they pursued a traditional way of life on this land was, he believed, beyond dispute. And when he combined the testimony of the various scientific experts with that of the trappers and hunters and fishermen, he could not help but conclude that the land would be significantly altered by the massive hydroelectric project. The effect on the way of life the old Crees and Inuit had described to him in their own language would be nothing short of "devastating," Malouf concluded. Furthermore, he had a great deal of difficulty comprehending the arguments of the James Bay Development Corporation regarding the extent of the financial loss incurred by calling a halt to the work. The numbers did not make sense.

"In addition," he said in his slow, even voice, "I find it difficult to compare such monetary loss to the damages which such a large group of people will suffer. The right of petitioners to pursue their way of life in the lands subject to dispute far outweighs any consideration that can be given to such monetary damages."

The Natives had a right to their court injunction, he said. The work on the James Bay project would cease immediately, by order of the Superior Court of Quebec.

Billy Diamond and Robert Kanatewat could not believe it. Nor could Charlie Watt and Philip Awashish and Ted Moses. The little meeting the Crees had called in Mistassini had succeeded in blocking the "Project of the Century." James O'Reilly sagged in his seat, totally drained, exhausted from the toughest court battle of his life.

In Ottawa, Indian Affairs Minister Jean Chrétien took an opportunity to rise in Question Period and twist an answer into a great ovation from his own government side. He had been under fire for providing federal funds to Indian groups to fight their own cases rather than going to battle for them, and this was the first concrete example of his strategy working. "Excuse me, Mr Speaker," he said to a laughing Lucien Lamoureux, "but after five years, four months and ten days in this job, I thought I could have a few moments of satisfaction." The Malouf decision, he said, had given him his happiest day since Prime Minister Pierre Trudeau had appointed him to the Cabinet.

But Robert Bourassa was hardly so pleased. In a curt, two-paragraph statement, he announced that the James Bay Development Corporation would be appealing the injunction and would be asking the Quebec Court of Appeal to delay it until such an appeal could be dealt with. This would be done, he promised, "as soon as possible."

The following morning, when James O'Reilly came late into his downtown office, there was a short note waiting for him on his desk.

"What a magnificent victory for you," it read, "for the Native people, for us, for justice, and for dear old Dicey! My heartiest congratulations to you and your team. No matter what happens now, a mighty blow has been struck for the citizens and against the overmighty state. Now you can rest on your laurels and murmur, *'Et maintenant, Seigneur, vous pouvez fermer mes yeux,'* but I know you won't. As a verse in the Bible says, 'The wicked flee when no man pursueth,' to which an older preacher used to add, 'But they make better time if someone is after them.' That's you."

It was initialed "FRS." Frank R. Scott, poet, constitutional expert, human rights advocate, minority fighter, former dean of law, McGill University—and secret strategist for the James Bay Cree court battle.

Malcolm and Hilda Diamond's three youngest boys: Billy in the middle, with Albert on the left and Stanley on the right, Christmas, 1959

Hilda Diamond preparing meal of moose nostrils, 1971.

Photo by Brian Willer

Malcolm Diamond, 1981

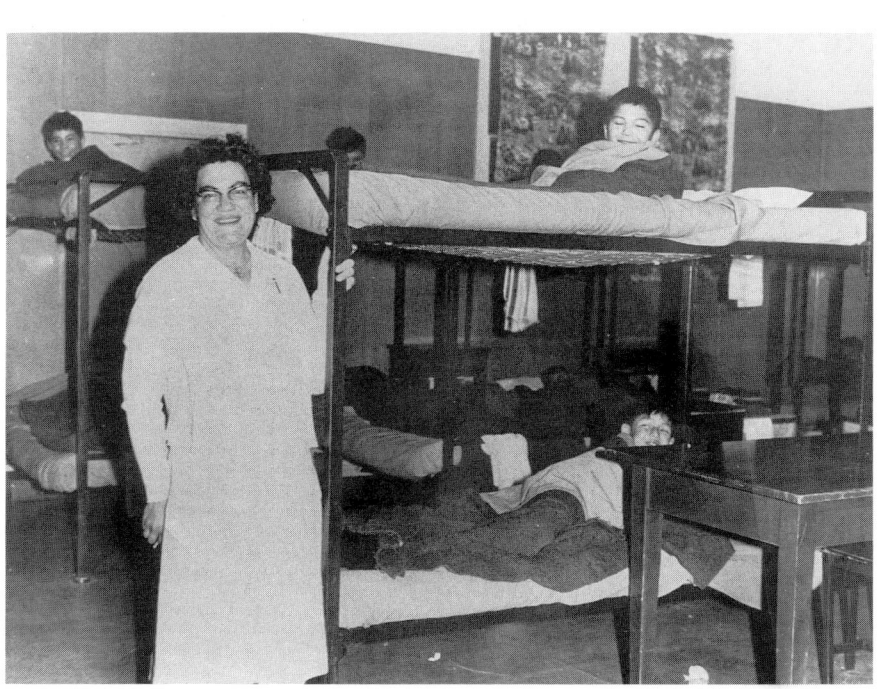

Photo courtesy of Cree Regional Authority

Boys' dormitory, Indian residential school at Moose Factory circa 1957

Jean Chrétien, then Indian Affairs Minister, jokes as Billy Diamond signs an agreement in principle, 1974, after the initial round of negotiations with federal and provincial governments.

The family in 1981. Clockwise, from top: Elizabeth, Lorraine, Philip on Billy's knee, Sandy and Ian

James Bay Crees and supporters protest Quebec Premier Robert Bourassa's announcement of the "Project of the Century", 1971.

The *Maclean's* cover story that was tabled at the first United Nations Conference on Indigenous Peoples and Land, Geneva, Switzerland, 1981.

Cree delegates at the United Nations Conference on Indigenous Peoples and Land, 1981. Grand Chief Billy Diamond is fourth from right, second row.

John Tait (far left), Indian Affairs Minister John Munro, Billy Diamond, Bob Epstein, and Parliamentary Secretary Raymond Chénier during the tabling of the Tait Review, 1982.

Grand Chief Billy Diamond makes presentation of Cree snowshoes to Pope John Paul II, 1981.

Quebec Premier René Lévesque jokes with Grand Chief Billy Diamond at a Cree reception in Quebec City, 1982.

Chief David Ahenakew puffing on a peace pipe at the beginning of the First Ministers Conference on the constitution and aboriginal rights held in Ottawa in March 1983. Grand Chief Billy Diamond is looking over Ahenakew's shoulder and George Erasmus is on the far left.

Aerial shot of Anglican Church mission, Waskaganish, Quebec. The original Diamond shack was located to the right rear.

Sandy Diamond in Waskaganish classroom with first Cree Lexicon textbook, published in 1987.

Government of Québec photo

Premier Robert Bourassa presenting the Ordre National du Québec to "businessman" Billy Diamond, 1987: "I was taking back my father's honour."

Former Waskaganish chief Simeon Trapper with Cree-Yamaha canoe, 1988

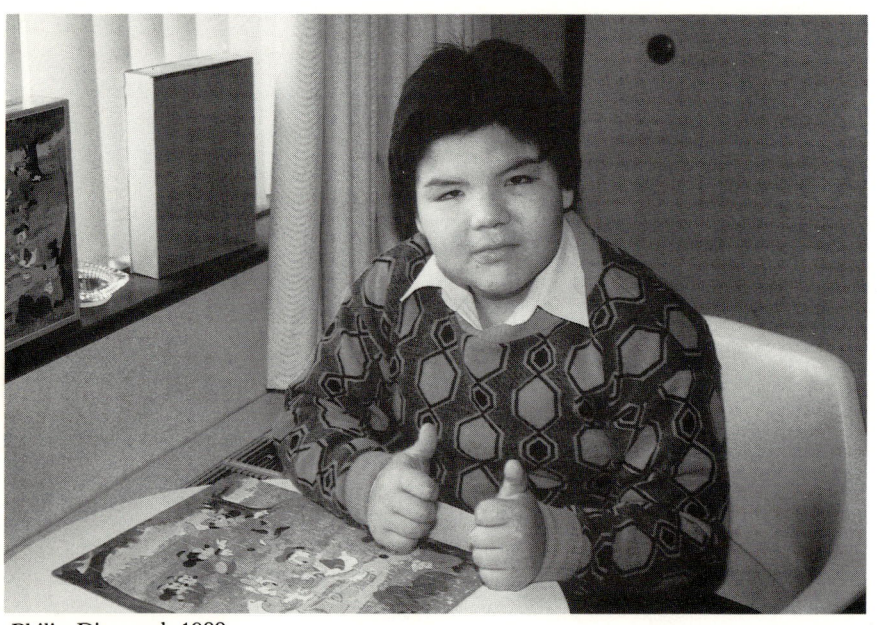

Philip Diamond, 1988

CHAPTER NINE

ENTER JEAN CHRÉTIEN

Jean Chrétien had tried to stay on top of the situation throughout 1973, though it had been a difficult year for him. Indian Affairs had gone from being the Cabinet portfolio of oblivion to a post as much in the news as the ministries of his front-bench colleagues, and Chrétien had been working himself close to a state of exhaustion. The Nishgas of British Columbia had managed to get the first comprehensive land claim all the way to the Supreme Court, and while they had not managed to win the case, a split decision had meant that land claims could no longer be as easily dismissed as Maître Geoffrion had wished when he first went up against the James Bay Crees. Furthermore, a grand plan to move oil and gas through British Columbia's Mackenzie Valley by pipeline was beginning to arouse public sympathy for the Natives, who vehemently opposed it. And, of course, all year long the Malouf hearing in Montreal had been producing newspaper headlines and sympathetic editorials.

In February, a twenty-three-page memo had leaked out of the office of Donald Macdonald, then minister of energy, mines and resources. The memorandum had spelled out the federal attitude toward the James Bay fight with Machiavellian heartlessness. In the memorandum, there was no evaluation of whether getting hydroelectricity from James Bay was a good or bad idea. Instead, the emphasis throughout was what the project meant in cold, political measure. There was intense concern over maintaining a firm, trustful relationship with the Quebec Liberals in this time when Confederation was so delicately balanced. There was the unmistakeable message from Quebec that Ottawa should butt out when it came to dealing with the Indians of James Bay. There was fretting over what the project meant in macroeconomic terms and how the "critical bunching" of Bourassa's investment schedule could seriously affect both the value of the Canadian dollar and the balance of payments.

It did not take a keen eye to read between the lines: a quick and easy settlement would be best for all, with no rocking of the federal-provincial boat, please. It is indicative of the sensitivity Ottawa felt toward Quebec at that time that neither the New Democratic Party nor the opposition Conservatives elected to press the government on the memorandum. The issues it outlined were quickly raised, quickly dropped, quickly forgotten.

Nineteen-seventy-three was also the year in which fighting once again broke out between Israel and the Arab countries in the Middle East. After a few initial gains, the Arabs were pushed back with severe losses. And such was the anger of the Arab states toward those who had supported Israel that oil shipments were cut off to the United States, Europe and Japan, thus precipitating a worldwide energy crisis. Robert Bourassa's mad scheme to turn James Bay into a turbine suddenly seemed enormously sensible to federal politicians who, for the first time in history, were worried about North American energy supplies.

With all these considerations, Chrétien was working furiously behind the scenes to arrange a prompt, gentle settlement of the James Bay claim. It was a plan that took a considerable step forward when the federalist Chrétien managed to manipulate the provincial political scene so that his own man was suddenly at the centre of the negotiations. Premier Robert Bourassa, seizing the opportunity created by the sudden shift of sentiment toward supporting alternative energy projects such as his James Bay dream, had called an election for the fall and had come to Chrétien looking for candidates the federal Liberal might recommend.

"I said to Bourassa, 'I have the perfect candidate for you,'" remembers Chrétien. " 'He's trilingual, French, English, Italian, a lawyer, smart—and his name's John Ciaccia.'" On the surface Chrétien appeared to be a fool squandering his wealth, offering up his deputy minister, his key departmental advisor on Indian land claims, and asking for nothing in return except that Bourassa consider Ciaccia for a Cabinet posting. Bourassa liked the sound of it. He approached Ciaccia about running and Ciaccia asked for forty-eight hours to consider. Ciaccia then went off to discuss the opportunity with his minister, Chrétien, who reacted with suitable surprise, which quickly dissolved into pleasure and encouragement. Ciaccia would never know how his minister had meddled in his own political career.

But Chrétien wasn't finished. He went back again to Bourassa, insisting that Ciaccia would need a safe, certain seat before he would agree to take such a leap of faith. Chrétien had just the seat in mind, too, the riding of Mont-Royal, the provincial equivalent of the traditionally Liberal riding held then by Prime Minister Pierre Trudeau. Bourassa offered Ciaccia the seat, and Ciaccia accepted.

"Trudeau gave me hell," says Chrétien, "because I was interfering in his riding. I just said 'Pierre, it's not me—Bourassa said, "Give me a good candidate." ' "

Ciaccia won easily, and the moment Bourassa named his Cabinet, Chrétien was back on the phone reminding Bourassa of his commitment to make Ciaccia a Cabinet minister. Bourassa countered that it was only a commitment to consider him as a rookie member. No problem, said Chrétien, he had the perfect suggestion. Malouf was about to come down with his decision. The negotiations with the Crees would have to begin sometime soon, so Chrétien suggested, "Why don't you name John Ciaccia as your negotiator?" That, too, seemed like an excellent idea to the premier of Quebec, who thanked the minister of Indian affairs and northern development. Chrétien said he was glad to be of some help.

After Ciaccia had received his assignment from his new boss, he came back to Ottawa for a friendly meeting with Chrétien. Ciaccia said he was worried, concerned that he would not know what to do. Chrétien laughed. He reached into his desk drawer where he had deliberately placed the confidential memo Ciaccia had written that summer—the memo that contained virtually the exact points that Billy Diamond had dictated off the top of his head while Jim O'Reilly scribbled—and pushed it across the desk at Ciaccia.

"What's that?" the new provincial member from Mont-Royal asked, reaching to pick it up.

"It's what you recommended when you were working for me," Chrétien said. "It's all there."

Ciaccia could only laugh at the irony. "It was an Italian that created this situation," he said to himself, thinking of the events Christopher Columbus had set in motion nearly five hundred years earlier, "it had to be an Italian that helped solve it."

The two Italians, however, were more than centuries apart. Christopher Columbus had believed that the "Indios" he discovered must be "made to work, sow and do all that is necessary and to *adopt our ways*." Ciaccia believed nothing of the sort. Canadian Indians, he believed, had their own ways, and had a right to preserve them. However, in Quebec City he held a minority opinion.

"It was like climbing walls," he says. The distance between the memo Chrétien had spun across the desk at him and the current thinking of the provincial government seemed, at times, too wide to breach. Paul Desrochers, Bourassa's key advisor at the time, was generally sympathetic to striking a deal, but he was convinced that $20 million would more than pacify the Indians. As for the others around Bourassa, they were convinced the Natives had no rights and, therefore, no right to hold out their hands.

Ciaccia went his own way, using the memorandum as a basis to construct a watered-down version of what Billy Diamond had envisioned. The offer was approved by an anxious Bourassa and presented to the Indians of Quebec Association on November 19, only four days after the Malouf decision. Done in haste, the meeting revealed a fundamental error that had nothing to do with the actual content of the document. Chrétien and the province had been involved in drawing up the offer, and the Indians of Quebec Association had been brought in to receive it—but no one had thought to ask the Crees and Inuit to come along to the meeting and say what they thought.

The three groups gathered in the Hilton Hotel near Montreal's Dorval airport, which suited Chrétien, as he could drop into and out of the meeting virtually unnoticed. Chrétien stood firmly behind the offer John Ciaccia was presenting to Andrew Delisle of the Indians of Quebec Association, and he wanted it known that Ottawa favoured a prompt settlement. He even had a master plan which he presented to the IQA lawyer, James O'Reilly, at the meeting.

"My idea was for them to lift the injunction voluntarily," Chrétien says. It was believed by all that Bourassa would get his way and be allowed to appeal, so why not have the Crees move first? They could voluntarily suspend the injunction, but keep it legally alive so that, in Chrétien's words, "they would have a club over the head" of the province and the development corporation. But O'Reilly didn't bite. In his opinion, it was far better to have the case dealt with properly in appeal. The courts would decide. Chrétien said they were "crazy" to think it would go their way, but he could not force them to take his advice. All he could manage was one self-satisfying, bitingly sarcastic line to O'Reilly: "Are you for the Crees or the trees or the fees?"

The proposal Chrétien so favoured contained eleven short points. (1) Land would be set aside, in reserves if the Natives desired, at a ratio of 640 acres per family of five. (2) Hunting and fishing for personal use would be permitted at all times, but trapping would be subject to provincial regulations. (3) $40 million in cash would be payable over ten years, plus royalties from all resources could conceivably rise to a ceiling of $60 million. (4) The money would be put into a Native development corporation. (5) There would be new programs introduced regarding tourism, a guaranteed minimum income for those who wanted to follow the traditional ways of life, and training programs for new employment. (6) Certain modifications to the project might be possible. (7) A committee on the environment would be established. (8) The band councils would govern the reserves, and one Native from each council would serve on the general council of the James Bay Development Corporation. (9) The Native development corporation would be exempt from income taxes for ten years. (10) Only those Indians and Natives currently living in the territory would be eligible. (11) A formal agreement would be signed by the federal government, the province and the Natives involved.

Word of the secret offer—the second secret offer made through the Indians of Quebec Association in the space of three months—leaked through to Rupert House when Chief Billy Diamond was settling Elizabeth and their new baby boy back home. He blew up in anger when the call came in. A helicopter was hastily chartered to get him out of Rupert and he arrived in Montreal in time to meet with Andrew Delisle and Max Gros-Louis of the Indians of Quebec Association.

"I demanded to know if there had been a meeting," he says. "And the answer was 'Yes.' I was furious at our leadership and I was stunned by what they had done by secretly speaking to the government on our behalf without even telling us. And I was mad at Chrétien for initiating any discussions. I said the Indians of Quebec Association could not make decisions on their own. Malouf had not handed down his decision to the IQA, but to the Cree chiefs and the

Cree elders. And because of that, the Cree chiefs would have to make any decisions on a deal."

Billy Diamond flew back up north with a copy of the eight-page offer. Already, the celebrations of the previous week were falling apart. Bourassa had not only made good his promise to appeal, but within a week the James Bay Project was right back on track. The government and corporation lawyers were able to convince Judge Jean Turgeon of the Quebec Court of Appeal not only to permit an appeal, but to use a provision in the Quebec Code of Civil Procedure to suspend the injunction without so much as a further hearing. The Malouf decision, in effect, was immediately overturned.

The Crees were quickly falling out with the Indians of Quebec Association. President Andrew Delisle said it made sense for Chrétien to negotiate with the province on their behalf, but Robert Kanatewat, by now a vice-president of the IQA, insisted that only the Cree people could decide what was best for them.

James O'Reilly—at that time being paid by the IQA to work almost solely on the Cree question—knew only that an injunction under suspension was similar to no injunction at all. And though the James Bay Development Corporation had flown its workers out immediately after the injunction, the work camps were already filling up again. He knew that by the time a proper appeal would ever be heard, the balance of inconvenience would have shifted dramatically in favour of the government and the corporation. O'Reilly began to think that the only way out was to take the case as quickly as possible to the Supreme Court of Canada.

O'Reilly sought and gained permission to appeal the curious judgment of the Quebec Court of Appeal. It would take place in Ottawa in the first week of December, and rather than having only the usual fifteen minutes that are allowed and a minimum of Supreme Court officials, the Crees would have two days to argue their case, and five senior judges of the Supreme Court of Canada would sit in judgment.

The week of the Supreme Court hearing, five hundred Crees and white supporters marched on Parliament Hill carrying placards with everything on them from simply "Boo Bourassa" to "Electricity Is Clean—Justice is Dirty, Dirty, Dirty." It was a far angrier demonstration than usual for the Hill, and the tension in the ranks of the Royal Canadian Mounted Police was palpable. The crowd began to get unruly. Some of the demonstrators jumped into the chill water of the Centennial Flame fountain, leaning over to burn copies of the Malouf injunction in the eternal flame of the Canadian government. Others began pushing against the barricades.

"It was scary," remembers Matthew Cooncome, then a nineteen-year-old Cree university student who was standing at the front of the demonstrators with his girlfriend. "We got pushed up the steps and the guards up there pushed and hit us back. She fell down and I started swinging. I knocked the hat off one Mountie and they grabbed the guy standing next to me and beat him up. It was the first time I ever saw brutality like that, and it shocked me. Here was a government that is supposed to protect us—our *trustee*—but here is that government's army trying to suppress us."

The Crees fared little better a few hundred yards west along Wellington Street in the Supreme Court building. James O'Reilly tried to fit in as many of the original arguments as he could, but the two days quickly ran out. There was no Jacques Beaudoin around to deliver a gut reaction as to how the case had gone, but O'Reilly knew when he was packing away his legal documents that it had not gone as well as it should have.

On December 21, the Supreme Court announced that it would refuse the Crees permission to appeal. There was small comfort in learning that the decision had been split, with three of the justices holding that suspension of the injunction was within the discretion of the Quebec Court of Appeal, and two—Justices Martland and Ritchie—convinced that there were fundamental issues involved in this case that warranted a full airing in the highest court in the land.

The Cree chiefs gathered in Val d'Or in the second week of December to decide what they would do. The key officials of the Indians of Quebec Association were also on hand, and the anger was apparent whenever either Billy Diamond or Robert Kanatewat referred to the IQA, but the fact remained that an offer was on the table and would have to be dealt with. Diamond went through the eleven points line by line, insisting that it was a dreadful offer. Nowhere could he find any mention, let alone recognition, of Cree rights. The health situation had not been addressed. The land promises were inadequate, the trapping offer an insult, the money meaningless. Kanatewat agreed with Diamond on every point.

The meeting was interrupted by word that a call was on hold for Chief Diamond. The caller was Jean Chrétien, the minister of Indian affairs.

"*Billy!*" Chrétien shouted when Diamond took the receiver. "I understand you have an offer from Bourassa."

"Yes."

"It's a good offer, Billy—you should take it."

Diamond was cool, denying the value of the proposal.

"I'm telling you, Billy, it's the best offer any Indian in Canada ever got."

Diamond began to detail the problems he had found with the document, but Chrétien cut him off.

"*I'm coming up!*" he shouted.

Less than two hours later, a white government jet was taxiing into the Val d'Or terminal. Chrétien was met by the only one at the Val d'Or office of Indian Affairs who happened to be wearing a tie, and he was whisked off quickly to the gathering where Billy Diamond once again proceeded to outline the many problems the Crees had with the proposals. But Chrétien's determination to settle this threatening issue could not be diminished. It could all be worked out later, he argued, but Diamond disagreed. "We must be sure *now*," he argued. Chrétien persisted, countering that if the Crees seized the opportunity now, he would himself lean on Bourassa and this whole mess would be cleared up in a matter of a few days. The Crees said they would have to think about it. First, they wanted to go for lunch. Chrétien, anxious that they keep discussing the matter, ordered lunch to be brought in at his expense from the Kentucky Fried Chicken outlet. He continued talking through the entire meal, but could not convince Diamond to budge. The Crees would not accept the offer.

Chrétien left in a foul mood, and without paying for the chicken. "We sent the bill to his office," says Ted Moses, who was at the meeting, "but they just sent it back."

For two years the Crees had been blessed with favourable public opinion. It had been formed by veteran journalists like Boyce Richardson and James Stewart and a bright, sympathetic young reporter for the huge Southam News chain, Bill Fox, who would later become Prime Minister Brian Mulroney's communications director. The goodwill had persisted throughout the Malouf hearing, had intensified when the injunction was overthrown and heightened during the march on Parliament Hill. The Crees had known nothing but applause from the public, and in 1974 were stunned to learn first-hand just how fickle that love can be.

From seeing whites climb into the Centennial Flame fountain to burn documents in their support in December, the Crees turned in

January to open-line shows where they themselves were under fire. "Do they all want gold-plated snowmobiles and mink parkas for the squaws?" one irate caller asked. And the lines were lighting up with more vindictiveness to come. The cause of this sudden switch lay in changes in strategy by both the provincial government and the federal politicians, a tandem shift that the Crees were convinced was far from accidental. Early in the last week of January—just as the Cree leaders were beginning a tour of the eight villages to discuss the secret offer with the people—Premier Robert Bourassa called a Friday afternoon press conference and dramatically revealed the contents of the November offer.

Bourassa's encounter with the media was brilliant. Once he had highlighted the $100 million in cash and the two thousand square miles that would be given to these deserving Natives, he said that for two months he had not received as much as an acknowledgement from them. He could not understand why, particularly when he had made it perfectly clear that the offer was "open to negotiation." When Bourassa's officials were pressed as to why the premier would go public without first informing the Crees that he was about to do so, they contended that every effort had been made to reach the other side. Bad telephone connections were blamed, a "misunderstanding." The Crees who might have told the other side of the story, of course, were all gathering in Fort George to talk about the proposals in private.

After a weekend of mounting public opinion against the Crees, Jean Chrétien stepped forward on the day the Cree leaders were travelling between the remote coastal villages of Paint Hills and Eastmain. Unless the Indians were prepared to accept the Bourassa offer as a basis for negotiations, Chrétien announced, he might be forced to cut off federal aid to the Crees and Inuit. "It's the best offer ever made to Indians anywhere in Canada," Chrétien said, "certainly the best offer by any provincial government." The federal minister wanted to make it clear that he was on the side of the Natives, that he himself had always believed that the original inhabitants of the area had rights. "But," he added, "if they are completely unreasonable in their demands, the cutoff may be necessary."

Without the federal funding Indian Affairs had been providing, there would be no lawyers and no experts to argue the Native case, and not even enough money to permit the Billy Diamonds and Robert Kanatewats and Charlie Watts to do it on their own. The Crees and Inuit were effectively checkmated. Chrétien later backed down when the opposition and editorials attacked him for threatening the Natives' right to appeal, but the point had been made, and the effect was immediate: the Crees and Inuit were put on the defensive.

And that, of course, is precisely what both the federal and the provincial officials wanted. "I was at wits' end," remembers Ciaccia. "I didn't know what to do." Bourassa's willingness to go public with the offer and then Chrétien's timely threat was, he hoped, a chance to bring about "a breakthrough—but the Native people were *very* upset."

"The Inuit and Indian people have occupied the land for centuries," an angry Charlie Watt said, "and they are now being asked to give up this right in a period of months." But it was Billy Diamond who captured the headlines with a single, succinct phrase. "Abraham Martenhunter, of Fort George," he said, referring to an old Cree hunter, "has stated that the Indian lands are not for sale, not for millions and millions of dollars."

The Crees had gone to Fort George to consider their options. Robert Kanatewat and Billy Diamond were offended by the Indians of Quebec Association for what they perceived to be an obsession with the monetary portion of the Bourassa offer. "Many whites feel the Cree only want the money," the Rupert House chief said, "that they don't really want to stop the project."

When the people of Fort George spoke, it became obvious that money was a minor consideration compared to land and the right to use it as they themselves decided. They could not understand Bourassa's offer of two thousand square miles when Justice Malouf had said they had rights over hundreds of thousands of square miles. As for the money, many of the elderly Cree could not even understand the offer, for there was no word in the Cree language for "million." Their numbers only went up to one thousand.

What came out at the Fort George meeting was a public acceptance of what the Cree leaders had always known privately: that the project would never be stopped. It was James O'Reilly's task to stand before the crowd and explain that, despite Malouf's ruling, the Fort George River would one day be dammed up and flooded, just as Robert Bourassa had stated three years earlier.

"White man will come anyway because he wants this land," O'Reilly told them. "And what white man wants, he gets."

"It was the hardest thing I ever had to do in my life," says

O'Reilly, who fifteen years later could not forget the sight of the shattered villagers filing silently out of the meeting and into the Fort George night.

It was up to Billy Diamond to convince the people that they now had no alternative but to negotiate, just as John Ciaccia had hoped. "When a man wants to cut wood," the young Rupert House chief said, "he does so when his axe is sharp and strong so that he can cut as much as possible. Well, the judgment is our axe . . . . It is in our favour and it is strong, very strong: we still have that judgment." As O'Reilly, Diamond and Kanatewat spelled it out in Fort George and in each of the other villages in an exhausting mid-winter tour, the Crees of James Bay had three options: they could continue pursuing justice through the higher courts and ignore Bourassa; they could stop the legal actions and negotiate; or they could continue working through the courts and talk at the same time. And once the people of Fort George, the village to be most affected by the project, had elected to go with the third choice, all the other Cree villages were quick to follow suit.

"Maybe we better obey these people we call our leaders," said Samson Lameboy, a member of the Fort George village council, "and let them continue to fight in the way they think is best.

"Get enough land so our children can survive when their time comes to hunt and fish," he added, turning from the audience back to the leaders. "That must be our main priority."

CHAPTER TEN

AGREEMENT

If the Crees had begun to feel as if they were losing public sympathy, they were right. A national poll taken in January 1974—just before the difficult times with Jean Chrétien—showed that Canadians were split over the James Bay issue. While 65 percent of the country was aware of the battle between the Natives and the government, 41 percent of the informed public felt the Indian land should simply be expropriated if it was felt to be in the interest of the country at large. Slightly more disagreed, but the fact that four out of every ten Canadians had little or no sympathy at all for the Crees was disturbing news indeed.

The problem, everyone knew, was the perception of greed. Ever since Bourassa's brilliant press conference and his suggestion that the Crees did not have the good manners to respond to an offer of $100 million, the view had taken hold that the James Bay Crees were simply holding the country up to ransom. "The biggest error in the popular perception of what happened is that money was the key," says John Ciaccia. "Money, as a matter of fact, was the last thing discussed and the quickest thing settled. Hunting and fishing was by far the hardest. I quickly came to the conclusion that the Native problem was not an economic problem, but a cultural problem. It took thousands of years to produce them, it took thousands of years to produce me. And we sort of ridicule them, saying all they ever want to do is go hunting and fishing. But that is like reading for us. They get upset about restrictions and licences and provincial regulations for hunting and fishing and I say, well, what if we had to have a licence to read, how would we react?"

Ciaccia tried to appreciate the Crees' obsession with hunting and fishing rights, but it did not prevent the early negotiations from bogging down on precisely these issues. The two Crees chosen to act as chief negotiators—Ted Moses and Philip Awashish—were, in fact, the two young leaders most closely identified with the bush life, and every Cree involved in the talks was acutely aware of the sentiment back home that had been so neatly expressed by Samson Lameboy. But Moses and Awashish were still expected to work hand in glove with the Indians of Quebec Association, and the IQA, in the young negotiators' opinions, suffered from two preoccupations. The first was that it was not possible to separate the rights of all Quebec Indians from the rights of the Crees. And the second was money.

In early April 1974, the Cree chiefs gathered again at Fort George for a progress report. Nothing whatsoever had been done about land. Moses and Awashish were frustrated, embarrassed that they had nothing to show for more than two months of talking, and by the end of the meeting the other chiefs had turned to Billy Diamond and asked him to take over the negotiations.

They were asking a very sick man. The drinking had continued even after the marathon hearing in Montreal. Chief Billy Diamond was overweight and worried about himself. While others thought he had developed a dramatic technique of blinking hard and rubbing his eyes when he spoke, the truth was that he was beginning to see double. Rubbing seemed to make it go away, at least until the next meeting, and he had told no one, not even Elizabeth. Still, he accepted the appointment, and moved quickly, with a cold efficiency. At the end of the Fort George meeting, the Crees of James Bay formally told the Indians of Quebec Association that they were changing their agreement. The IQA no longer had a clear mandate to negotiate on their behalf. From now on, Cree interests would have to be given priority over general claims. The Cree leaders were also going to become more involved in the financial aspects of the continuing battle.

Since Chrétien had issued his threat to cut off funding, the Crees had been tallying that amount and trying to check the total against what the IQA had done for the Crees. So far, $709,195 had come from the treasury to the IQA to help the Crees prepare and fight their claim, but the Crees could not in their wildest imaginings see where such a large sum had gone. Nor, apparently, could the House of Commons Indian Affairs Committee, which had just met and decided to ask the IQA for an accounting of the money spent fighting the project.

As for the legal situation, it was not very promising. Technically, the Malouf judgment still stood, but the government had managed to turn it into an inoperative ruling. After the Supreme Court had said no, barely, to the appeal of late December, in mid-February the Natives had returned to the Quebec courts to ask that the Malouf injunction be put back into play until the appeal was complete, as would normally be the case. Justice Marcel Crete refused. And when the Crees turned again to the Supreme Court in April, hoping the high court would hear another appeal, this time on the Crete ruling, the legal avenues suddenly dead-ended when the Supreme Court refused.

Ironically, the work on the James Bay project did come to a forced halt toward the end of March, but it had nothing to do with the Crees or the courts. Union squabbling at the LG2 dam site up the Fort George River eventually boiled over into a full-scale riot on March 21, and overnight the operation was closed down and a full evacuation undertaken. Although the first word that came out was that a foreman had chopped off a worker's hand with an axe, the incident that had sparked the riot had been nothing more than an unpopular American supervisor telling a group of French Canadian workers that they knew "fuck all" about how to build a dam. No matter, by the time tempers had settled, rampaging workers had set the $5 million construction site on fire and a union organizer, Yvon Dupuis—a former professional boxer—had driven a bulldozer over the main generators, destroying the energy source for the project. Work was effectively suspended until late May.

Billy Diamond knew that this was nothing more than a temporary hiatus, more dramatic than the Malouf decision, but in the end equally ineffective. There would be no stopping the damming of the Fort George River. He began to place his hopes on Bourassa's negotiator, rather than the courts, John Ciaccia was different from anyone the Crees had ever dealt with before from the provincial government. He listened. He seemed to care. He also came with a direct line to Jean Chrétien, the minister of Indian affairs, and though there had lately been bad feelings between Chrétien and the Crees, they still respected him. Somewhere down the line, the federal government would surely come into play in this battle, and it was important to remember that Ciaccia and Chrétien were once on the same side, and had become good friends in the process.

For weeks Billy Diamond, John Ciaccia and their lawyers, experts, bureaucrats and advisors discussed the land settlement, but failed to make even the slightest progress. The government officials were resisting any massive handover of territory, and the Crees were simply not willing to agree to the 640-acre-per-family offer from Bourassa.

On May 23, a glorious, still, spring day with the sun full of summer's promise, Ciaccia invited James O'Reilly and Billy Diamond out to his Beaconsfield estate just outside Montreal. He had no idea what would happen, but it was a good chance to leave behind the bureaucrats and enjoy a cold beer in the shade by the pool. Unfortunately, the leaves on the elms weren't yet fully out, so the shade was meagre, and O'Reilly and Ciaccia ended up with severe sunburns. But that was a small price to pay for what was gained in that single afternoon.

Ciaccia had begun the informal session by stating what was already known: the Crees were asking for too much land. The Quebec offer was two thousand square miles and the offer was final. The Crees were demanding sixty thousand square miles—an area larger than Greece—and were refusing to budge.

"It doesn't have to be all the same type of land," Billy Diamond suggested as the sun shone ever hotter over the St Lawrence River. "Why not have different categories?"

"Go on," said Ciaccia. "I'm listening."

Diamond lit the pipe he had recently started to smoke, convinced it made him appear older, wiser and more sophisticated. He drew slowly, hating the taste but loving the image. "Why not have land set aside for reserves, as you've already suggested? And then why not have some land set aside for provincial land? And why not have buffers in between, different categories of land where Natives have different rights? In return, it will be less than sixty thousand square miles, but for us the government will have to recognize the rights of Crees in the entire territory."

Ciaccia thought about it for a while. "You know, that might work."

Diamond thought he could convince his fellow chiefs, but the province would have to throw in a sweetener, as well, and that would be some kind of revolutionary new program that would be roughly similar to a guaranteed annual income—a phrase that instantly strikes terror in the hearts of Canadian politicians.

"I'm tired of people saying our way of life is dead," Diamond said as a fresh beer was cracked open on the patio. "We need an incentive program to go back to the land, something that would be greater than welfare, but won't make you rich." Diamond insisted, further, that the program would have to be funded entirely by the province.

By the end of the afternoon, with the line between the fair-skinned O'Reilly's neck and collar as sharp as the bite in a ripe apple, they had talked about separate land categories, an incentive program for hunters and trappers, economic development, health, education and even money. "It was an historic meeting," says Diamond. "We broke all the ice that afternoon. A few days later we met again formally with Ciaccia and he announced to the room that a way had been found to break the impasse. He announced that the Crees would have an incentive program to get back to the land. He said that a Native development corporation would be established. He said there would have to be different categories of land established. Category 1 lands would belong exclusively to the Crees, 1A lands would be under federal jurisdiction, 1B lands would be under provincial jurisdiction and Category 2 lands would be for the exclusive use of the Crees. He said the Government of Quebec would recognize the rights of the Crees over these lands.

"The provincial officials were caught entirely off guard. We knew we had a coup."

Negotiations continued all summer, but the meetings were never again as simple and friendly as the one that took place around Ciaccia's pool. At one point, Ciaccia and the provincial negotiators became convinced there was a large gap between what Billy Diamond and James O'Reilly were saying the Crees wanted and what the Crees back in James Bay really wanted. Diamond challenged him to go up and see for himself, and Ciaccia agreed, deciding on an early summer trip into the village that would be most affected, Fort George.

Passing over Matagami, the government pilot received an urgent radio call from the Matagami chief of police, insisting that they land. When they did so, the chief advised them that they would not be going ahead to Fort George because an informant in the village had called to say if Ciaccia landed there was going to be violence. Ciaccia argued that not only did the Matagami police have no authority in Fort George, but the village chief, Robert Kanatewat, was waiting for them to land.

"No, he's not," the policeman said. "Kanatewat's off hunting."

Kanatewat was indeed off hunting, driving at that moment on the gravel road stretch heading toward the junction that would take him to Mistassini. His family were in the truck with him, and one of the kids shouted out that a police car was bearing down on them with its lights flashing and siren on. They pulled him over, hauled the Fort George chief over to the police car and handed him the radio, saying John Ciaccia was on the line. Ciaccia was outraged. Where was Kanatewat? What was all this talk about Ciaccia being taken hostage if he dared to land in Fort George? Why were the police holding him back? Kanatewat had to turn his back on the curious policemen as he spoke into the microphone. The words they could hear: serious, concerned. The smile they could not see.

"We had this plan," Billy Diamond remembers. "We were going to throw Ciaccia to the dogs. We'd gone up and pumped up the people. We told them Ciaccia was awful, the government of Quebec was awful. We said we didn't think they'd ever trap again. That fired them up. They were mad at us. I said, 'Don't get mad at us, get mad at Ciaccia.' 'Where is he?' they wanted to know. 'We'll get him up here,' we promised." And now he was on his way.

"I told the Matagami police chief that the only way anything would happen was if Ciaccia arrived up here with a slew of police," says Kanatewat. "But if he agreed to put Ciaccia under my care, I would take full responsibility. Ciaccia came back on the line. 'Are you *sure*?' he wanted to know. I said, 'I assure you, nothing will happen.'"

Kanatewat hurried back to the village and put the rest of the plan into motion. Kanatewat would not do any of the speaking. Instead, the elders and some of the youngsters would ask the questions. Ciaccia continued on to Fort George, landed, and attended without incident the school meeting, where one after another, Cree elders and youngsters stood and let him know that they not only wanted everything their chief and the chief of Rupert House was asking for, they wanted more.

Afterwards, the entire band council formed a security phalanx around Ciaccia's group and escorted them to the motel where they would spend the night, the dark concealing the wide grin on Chief Robert Kanatewat's face but not the giggles that burst from his throat every so often as he saw the nervous visitors to their safe haven.

After John Ciaccia's trip to Fort George, negotiations began to move smoothly once again. No one doubted any longer that Diamond, Kanatewat, Moses and Awashish spoke for the Crees still back on the land. The problem now, however, was with the Indians of Quebec Association. IQA loyalists had long been turning on the Crees for moving so quickly toward a deal that would do nothing for other Quebec Natives, and the Crees had become more and more vocal about what the association had done with the money they'd obtained from Chrétien.

On August 8, 1974, the Cree chiefs gathered at the village of Eastmain and took the first step toward a full break with the IQA. They reviewed all the negotiations, agreeing that what they had so far from Ciaccia could form the basis for an agreement-in-principle. They talked about what the IQA had failed to do for them and, the following day, formed the Grand Council of the Crees of Quebec—the first formal political body in the entire history of the Crees of James Bay.

Albert Diamond, Billy's young brother who had been doing well at university, was recruited to oversee the finances. Abel Kitchen, just out of school, was put in charge of setting up a regional support system for the Crees that could one day evolve into self-government, and Billy Diamond, obviously, was to become overall leader. He would soon be given the title grand chief, but the Crees would wait until the upcoming IQA annual general meeting to make it official.

"It was ugly," Billy Diamond remembers of the IQA gathering. "Very painful. A lot of good friendships died that day." The Crees informed the association that they were striking out on their own, and James O'Reilly, the longtime IQA lawyer, would be going with them. The Crees also wanted a full audit of all the money that had been received from Ottawa for the Cree battle, and they wanted a cheque immediately for the remainder. "I was given a cheque for $26,000," recalls Diamond. "I handed it over to Albert and said, 'Let's see what we can do.' We had $2 million worth of bills to pay!"

It put the new Grand Council in an awkward position. With an agreement about to be reached, they needed to blitz the communities again before signing anything, but they had no cash to pay for the travel. In desperation they turned once again to the enemy, the James Bay Energy Corporation—a subsidiary of the larger development corporation—and the company graciously arranged for a single-engine Otter to take them into the villages.

The mounting bills were a grim reminder that money mattered, even though the Crees preferred to discuss hunting and fishing rights. But still, the issue of compensation was left deliberately to the end. The problem was *perception*. How would people view it? They already knew from experience that money was the one part of the deal everyone seemed instantly to understand, and also have an opinion on.

"Billy has an understanding of things," says Ciaccia. "It's uncanny. Never underestimate Billy Diamond. When it came to money, I said to Billy, 'I have a real political problem here. We cannot afford to have the public think we are creating millionaires of every Cree. If the public perceives we're creating millionaires overnight, I won't be able to sell it.' He understood perfectly."

They negotiated all through the summer, often in marathon sessions that saw the best weather pass without them even walking through it. And by September the pace was again beginning to take its toll. Robert Kanatewat, who had been attempting to get back home to Fort George every weekend, found during one visit back home that he had lost touch. "I was playing with my son," Kanatewat remembers. "He was about five at the time, and we were playing rough, having a little fight, and I accidentally hurt him and he started crying. 'Daddy,' he shouts, 'go on home!' He thought I wasn't in my home. He thought I lived somewhere else."

The same thing was happening to John Ciaccia. He'd leave the house at dawn and often not be back until three o'clock the following morning, and then up again at dawn for meetings. Well after midnight one night he went and stood at the bedroom doorway of his own son, Mark, who was then eleven years old. He was watching when the boy stirred and sat up, half focussing on the shadow in the doorway. "I think you're my father," the boy said, and then fell back down into the covers.

As for most of the others, they didn't even attempt to maintain a home life. The Crees were virtually living full-time in Montreal's downtown Holiday Inn, working from daybreak to well past midnight on the details of the agreement-in-principle. Ted Moses had happened to mention he'd like a week off to do some early goose hunting up at Eastmain, and the idea struck Billy Diamond as perfect for them all. He and Albert would come along. It would be good to get back to the bush.

But they never made it. They flew up to Val d'Or, with the Nordair stewardess running constantly between the bar and their seats, serving wine, followed by expensive cognac to satisfy Billy's insatiable appetite for the liqueur, and they went from the airport directly to the Moose Hotel, closing it down at three in the morning. Then they stayed around while Billy bought a bootlegged bottle from one of the bartenders. They stayed up all night drinking.

In the morning they could not get out of Val d'Or. The airport was fogged in and the planes wouldn't be moving all day. Billy suggested they head off immediately for another case of beer, and before the day was out, they had retraced perfectly their tracks of the previous night, closing down the Moose, bumming a bottle or two and drinking on in their hotel rooms.

When the weather broke and they were able to fly, Elizabeth Diamond came out to the Rupert House airstrip to welcome her husband home. She burst into tears at the sight of him. She got him back to the house, began pouring coffee into him and put out the word for neighbours and friends to come over. John Whiskeychan came from the Pentecostal Church and led prayers, and though Billy Diamond sat groggily listening, he was far more worried about the state of his health than the state of his soul. The double vision was back worse than ever. He was on the verge of signing an agreement that he, more than any other Native, had created from scratch, an agreement certain to change the James Bay Crees forever. If it failed to deliver what the people were hoping for, he saw no chance of turning back. He would have failed his people as surely as Joseph Brant had failed his. The agreement would be forever.

But he did sober up, and would stay sober for the remainder of these negotiations. When he wanted to relax, he would reach for his new pipe instead of another beer, thinking a pipe was more in keeping with a leader's image than the cigarettes he had been smoking off and on since high school. Elizabeth thought his pipe was phoney, and told him so. He stopped smoking as much but kept the pipe in his pocket because he liked the feel of it in his hands. He had no idea then that the silly affectation would soon save his life.

There seemed to be no time to get his personal life back on track. The pace quickened in October, with federal government officials showing up in Montreal and now beginning to worry out loud about all the concessions that Ciaccia seemed willing to make to the Crees.

Ciaccia, in the meantime, set out for Quebec City with a rough draft of what would become the agreement-in-principle. Although he felt confident, to make himself feel even more sure, he put on his best suit and decided to drive himself in his classic Jaguar. He thought that, for once, a treaty was about to be signed that would not come back to haunt both sides.

Robert Bourassa was waiting for Ciaccia in the same Cabinet room where Malcolm Diamond had been prevented from making his feelings known. But this time the entire Cabinet listened carefully, and when Ciaccia had finished his presentation, every one of them, Bourassa included, broke out in applause. Ciaccia was elated. He left the Cabinet meeting and walked out into an early snowfall. The storm grew worse on the drive back to Montreal and made visibility difficult. Then the Jaguar blew a tire, then a second, and Ciaccia, finding he had no jack, had to wait until the provincial police came along and helped him change both tires. Still, he arrived back in his Beaconsfield home happy and content, and for the first time in months slept soundly on into the morning.

But even after the Cabinet had given its initial approval, there was much to do. The pressure intensified to the point where, during the last few weeks, Billy Diamond changed his room at the Holiday Inn daily to circumvent the midnight calls and persistent knocks on the door. They set a November 15 deadline for signing of the agreement-in-principle, and refused to budge when the federal officials began talking about needing more time.

On October 28 the federal Cabinet had met in Ottawa to discuss the agreement-in-principle, and according to confidential Cabinet document 594-74, they had concluded that "on balance, the current Quebec offer can be considered fair and, if anything, on the generous side. Certainly, if it had not been for the Hydro Project and the ensuing court action, the requirement of the 1912 Boundaries Extension Act that the Quebec government treat the Indians in the same manner as had the federal government heretofore, would have resulted in a much less generous settlement." Ottawa's concerns were simple: there would need to be some assurance that the settlement would be binding enough that it would "ensure real and lasting benefits" and, it was briefly noted, "It is impossible to predict with any certainty future financial implications arising out of any James Bay settlement."

Two days before the deadline, Billy Diamond, Philip Awashish, Robert Kanatewat, Ted Moses, Peter Gull and other Cree negotiators sat down for a strategy meal and decided that the only way to force the government's hand was to move first and have the bureaucrats scramble to follow. They then met with Charlie Watt and Mark Gordon of the Inuit side and decided on a course of action. They would wait until the evening before the deadline and then put out a short press release announcing the agreement-in-principle. The excuse for the press release, they would argue if the government asked, would be nothing more than the Crees and Inuit letting the media know where and when the Crees would be holding their press conferences. But, in fact, there was no agreement-in-principle at the time that the Native press release announced it. They waited deliberately until "happy hour," to put their release out on the fax machine to the various news services. Then they switched rooms in the hotel again, and conveniently could not be found for further comment.

The Crees had no idea when they went to their new rooms that night that the whole deal was on the verge of falling apart. Ciaccia had been called at his home close to midnight by the Cabinet secretary and told that one minister was changing his mind about the deal. He wouldn't spell out precisely who, but Ciaccia had no trouble guessing—Justice Minister Choquette.

A few phone calls later and Ciaccia had arranged to meet with Choquette in his Montreal office at 9:00 A.M., and he then spent from midnight to shortly after 4:00 A.M. jotting down notes on what he would say. "I don't even remember what the points were now," says Ciaccia, "but I do remember explaining to him why it was important. By ten I had him convinced enough to say go ahead. I ran from his office over to the hydro office where the signing was to take place and my signature was on the agreement by 11:00 A.M. It was a rough night."

Choquette really had no choice, as the morning headlines had already gone with the Cree and Inuit press releases and were announcing that the agreement had been reached. "Natives accept $150 million," the main headline in the Montreal *Star* read. The Crees and Inuit would get the first $75 million within the first ten years of the agreement, and a further $75 million in royalties from hydroelectric projects spread out over an even longer period. Far back in the turn pages it was also reported that Natives would receive exclusive rights to fish and hunt and trap in most of the 65,130 square miles affected by the project.

The money, as Ciaccia and Diamond had expected, was where the *perception* would be. It worked out, the papers said, to about $15,000 for each Native, not an outrageous figure and not one, anyway, that would be going directly to anyone. The key points of the agreement—like the land rights—were overlooked and ignored in the first flush of reaction. Modifications would definitely be made to the project. Burial sites would be marked and, if possible, moved prior to flooding. Financial aid would be forthcoming to trappers. Natives would have extensive governing powers. School boards, police and health groups would be established.

Premier Robert Bourassa came to sign for the provincial government, and Judd Buchanan, the new Indian affairs minister, came to sign for Ottawa, as did Jean Chrétien in his new position as president of the Treasury Board. Charlie Watt signed for the Inuit, and Billy Diamond—wearing a checkered suit that could have graced Nathan Detroit in *Guys and Dolls*—lined up to sign for the Crees, but stopped suddenly when he couldn't find a pen.

"Might as well borrow your pen," he said to Chrétien, "since I've already borrowed your money."

But it wasn't all laughs. "We realize," the new grand chief of the James Bay Crees said at the press conference that followed, "that perhaps we will disappoint the public by signing an agreement-in-principle with the Quebec government. We realize that many of the friends we have made during our opposition to the project will label us as 'sell-outs.' However, we have come to a decision together, and we intend to carry out that decision, and we also consider it a great victory—a big victory for us because there are only seven thousand Crees and there are six million Quebeckers in this province. It is also a big victory because there are not many people that can persuade the best engineers in the world to change the location of a major dam, and to change their plans such that our way of life will be less harmed."

But he was right, the agreement-in-principle would not please everyone. George Manuel, the British Columbian then serving as president of the National Indian Brotherhood, immediately attacked the cash settlement as inadequate. "It represents $3.03 an acre," Manuel calculated, "and that's not enough."

The biggest kick was yet to come. Andrew Delisle, the president of the Indians of Quebec Association, waited two weeks and then—with George Manuel standing beside him—declared that the Crees and Inuit had been "duped" into signing the deal. John Ciaccia and James O'Reilly, he said, were part of a conspiracy to cause a split among the Quebec Indians. And he even dropped a broad hint that the James Bay Cree leaders may have been bribed.

But Billy Diamond was not even around to hear the accusation. The day after John Ciaccia had opened up his magnificent, old-world-style home to a Cree square dance that went on until dawn, the grand chief of the celebrating Crees caught a flight north and then north again to Fort George, where he checked himself directly into the hospital. His double vision had become almost constant. He hadn't slept at night for weeks. But it was all put down to nerves and exhaustion, and a week later they sent him home to Rupert House, where Elizabeth was waiting with two children who couldn't remember what their father looked like.

A week after he arrived home, Billy Diamond set out with his nine-year-old nephew, Bentley, to do some ptarmigan hunting. They went by snowmobile, staying close to the shore as the weather had been cold enough to form ice but had not lasted long enough for the ice to extend out into the bay. It was a quiet, relaxing break. By mid-afternoon they had shot eight birds. But a blizzard came up unexpectedly, wiping out the trails and forcing them to try making their way along the new ice, using the shoreline as a guide to show them how far out they could venture.

The new snow had also covered the weak spots, however, and they had barely set out when the ice cracked and gave way under the skidoo, sending the boy spilling out across onto safe ice and the heavy man and the machine straight down into the black water. Billy lunged and landed his arms onto the good ice, but could not pull himself up. Nor could the small boy help. And the water was seeping into his clothing, adding weight, sucking him back.

Keeping one hand firm on the ice, he felt in his pockets for something to help him gain a better purchase, finding only the cursed pipe Elizabeth had laughed at.

"Stay back!" he shouted to Bentley, who was crying and trying to crawl to his uncle.

The boy moved back, howling. Billy fell silent, breathing deep to cap the rising panic. Then, over a painful, frightening quarter-hour, he began the awesome crawl out of the hole. The stem end of the pipe he was able to use as an ice-pick, stabbing it into the ice and drawing himself ever higher until, at last, he could loop a leg over onto the surface and roll away from the black hole.

With the sobbing boy helping him, and his freezing clothes beginning to grind as he walked, Diamond made it into the bush, where they were able to get a fire going and take off his clothes. Eventually, another hunter came along and offered help, but Billy Diamond refused to budge. Instead, he sent the boy back with word that he would be along later. He would wait for the tide to go out and either haul his skidoo out or mark it so they could retrieve it later.

When the boy and the hunter got back to Rupert House and word got out, the village went into a panic. Old Malcolm Diamond organized a rescue squad of snowmobiles and they set out in the dark to bring in the first grand chief of the James Bay Crees, the man who had just gained the Crees right to territory larger than New York state and come back to the village waving a piece of paper he claimed was worth $150 million.

When they found him, the grand chief of the James Bay Crees was standing smoking his now-beloved pipe, savouring the taste of life and wondering how the hell he would ever pay for a new skidoo if it rusted up from the salt water.

CHAPTER ELEVEN

JAMES BAY AND WOUNDED KNEE

"Still want to change the world!" Billy Diamond scribbled across a blank page in the binder with the army camouflage design that he carried during the final negotiations. Twice he underlined the word *world*. "*Determined*," he wrote, and underlined it for emphasis, "*to do a lot more.*"

Barely a week after the premier of Quebec and the grand chief of the James Bay Crees had signed their names to the agreement-in-principle, the Quebec Court of Appeal announced that it had come to a decision on the Malouf injunction. Mr Justice Jean Turgeon—the very man who had suspended the injunction a year earlier—now had a few more points of law to put forward on behalf of himself and the four other judges on the appeals panel. Justice Malouf—Turgeon and his colleagues had determined—had been hoodwinked by "emotion and romanticism." After reviewing the arguments of the James Bay Development Corporation and the government, the panel had come to the conclusion that "the Indians and Inuit had abandoned the way of life of their ancestors and have adopted that of the whites."

When the appeal court judges weighed the evidence of those who worked in Hudson's Bay Company stores against that of the Cree and Inuit hunters, they concluded, "The Native people eat as do people inhabiting the urban centres." As for the Native claims that they were following a traditional way of life, the corporation offered, as proof that the Crees had adopted European ways, a selection from the *Jesuit Relations* (1633–1677) that described the Crees as "lively, always in action, always dancing or singing. They are brave and love war." And as proof that the Inuit were hardly traditional in the twentieth century, the corporation offered up a 1720 Dutch publication that claimed the Eskimos are "so wild and so intractable that no one has been able up to now to attract them to any commerce. They make war on all their neighbors, and when they kill or capture some of their enemies, they eat them raw and drink the blood."

The most intriguing piece of new evidence came from an anthropologist hired by the corporation to paint the project in a better light. "The James Bay project," Paul Bertrand argued, "presents for the Indian culture its main cohesive tool, and the salutary shock that will permit it to rediscover its identity and its personality."

When the other anthropologists read this, they were outraged. The Crees were furious. The lawyers were appalled. But a decade later, Bertrand—even if he had damaged the Crees' bargaining position somewhat—would prove to have been prescient, if a trifle blunt, about the "salutary shock" of the "Project of the Century." Before the endless battle against the James Bay Project would be over, the fight itself would have created the Cree Nation, and the prospect of more wars to come over the waters of James Bay would substantially sustain it.

In December it was back to the bargaining table, this time to deal with intransigent government departments, rather than a flexible, accommodating John Ciaccia. The Crees engaged a professional financial planner—Montreal's Norman Hawkins—whose first task was to meet with the new grand chief and explain to Billy Diamond what an expense form was.

There was also the matter of the lawyers, and the Crees decided on a bonus of $900,000 which would be split among several lawyers, including James O'Reilly. Twenty-five percent would be designated for the estate of Jacques Beaudoin, who had not lived to taste the victory he had predicted. The Crees then went to the Canadian Imperial Bank of Commerce and, using Bourassa's offer as collateral, secured a loan that would take them through the final negotiations.

Much of the money was spent travelling back and forth between the eight Cree communities and Montreal and Quebec City, where the final negotiations were taking place. Each Cree village had to be visited. There, they would go over the agreement-in-principle in detail and then find out what local problems had yet to be discussed back at the negotiating table. It was a time of great confidence for the village Crees, and they did not shy away from demanding that the most minute details be ironed out. As hunter Billy Ottereyes said at a Waswanipi band meeting held at Matagami, "The white man used to scare us, but now it's the other way around."

The negotiation of a final agreement was very different from the work that went into the agreement-in-principle. "It was a restricted group at first," says John Ciaccia, who continued to lead the negotiations for the province. "But now there was something like twenty-seven government departments being directly affected. We had to move the process into a parliamentary committee room that would hold forty or fifty people, and the first problem we had to overcome was everybody demanding to know why they hadn't been involved before. I felt a bit sheepish sitting there with all these deputy-ministers and directors and having them all looking at me like that. I had to explain the agreement and then I had to convince them why it had to be like that."

Ciaccia's most valuable argument was a simple twist on the prevailing sentiment in Quebec, where the Parti Québécois was rapidly increasing in popularity and separation from Canada was fast becoming a possibility. Whenever Ciaccia spoke of the Crees or Inuit, he spoke as if they were dealing not with acres and medical services but with "the cultural identity and survival of a people." Just as the six million of Quebec were anxious about their survival in an increasingly anglophone Canada, so too were the ten thousand Cree and Inuit Natives of northern Quebec trying to confirm their special identity within the province. "It's the same principle," Ciaccia argued, and, for the most part, it worked magnificently.

The battle over land was, as expected, the toughest fight of all. The Crown corporations—Hydro-Québec, the James Bay Development Corporation and the James Bay Energy Corporation—were determined that the maximum amount of affected land be limited to five thousand square miles, whereas the agreement-in-principle had settled on sixty thousand square miles, the difference in area being equivalent to the difference between the state of Connecticut and the state of Illinois. All Ciaccia could manage at the start was to have the corporations agree to leave it up to the government representative for lands. Both would make their presentations, and the bureaucracy would decide.

"They prepared their charts," Ciaccia recalls. "They had this big map with the five thousand square miles pencilled in and then the sixty thousand coloured in in red to really scare the shit out of everybody. The charts were up, all ready for the big meeting. I went in the night before and saw the guys in lands. I said, 'Look at all the green space here. I'm sure you guys don't want to see the whole North paved over eventually. Just remember, you're the guys in charge of category 2 lands—the more you have, the more control you'll have.'" Ciaccia talked about the importance of the provincial officials serving as "custodians" of the land, and how they couldn't always be there, but the James Bay Development Corporation was now there permanently. The following day the decision was tabled: sixty thousand square miles.

The second big obstacle was self-government, which was one of two points Grand Chief Billy Diamond was absolutely insistent upon—that and the removal of the LG1 dam from its location near Fort George. The dam location was an engineering problem, but self-government struck at the political fibre of the country. "I had less problems with Quebec City on that one than I did with Ottawa," says Ciaccia. "Ottawa said, 'You can't let *them* decide how they're going to spend that money.' I went to Chrétien. I told him the same guys who used to put obstacles in my way when I was here are putting obstacles in the way now, and if you don't do something, they're going to scuttle this agreement. Chrétien called a meeting, and did he give them a tongue-lashing."

For the most part, however, it was a quiet, if uneasy, time. The negotiations were mind-numbing, the hours required exhausting. He had become obsessive about the agreement, at times lost in his room, filled with crippling doubts, at other times manic about what it would do for Crees. At home his conversation became so dominated by the agreement that Elizabeth found it difficult to talk to him—but, then, she was just glad to have her husband back, if only for a while.

The dilemma of Grand Chief Billy Diamond was never so perfectly illustrated as in the fall of 1975 when, during the closing weeks of the final negotiations, the Indians of Quebec Association and the James Bay Development Corporation found themselves on the same side, cursing the entire process. The corporation broke its three-year silence on the battle by holding a special "information day" headed up by the corporation chairman, Robert Boyd, who immediately blamed the news media and "certain intellectuals" for tipping the balance in the favour of the Natives. "Dialogue with the population became extremely difficult, even impossible," Boyd complained. He argued that the project's very simple objective—to satisfy Quebec's energy needs—had been clouded by "politicization" issues such as Indian and Inuit rights.

At the same time, the IQA was fighting the negotiations from another angle. Andrew Delisle declared the negotiations illegal, saying the province had no right to negotiate what should be a federal concern and claiming that Indians were opposed to the final signing. Court injunctions were even sought by Montagnais Indians and a dissident Inuit group to prevent the signing, but neither the Superior Court of Quebec nor the Federal Court of Canada would accept their arguments.

The federal Cabinet met on October 23 to discuss the final agreement. Clearly, the Ottawa politicians were worried. "There are several key issues which may pose difficulties," the confidential memorandum to Cabinet prepared by Judd Buchanan began, and fourteen pages later the concerns were still being raised. The speed with which Ciaccia, the Crees and the Inuit were moving was alarming Ottawa considerably. The deadline, Buchanan wrote, "promises to lead to hasty and ill-considered decisions on the wording of the Agreement which may act against the long-term interests of the federal government and of the native people."

Indian Affairs had come to the same conclusion about the agreement that was delighting Billy Diamond. The Cree settlement, the bureaucrats reported to Cabinet, "will completely supersede the Indian Act as far as the Crees of Northern Quebec are concerned." The Crees would become the first Indians to move out from under the smothering, overly protective and often damaging legislation that, up until now, had completely controlled the government dealings with Indian bands. Would the Crees, for example, still be able to claim exemption on personal income tax? Did Ottawa have the courage to deny them this historic perk? Was there time, the memorandum wondered, to iron all this out before the unrealistic signing deadline upon which the Crees were insisting?

On November 4, with only a week to go before the final signing deadline, the grand chief of the James Bay Crees was summoned to Quebec City to appear before the National Assembly as a witness. Under pressure from the corporation and the Indians of Quebec

Association, certain members of the assembly were insisting on going over the agreement line by line and talking about a possible delay in the process. Diamond listened to what they had to say, but then, rather than argue the point, told them: "Gentlemen, I am the Cree leader. These are my chiefs behind me. I'm going to sign. You have until midnight November 11 to sign. You're going to have to make up your minds, and if you don't sign, it's going to be back to court. I'm not going to listen anymore."

A hastily scribbled note was dropped on the chief's papers as Billy Diamond gathered up to leave. "Don't get mad!" Ciaccia had written. "You're going to piss them off." Diamond turned the note over, scribbled, *"Piss on them!"* on the back, sent it back to the squirming Ciaccia and walked out of the room, with all the Cree chiefs trailing behind him.

To emphasize his point about the deadline, Diamond chartered two aircraft to leave Quebec City in the early hours of November 12. Within twenty-four hours of the deadline all Cree would be back in their home villages—either with the signed agreement or else with nothing. Whatever happened, they would negotiate no more.

"When we do go home," he had told the natural resources committee while in Quebec City, "we are not coming back. We are prepared to tell our people we will not speak to the representatives of the government of Quebec again, and I doubt very much if our own population will extend their mandate."

"Everybody thought he was fooling," says John Ciaccia. "But I knew he wasn't." Even so, the government did check out the bookings, confirming that Diamond did indeed intend to leave the moment the deadline passed.

By the time the final day came around, there was still much doubt as to whether or not there would be a signing. Charlie Watt of the Inuit wanted a specific ratification clause, and appropriate wording had to be found so the Inuit and Crees could have "consultation and confirmation" meetings in their communities—though the Cree leaders had already done this and each had been given power-of-attorney by his own band. A ratification agreement was included, however, and though the Inuit had some dissenters when they returned the details to the communities, the Crees voted 922-1 in favour, the lone dissenter being Billy Sagamish of Waswanipi, who didn't seem to feel any obligation to the chief who had once bailed him out of jail.

On the night of the tenth, the Crees held a party in Montreal. For most of the night they danced and drank, and at dawn 125

Crees—most of them hung over, all exhausted—piled into buses for the two-hour ride to Quebec City, where the signing was scheduled to take place. Their grand chief, however, flew, claiming he needed the extra rest.

When they arrived in the provincial capital, they were informed that the committee was still meeting, still going over the proposed agreement clause by clause, and might like to further question the Cree leader on the details. Diamond refused. "Tell them we're not here to meet with them," Diamond told the Cabinet secretary, Jean Cournoyer. "We're only here to sign." The Crees then left the Salon Rouge, where Cournoyer had asked them to wait, and went over to the Concorde Hotel, where they moved into suites and the elderly were able to lie down and rest. Word did not come back from the National Assembly until 8:00 P.M. "Yes. We are going to sign."

But there was still a delay. The new minister of Indian affairs, Judd Buchanan, could not be located. Word finally came that he was on a government jet coming in from his riding in London, Ontario. At 11:30, the books were opened and the pens readied, and though a photograph of a wristwatch indicates the deadline had passed by ten minutes when Grand Chief Billy Diamond moved to the document, in a moment his practised flourish was drying and the James Bay and Northern Quebec Agreement—the first modern, comprehensive treaty to be signed since the Supreme Court of Canada had indicated that there might be such a thing as aboriginal rights—was a historical fact and a legal document, duly signed.

There was no time for anything other than brief handshakes and small talk. Outside the Assembly the buses were idling for the ride to the airport, and already Cree elders were hurrying out, anxious to get back to sleep and eventually home. Billy Diamond spoke briefly with Bourassa and Buchanan and Ciaccia, then left with James O'Reilly, walking into the chill night air and then up into the first bus to the sound of an enormous cheer that took several minutes to die down.

But when all was quiet, a voice from the back of the bus asked the obvious question. "Now that we've signed, *what do we do next?*"

At a press conference in Montreal on the treaty, Billy Diamond tried to downplay any sense of victory the Crees might have felt. "The Cree people all understand that the province must be allowed to build the hydroelectric project in the James Bay area," he said. "We realize that many of the friends we have made during our opposition to the project will label us sell-outs.... I hope you can all understand our feelings, that it has been a tough fight and our people are still very much opposed to the project, but they realize that they must share the resources."

"By most counts," the *Financial Times of Canada* reported, "the provincial government came out the clear winner. For $225 million (of which $33 million will be paid by the federal government), plus recognition of native peoples' rights on some 61,000 sq. mi. of territory, it gets a virtual free hand to develop the rest of Quebec as it sees fit. The money involved amounts to only about 2 percent of the cost of the $12 billion James Bay hydroelectric project, and the territory allotted to the Native people is only about 15 percent of the region."

The Crees and Inuit, however, had placed land as their highest priority. They now had Category 1 lands, which would mean exclusive control over 2,020 square miles for the Cree and 3,205 square miles for the Inuit. True, the Crown would have mineral and subsurface rights, but there could only be development with full Native consent and involvement. Category 2 lands would include 25,030 square miles for the Cree and 35,000 square miles for the Inuit, land which would be for the exclusive hunting, fishing and trapping of the Natives. Any development on these lands by the province would require both compensation and replacement.

It was an enormous amount of Canadian real estate when one took into consideration that the total area covered 65,300 square miles, or 41,792,000 acres, for a population of some 10,000 Quebec Natives. The entire population of registered Indians in all of Canada at the time—roughly 250,000 people—were living on reserves totalling barely 6 million acres.

In addition, the Cree Indians would have something that no other Indians in Canada enjoyed: a guaranteed-income scheme for hunters. For the Indian negotiators, it was the incentive scheme, not the cash, that was the cream of the agreement. But, of course, no one wanted to talk about the plan to keep hunters in the bush. They wanted to talk dollars, big dollars. The amount of money the papers were concentrating on—$225 million, of which the Crees would be getting $150 million—mostly involved cash, and the payments would be spread out over a long period. Instalments over the coming ten years would add up to $75 million, and a further $75 million would be paid out when the James Bay hydro project began operation. A final $75 million would be put up in twenty-year

Quebec bonds which would be issued in five-yearly instalments. But everyone who was deeply involved with the deal—from John Ciaccia on the government side of the table to Billy Diamond and Charlie Watt on the Native side—knew that the *true* value of what they had signed could not be broken down so easily.

There was a remarkable difference between the treaty of 1975 and those Duncan Campbell Scott had arranged on the other side of the bay in 1905. When Scott handed out the initial payments of $8 per Indian, he noted in his journals that there were Indians "who thought they had received more in eight ones than some of their fellows had in four twos." The Natives on the east side of the bay in 1975 showed rather more financial acumen.

"It was not in the Cree interest to show how much money the agreement was worth," says James O'Reilly. "We're not that crazy." Adds Ted Moses: "There was a deliberate intent to avoid talking about it."

"We originally talked about caps on services, ceilings on health and services, those sorts of things," says Billy Diamond. "But we knew someone would add it up. We had to take the risk and hide the money in programs like the Income Security Program. That program didn't even exist when we signed the agreement. It had to be developed, then drafted as legislation, then passed. But it was a risk we had to take. We knew we had to hide the money. We knew it might be used against us at some time, but we had to chance it."

Those services, according to Norman Hawkins, the Montreal-based Cree accountant, are now worth approximately $80 million a year to the Crees—costs which, had they been tallied up in the aftermath of the signing, would have soon tacked another $1 billion to the agreement, with the value rising annually. Warren Allmand, the minister of Indian affairs who would introduce the legislation to formalize this agreement in law, would later refer to the treaty as a "Trojan horse," only half in jest.

At the Montreal news conference, the actor in Billy Diamond built a look of pain and sadness on his face as he shook his head and told the gathering that the agreement was the best the Crees could do, considering the circumstances.

The James Bay and Northern Quebec Agreement of 1975 had taken nearly two years of exhausting, high-level negotiation to hammer out. In contrast, Duncan Campbell Scott and his fellow travellers would often scribble out their treaties in the evening and present them *de facto* in the mornings, handing out a few dollars to the likes of Charles Wabinoo of Attawapiskat, who pulled a crucifix from his shirt, kissed it, made the sign of the cross toward Scott and said, "From my heart I thank you." Chief Billy Diamond thanked no one.

One hundred and thirty-eight years had passed since Peter Jones—a halfbreed Methodist minister—had been sent by the Mississauga tribe to England to ask the Queen for title to the lands on which the Mississauga were settled, and had been summarily turned down. But now the Crees of James Bay had title to a land area half as large as Belgium and full rights over a chunk of Quebec significantly larger than Greece. They had forced a dam location to be moved and had demanded the rebuilding of one village and the creation of another. On a more personal level, Grand Chief Billy Diamond went to bed that night convinced that he had not turned into a modern Joseph Brant.

Even so, the cheers that had greeted Billy Diamond as he boarded the bus outside the Quebec National Assembly were hardly shared by all. The Indians of Quebec Association did call the signing a "sell-out." And the criticism of the better-known Canadian Native leaders—George Manuel and Noel Starblanket in particular—continued; in their opinion, the final agreement was just as bad as the agreement-in-principle they had ridiculed a year earlier.

"It was naïve, maybe," says John Ciaccia, "but I thought the agreement would get a better reaction. I was hurt. I knew the time that had been spent, the efforts, the lengths to which the governments had gone beyond what would be normally expected. But unfortunately, there just wasn't any realization of what the agreement meant." In part, the problem was the general atmosphere in the country concerning Native rights. Rather than hailing what the Crees and Inuit had received, leaders concentrated on what had been lost, and that was the extinguishing of whatever aboriginal rights the Crees and Inuit might have had a claim to in exchange for new rights outlined in legislation. And even though the editorial page of the *Globe and Mail* hailed this "landmark" treaty as "the first agreement with native peoples in Canada which recognizes what is sometimes referred to as aboriginal rights," the point was lost on others.

By agreeing to extinguish such rights, other Natives contended, the Crees and Inuit were damaging aboriginal claims that might exist elsewhere in Canada. Billy Diamond argued that he did not give up any traditionally held rights. All he did, he contended, was to give the government the right to build a dam. But this argument did not wash with the more militant leaders, particularly George Manuel of British Columbia. And in Diamond's heart, he knew that Manuel had a point: the Crees and Inuit had agreed to extinguishing vital rights. But what his mind had convinced him, just as Charlie Watt's mind had convinced him, was that it was a case of either volunteering to extinguish them or waiting to drown. The "Project of the Century" was, from the moment it had been announced, unstoppable.

Two well-known British Columbian Indian leaders—George Watt and Nishga chief Rod Robinson—were quick to come to Billy Diamond's defence and invited him out to the West Coast to talk about the treaty. "We wanted to hear it from the horse's mouth," says Watt. "He came out and destroyed everything Manuel and his sons were going around saying about James Bay." Robinson felt the same way: "The James Bay Agreement was good. These were difficult circumstances and we appreciate that. We gained a lot of valuable experience in negotiations from Billy Diamond. It's only once in a while that a person of this calibre comes along, and it takes tremendous leadership to bring about something like that."

But Watt and Robinson were in a minority position. The moment belonged to the militants, and they did not talk about what had taken place on paper in James Bay, but what had taken place under siege at Wounded Knee. The Crees, knowing that no one was interested in hearing about a success story that had the unfortunate stigma of no formal recognition of aboriginal rights, shut up completely. "The Crees went into a closet," says Billy Diamond. "They had been ridiculed and belittled for signing an agreement with a government. They were made to feel ashamed for what they had done."

And then, less than six months after the signing of the James Bay Agreement, a virtually unknown Alberta Indian leader by the name of Nelson Small Legs, Jr., put a rifle to his head and killed himself, leaving behind a suicide note that said, "I give my life in protest to the Canadian government for its treatment of Indian people for the past 100 years." When the Small Legs suicide succeeded in galvanizing Native anger against the government, Diamond stayed silent. When the call went out across the country for the key Native leaders to come to the funeral–a spectacular show featured high on the agenda of the nightly news, no one called the grand chief of the Crees, and he was just as pleased, for he could not have gone.

"For a flashing moment he got everybody's attention," Diamond says, "and then he was forgotten. I was determined that no one would forget the Crees. We wouldn't come into the sky like flashing meteorites and then simply disappear. I considered Nelson Small Legs' suicide to be a tragic mistake. We couldn't bring him back to life, but we could learn from that failure. The Crees were ready to risk failure, but we weren't ready to accept failure. And when all the criticism hit us it just made us more determined than ever to try.

"We had to accept that we would be criticized. I had to accept that I would be ostracized. I was ready to accept that, but what I could not accept was the criticism from within my own self. I knew that the worst failure is the failure not to try, and I had to try, no matter what the consequences.

"But it was the encounter with AIM, the breakup of the IQA and the suicide of Nelson Small Legs, Jr., that all convinced me that there had to be a solution, and it had to come from within the Crees themselves. I could not use the tragedy of Nelson Small Legs to advance my own causes.

"It was sad and tragic what happened. I thought of going to the funeral but then I decided no, my fight is right here. It must be fought here and won here."

CHAPTER TWELVE

BIRTH OF A NATION

Shortly after the final agreement had been signed, Grand Chief Billy Diamond and Chief Robert Kanatewat of the Fort George band struck out on a private mission. They drove out the gravel road leading from Fort George up the La Grande River, keeping a promise they had made to each other during the long months of negotiations. They passed by the spawning grounds of the whitefish, the first site proposal for the main dam, and there they punched their fists out the open windows in victory, knowing that no dam would now be built along this stunningly beautiful twist of fast water. They passed by the shoreline where they had convinced the government of Quebec and the James Bay Development Corporation to spend $60 million on a brand-new, entirely modern Cree village to be called "Chisasibi"—"Big River" in Cree. On they drove until, some fifty miles upstream from the village of Fort George, they came to the LG2 dam site, the main power block on the La Grande River. And here, unnoticed by the construction workers, they walked to the highest point of the dam until they found the spot where, so many months before, Premier Robert Bourassa had come to pose for photographers and talk to the press about the progress of his "Project of the Century."

With the picture of the Quebec premier in mind, Robert Kanatewat moved to the edge of the dam and struck exactly the same pose as Bourassa, with the vast, still empty reservoir spreading out over the taiga beyond. Billy Diamond pretended he had a camera, but as he brought his hands up he cupped them and drew them around his mouth. Leaning back, the grand chief of the James Bay Crees screamed into the face of the imaginary premier with all the voice he could summon: "We beat you—you bastard!"

He shouted again, and Robert Kanatewat, laughing so hard that tears were running down his cheeks, turned and shouted as well. "We beat you—you bastard!—We beat you! We beat you! We beat you! . . . ," their voices lost on the work side of the dam to the growl of the bulldozers, and slowly fading on the reservoir side as the range of the human voice gave in to the sheer vastness of Robert Bourassa's dream.

Several years later, Grand Chief Billy Diamond would return again to the LG2 site, passing through on a fishing holiday that would take him farther north. Standing in a small airport terminal outside the construction town of Radisson, he paced below a gawdy, full-colour poster of the finished dam that said, *"D'un rêve à la réalité"*—from a dream to reality. Standing beside the poster with a handful of brochures, a public relations man offered the Cree chief an open invitation to tour the finished project: the prison-style fences, government homes, company trucks and cafeterias. Everything within sight and sound made it feel as if what Bourassa had written in his 1972 book, *James Bay*, had come true: "Quebec must occupy its territory; it must conquer James Bay."

By the time LG2 was completed and the first switch thrown on a dull afternoon in late October 1979, the sensation of seeing the main dam operating was only hinted at by its description: 16 penstocks leading to 16 turbines, the pent-up waters of the vast reservoir plunging through each 6-metre penstock and dropping 450 feet to boil past the turbines at a rate of 4 million tons per second. Those numbers and words told nothing of what one felt standing on the steel floor of the underground cavern that houses this monster, to stand and actually vibrate with the floor as the largest underground powerhouse in the world churns out enough power for a city of four million people. On the particular afternoon that Grand Chief Billy Diamond and his fishing party passed through in June 1983, Wilf Paiement—then considered one of the heavyweight contenders of the National Hockey League—took up the public relations man's invitation to visit this floor while a 600-ton rotor screamed over his head at 133 revolutions per minute—and instantly panicked.

"I've got to get out of here!" the Quebec Nordiques enforcer shouted. "This thing is scaring the shit out of me!" Paiement moved to the poured concrete walls for support, leaning to steady his legs, only to discover that the walls were literally bouncing with the force that was passing through. "Let's get *out of here!*" Paiement screamed.

But outside the shock merely changed from a physical to a visual one. Beyond the dam wall where Diamond and Kanatewat had climbed and shouted years earlier, the flooding was now complete. Where once there had been only freckles of open swamp surrounded by the black spruce there was now a series of reservoirs that took up a surface area half the size of Lake Ontario, the spruce now drifting sadly about the dark wash. Barges with open incinerators were working twenty-four hours a day, seven days a week, moving about the various reservoirs picking up the deadheads by crane and dropping them into their sparking cauldrons. It is another world, a world filled with floating incinerators, underground highways, bouncing walls, shaking floors, screaming turbines and vast waterfalls that thunder under clear skies and fill the air with a constant, reminding mist.

"We believe that only the beavers have the right to build dams in our territory," the Crees had argued in their very first statement against this project, but the beavers turned out to be poor competitors. When the flooding began, they built their lodges on higher ground, and when the flooding continued, their kittens drowned in those lodges. What beavers remained moved on to quieter waters.

The fish, however, could not stake out new claims. The flooding leached mercury from the land and the mercury entered the trout and the whitefish through the food chain. The Crees caught the trout and the whitefish and ate the fish and the mercury passed from one system into another. Eventually, tests done on certain older Crees in the area—Indians whose entire summer diet was based on fish—found mercury levels in the blood as high as twenty times what the World Health Organization says is acceptable. Before the tests were done, the symptoms of these older Crees—numbness of limbs, trembling hands, reduced peripheral vision, lack of coordination in muscles and eyes—had been dismissed as premature aging.

"I don't want to see the God-damned dam!" Diamond had yelled in the face of the public relations man in June 1983. "Your God-damned dam ruined my land!"

By 1979, when Premier René Lévesque pulled the switch that started those turbines turning, the James Bay Project had become the darling of Quebec. The world energy crisis had made the hydroelectric scheme seem sensible rather than foolishly ambitious, efficient rather than disturbingly expensive. And with a $400 million, privately owned paved highway running from Matagami to the LG2 site, as well as a landing strip that could accommodate everything from government jets to tourist package flights, it no longer seemed so isolated. The riot of 1974 was now forgotten, with people thinking not of the millions of dollars worth of destruction the rioters had caused but of what had come out of the tragedy: a clean-up of the Quebec construction unions, a better understanding between workers and management, and a potential Canadian prime minister from the province of Quebec.

It was the James Bay riot that made Brian Mulroney a household name in Quebec and propelled him to run for the leadership of the Conservative Party, losing in 1976, winning in 1983 and becoming prime minister in the Canadian general election of 1984. The James Bay riot had led to an official inquiry, with law professor Robert Cliche named by the premier to chair the investigation. Cliche had then chosen a favoured former student, Montreal lawyer Brian Mulroney, to be one of the three commissioners, and as the Cliche inquiry quickly became a daily soap opera about loan sharking, payoffs and criminal control in the labour unions, Mulroney soon emerged as the star of the show. Whether this was because he so exemplified integrity in the face of such deceit or because he played the Quebec press so brilliantly hardly matters: when it was over he was on his way to becoming prime minister.

It became impossible to be a Quebec politician and not become caught up, in some manner, with the James Bay Project. The Parti Québécois, which had opposed the project from the very beginning, found themselves voted into office on November 16, 1976, an election that shocked the rest of Canada but had been predicted in Quebec since the Cliche Commission, set up, ironically, by Robert Bourassa, had put a stamp of corruption on the provincial Liberals that Bourassa had been unable to shake. With the PQ victory coming almost exactly a year after the signing of the final agreement with the Crees and Inuit, and with construction moving rapidly toward completion of the first dams, a reassessment of the PQ stance on the James Bay Project became a matter even more pressing than the party's stated objective to separate from the rest of Canada.

Whereas Jacques Parizeau, the PQ's financial brain in 1976

—and, in 1988, its leader—believed Bourassa's scheme was "sheer delirium" when it was first announced, Parizeau's leader, René Lévesque, was never quite so adamant. Lévesque, after all, had been minister of water resources and of public works in the provincial Liberal government that had taken over the hydro industry in the early 1960s. And though he himself had railed against the constantly rising costs of the project, by 1976 he had softened his stance considerably. The move from Parizeau's "sheer delirium" to Lévesque's own sense that the project must go on was, in the PQ leader's opinion, nothing more than natural "evolution." Besides, Lévesque added with a self-deprecating grin: "Only idiots and asses never change their minds."

Three years after his election—on October 27, 1979, at 3:45 on a dull Saturday afternoon—Premier René Lévesque, looking a bit awkward in a white construction cap and surrounded by workers and politicians wearing buttons saying "I took part," pulled the switch that started the waters flowing. It was a day intended for easy celebration, but the mischievous Lévesque could not let it pass without a jab at Bourassa, who by this time had given up the leadership of the Liberal Party and dropped entirely out of the public eye. While Lévesque spoke of the project as "symbolizing the pride of Quebec," he went on to say that Bourassa's original decision to go to work on the dams was "strictly political." The "Project of the Century" was, in the new premier's opinion, "a political improvisation that could have become very unfortunate had not the price of oil quadrupled."

The remarks were intended to cause the slim man in the horn-rimmed glasses standing off to the side to squirm. But Robert Bourassa—appearing in public like a forgotten movie star—was generating his own surprising energy. He had arrived in James Bay unnoticed, coming merely to see the completion of something begun in another life, but when he had walked into the Radisson cafeteria that Saturday morning the construction workers had risen to their feet and cheered, whistling, stomping their feet, some even jumping onto the tables to get a better look at the man who had heard nothing but jeers for so long and then deliberately vanished from the public eye.

It was a pivotal point in Bourassa's life. At forty-six he had come to believe what was commonly said of him: that he would never again be elected to public office. But now, even as he stood in the eleventh row of the dignitaries assembled for the official throwing of the switch, there was a buzz in the room that Lévesque was blowing it and Bourassa was being reborn. The press took offence at Lévesque's attempts to claim all political credit for himself and the PQ. The workers obviously felt first loyalty to the man who had dreamed up their $1,000-a-week paycheques. The Friday edition of the Montreal *Gazette* was being passed around everywhere, with a huge, eight-column headline—"Bourassa's dream comes true"—and just as the first electricity was produced the moment René Lévesque's hand brought down the switch, a renewed charge also went into Robert Bourassa.

The strange, private man who was supposedly finished forever would be re-elected leader in 1983, and even though he would himself lose in the 1985 provincial election, his party would win hugely, and after an appropriate by-election he would once again enter the National Assembly as premier of Quebec—the culmination of one of the most amazing political turnarounds in Canadian politics.

In total, 375 guests had been invited to the Saturday afternoon ceremony. Nine of them were Cree chiefs, including Grand Chief Billy Diamond, who had last stood on this spot when he screamed *"We beat you—you bastard!"* into an empty basin of scrub spruce and swamp. Not one of the nine showed up. Nor did Charlie Watt of the Inuit, who claimed he had more pressing business in Fort Chimo.

"We still feel very much opposed to the project," the grand chief told reporters in Val d'Or. "We appreciate the invitation, but we feel our presence at the opening ceremonies would be construed as agreeing with the idea of the project."

Robert Kanatewat, who had stood that day shouting in vain with the grand chief, was not one of the nine Crees invited, even though his was the name on the legal case that began what led to the historic final agreement. In fact, Kanatewat was no longer chief of Fort George, which was now being rebuilt as Chisasibi seven kilometres up the river. He had faced up to his secret drinking problem and defeated it, but he was not prepared for what hit him shortly after the end of the long negotiations process. He was blamed for his own successes.

"I was turfed out as chief," remembers Kanatewat, who now runs his own transportation business in Chisasibi. "People believed that I was the culprit that let the government flood the land. Some of them even went so far as to say that Billy and I made a deal and had money stashed away from it. They believed that I tricked them."

No area was more affected than Kanatewat's Fort George. It was on this river that the dams were built, to Fort George that the press, the anthropologists and the politicans came to debate the project, Fort George where the key meetings were held and, in the end, Fort George that had to be moved off the silt island at the mouth of the river to higher ground when engineers determined that the seasonal flow would eventually erode the island away. It was here that the Bourassa dream was perceived entirely as a nightmare, and here where the reaction was most angry.

"When we said we were going to stop the project, that we *would* stop the project," says Kanatewat, "they had no sense of how big it was." From the beginning both Kanatewat and Diamond had known that the project would never be put off completely, that the best they could do was to have a significant say in how it was carried out. But many Crees believed that the two chiefs would merely head out into the bush and throw the whites off the Cree land, and that would be the end of it. When the project could not be stopped even by Kanatewat's great victory in the white man's courts, he was viewed as a failure for having been taken in by the white man's tricks.

And then, of course, there was the move to the new village. "It started almost as a joke," he recalls. "We had a band meeting and there was talk about a bridge to the island, just a bridge, and I said, 'Since they're having such a tough time, why don't we get them to move us? Our ancestors will have to move anyway once the dams are completed, so why not get it now when we've got the government on the run?' Right away, half said yes, but the other half were against it.

"And then I made my big mistake. At another band meeting about the relocation I said, 'Why don't we buy out the Bay?' That did it. There is still a strong sense among the elderly here that the Hudson's Bay Company saved our lives. If it hadn't been for the Bay, they say, we all would have died. These are people, don't forget, who believed all their lives that the things you got at the Bay—the grub, the tea, their flour—all was free of charge. All they had to give back was a few beaver skins when they came back in the spring. They had their own meeting, and in the summer of 1977, I was told to step down as chief.

"Two or three years later I got curious as to why they had all of a sudden decided they no longer needed my services. I knew where to ask—what was the *real* reason? They talked about me giving the right to the government so they could flood the land. They said I was the one who forced the move. I was the one who wanted to buy out the Bay. And they said, 'If you're going to do all that, what next?'"

What next ... the same question had been plaguing Grand Chief Billy Diamond since that unidentified voice from the back of the bus had shouted "*What do we do next?*" as the Crees left the National Assembly after the signing of the final agreement. There were offices to establish at Val d'Or—the most central point for transportation and communication—and staff to hire and enterprises to get underway. But above all else, there was an attitude to be changed. The war was not over with the signing; the battles were just beginning.

Billy Diamond had the firm Peat Marwick come in to the Cree operation for "consciousness-raising" sessions. They would talk about the concept of a self-sufficient nation for the Crees, about goals in general without worrying about the detail. The worrying about detail he left to himself, often late at night in the trailer he took over on the outskirts of the town—late-night brooding sessions with a bottle of scotch and a scratch pad of curious doodles. The secret, he told himself, would be to hire good people, the best he could find. He wrote down that he needed a "scrounger." Someone who would know the Department of Indian Affairs inside out and who would know "where the dollars were hidden in the desks." He went to the best departmental bureaucrat he knew at the time, John Ryan, who had devoted twenty years of his life to Indian Affairs, and talked him into giving up his pension and heading off to Val d'Or to work in economic development for the Cree Regional Authority—the new bureaucratic arm of the Grand Council of the Crees.

He also needed a "detail man" and advertised the position, drawing in an application from a California psychologist by the name of Robert Epstein, who had previously been working with Indians in Alaska. The Crees interviewed Epstein, were intrigued by his commitment to social issues, but hired him almost exclusively on the basis of a question put to him at the end of a two-and-a-half-hour interview.

"What would you say," Albert Diamond asked, "if we said we wouldn't hire you because you are a Jew?"

"I'd say," answered a visibly angry Epstein, "that you are fucking yourselves."

They assigned Epstein the task of establishing the Cree school board, though he later moved on—much to the relief of school workers who found his thoroughness relentless—to become Diamond's executive assistant and, a few years later, the Crees' full-time lobbyist in Ottawa.

They set up a Cree construction company, a housing authority, a health board and a school board. The young Cree leadership joined, *en masse*, the local Cisco Island Golf Club. "It's not me that gets lost in the bush," Billy Diamond complained to the club president, Joe Tremblay, "it's the ball—because it's *white*."

They bought cars and learned to drive, and within a matter of months not one of them had a licence that had not been suspended in court for various offences. At one point, when the Quebec police pulled over a weaving Cree car at four in the morning, the Crees tried to beat the charge by refusing to admit that any of those in the car were behind the controls, which led to the suspension of all six licences.

For the grand chief, however, it was not all golf and parties. Elizabeth and the two children moved down to the trailer in Val d'Or. Lorraine was now six years old, Ian was two, and toward the end of April, Elizabeth gave birth to a second boy who was formally named Sanford but known from his first day as "Sandy." It was a difficult time for Elizabeth, her territory pinched by the small trailer, her family hundreds of miles to the north, her children unsettled and her husband either too busy to help or else out of town.

Grand Chief Billy Diamond was busier in the post-agreement months than he had been in the months leading up to what most of the Crees felt would be the solution to all their concerns. But the agreement was only signed paper without legislation, and getting the James Bay Agreement turned into law now seemed far removed from the mere formality it had seemed on the night of the final signing. "We saw a strange change in people," says Billy Diamond. "The same people we had negotiated with through the agreement-in-principle and the final agreement were the same people that we had to deal with for the final legislation. The same people who had signed the agreement were now *against* the legislation."

The grand chief followed every avenue he could find to let people know that the governments had yet to follow through on the signed agreement. In June 1976 he appeared before Justice Thomas Berger's inquiry into the building of the Mackenzie Valley pipeline, and warned that the trust that had been built up between the Crees and the government could not be misused. "The Cree will certainly not misuse that trust," he told Berger. "However, if we do not have legislation on the James Bay agreement, then that trust has been misused and the Cree can claim the agreement has been breached. The Cree can charge that there has been a violation in the agreement."

John Ciaccia also spoke to the Berger Inquiry on the details of the agreement, and, much to the Crees' delight, said that whatever the Natives had signed away, "must now be replaced by proper legislation which will safeguard the Natives' rights granted in the agreement." But still, the summer of 1976 passed without a vote.

The diaries Billy Diamond kept during that time began to reflect his anxiety. Quebec had passed the appropriate bill in June but had refused to declare it law until the federal legislation had been passed as well. A mid-September Cabinet shuffle seemed only to set things further back, as Judd Buchanan was suddenly replaced as minister of Indian affairs by the former solicitor general, Warren Allmand. Shortly after his appointment, Allmand brought together Billy Diamond and Charlie Watt in his Montreal constituency office for Notre-Dame-de-Grâce-Lachine-East, and Diamond exploded, calling both Allmand and Watt "assholes" for not pushing harder. He then stormed angrily out of the brief meeting. But his outburst seemed to have no effect.

It would soon be a full year since the signing of the final agreement, yet nothing had been done in Parliament to bring the agreement into force. The parliamentary session was running down quickly. James O'Reilly, seizing an opportunity presented by a pick-up hockey game involving Montreal lawyers and a few politicians, deliberately cross-checked Allmand and suckered him into joining him in the penalty box, but even his pleading in this intimate surrounding accomplished nothing. Allmand's hands were tied. Everything to do with Quebec was on hold.

The problem, of course, was the Quebec provincial election. Just when John Ciaccia might have been counted on to pressure his old friend, Jean Chrétien, to lean in turn on Allmand and the rest of the Cabinet, the Bourassa government had put a moratorium on all outstanding issues until after November 15. And once the Parti Québécois had won the day, neither the Quebec bureaucrats nor the new ruling politicians wanted to concentrate on what the future held for a few Natives when the future of six million Québécois—perhaps the future of all of Canada—was suddenly up in the air.

Toward the end of that disappointing year, Billy Diamond made a checklist of how the year had gone. He put a large check beside such points as "better structuring of organization," but he put a large, angry "X" beside the point at the top of the page: "Legislation and regulations passed." He turned over a page and began scribbling the questions he was afraid to ask aloud. "How can the vision fail? What worries do you have? What forces will oppose you?"

There was nothing to do but go to Ottawa and fight. With Robert Kanatewat and the other band chiefs, Billy Diamond called a press conference in the first week of December and said that the lack of enabling legislation had left the Crees in a "state of limbo." They couldn't touch their money because the cash was being held in trust until the legislation was passed. They couldn't plan ahead. They couldn't start up their school board, their police force, the income security program. . . . He would sit, the grand chief announced, in the public galleries and scowl down at the members of Parliament until they stopped "insulting" the Crees by questioning Bill C–9, the proposed legislation. Parliament did pass the bill on second reading, and the legislation went back to committee for further study. Then, in February 1986, Noel Starblanket, the president of the National Indian Brotherhood, attacked Bill C–9 as being prejudicial against aboriginal concerns in the rest of Canada. But Diamond had another argument to present in the bill's favour, one that said nothing about other Native Canadians or even about other Canadians—but everything about what would have happened to a few thousand Cree if they had chosen not to fight, and eventually settle.

"I would see," Diamond told the committee as several critical members shifted uncomfortably in their seats, "the continuation of the harassment by game wardens in certain of our villages where our fishnets, our rifles and our moose meat and beaver meat were seized. . . . The trappers today would have never been compensated for what had been lost in respect of their trapping caches. Many surveyors in the area were taking artifacts and snowshoes and the tools that the Cree trapper needs, which he kept on his trapline.

Today, because of our intervention, there is a contract between ourselves and the James Bay Energy Corporation to secure claims for trappers who lost such tools.

"Also, I do not think there would have been any contract in respect of marking burial grounds for our own people. Our burial grounds are very sacred, and because the Cree people spoke we now have a contract whereby the Crees will be in a position to mark and, if they agree, to have a ceremony in respect of that burial ground. . . .

"I think my people would have lived in poverty and I think my people would have just disintegrated as our own people. Their pride would not have been regained and they would not have had any respect for themselves. . . . I feel the Crees would have been a totally forgotten people."

But they were not forgotten. Warren Allmand shortly introduced the bill for a third reading and it was easily passed, confirmed by the Senate and declared law. Quebec then declared its previously passed legislation law, put through a long series of ancillary bills, and on June 30, 1978, the last legislation was passed to make the 1975 James Bay and Northern Quebec Agreement law.

Grand Chief Billy Diamond took copies of all the legislation and laid it out on James O'Reilly's desk. What they were looking at was not a pile of government bills, he said, but a charter for the creation of a Cree Nation.

PART THREE

AIR

ᎠᏂᏕ

They were to make certain promises and we were to make certain promises, but our purpose and our reasons were alike unknowable. What could they grasp of the pronouncements on the Indian tenure which had been delivered by the law lords of the Crown, what of the elaborate negotiations between a dominion and a province which had made the treaty possible, what of the sense of traditional policy which brooded over the whole? Nothing. So there was no basis for argument. The simpler facts had to be stated, and the parental idea developed that the King is the great father of the Indians, watchful over their interests, and ever compassionate.

> Duncan Campbell Scott,
> Indian Treaty Commissioner,
> *The Last of the Indian Treaties*,
> an account of the Canadian
> government's negotiations leading up
> to the signing of James Bay Treaty
> No. 9, 1905.

CHAPTER THIRTEEN

PHILIP

It is difficult to appreciate how quickly change came to James Bay. Shortly after Robert Kanatewat was asked to step down as chief of the Chisasibi Band, he found himself visiting an old friend who had recently come off his trapline and used some of his hunter's income-security money to purchase a television set. Thanks to the new satellite dishes and video cassettes, the Crees were now watching the same programs as other Canadians in Montreal, Toronto and Vancouver, often with wider choices, and within a matter of months colour TV had become as essential to the average Cree household as the snowmobile.

From the moment Kanatewat walked in the door the television was on, the old Cree sitting directly in front of the screen and staring as intensely as if he were stalking the characters as they moved in and out of the scenes of a weekly series. When the fire ran low, the old man rose, snapped off the picture tube and raced outside, returning with an armful of split spruce. Only after he'd carefully stoked the fire did he reach out and turn the television on again.

"What did you do that for?" asked Kanatewat.

The old man turned, blinking, not understanding. "What do you mean?"

"Why did you turn off the television before you went out?"

"I didn't want to miss anything."

"Here was a modern agreement in a third-world situation," says Billy Diamond of that time. "Overnight, the Crees were expected to move into the twenty-first century. There was a lot of catching up to do and we were about to suffer the consequences of change."

The Grand Council continued to operate as the political organization while the Cree Regional Authority served the function of the public service, the Cree bureaucracy. Billy Diamond would continue as grand chief, surrounded by the young leaders who had emerged during the negotiations: Abel Kitchen, Albert Diamond, Ted Moses, Philip Awashish, Henry Mianscum. In essence, they were creating a government from scratch, and whenever they got word of a young, bright Cree, they would bring him or her down to Val d'Or and put the young person to work. They needed secretaries, heavy-equipment operators, teachers, social workers, policemen, accountants. Unfortunately, Diamond recalls: "We were quickly running out of Crees. Think of us as a town of a few thousand people. How can we possibly be expected to produce all our own engineers and doctors and lawyers and accountants and scientists?"

It meant that the consultants were now as much a part of the organization as the Cree leadership itself, a situation that infuriated certain Crees who believed the lawyers and other experts had been necessary only during the court case and actual negotiations. "Sometimes," says Albert Diamond, who supported his brother's belief in hiring the best help money could find, "it began to seem like there was another tribe out there somewhere called 'consultants.'"

Few of the outsiders were Indian, the key exception being Marsha Smoke, a young Mississauga Indian from the Alderville Band in southern Ontario who came to work as the director of administration for the Cree Regional Authority and soon began working exclusively for Grand Chief Billy Diamond. "At the time I was hired," says Smoke, "some of the other Indians I knew were calling Billy the 'Shah of the Crees.' But he was not up there being in the least bit extravagant—I couldn't believe when I got there that he was living in an old trailer." But he *was* there, often staying up through the night trying to figure out who he was. The double vision was back. But if he removed his glasses, pressed in tightly and rubbed, the problem would vanish for a few minutes until he repeated the action. Those who thought it was not affectation began to see it as a nervous habit, and they read into it that the grand chief's attention span was wavering if he removed his glasses while you were talking to him. His attention was indeed wavering, not because he was bored, but because he was scared.

The dizziness was also back, but alcohol seemed to ease the symptoms, and the drinking that he had always believed would cease once the pressure was off and an agreement signed simply continued unabated. His friends were quickly learning that any excuse to celebrate meant the distinct possibility of an extended binge. There was talk of other women, and as all who travelled with him knew, the grand chief never had to go looking; they were always there, lingering in the halls at the end of a meeting, sitting down to talk in a bar, attracted by that same curious magnetism that so easily captured the focus of the cameras, the point of the microphones.

Elizabeth Diamond heard the talk and said nothing. She lived in Val d'Or, but once the lights and shopping wore off, she came more and more to hate the city and the trailer park. Even though she was with him more now, she still felt that she was losing her husband, who was too often brooding, too often drunk, too often lost for the night. Other times he was the happy-go-lucky kid she had married nine years earlier, laughing and joking and hugging her just as he did on the morning of November 15, 1979—four years to the day after the signing of the final agreement—when she gave birth to their fifth child—a baby boy they decided to call Philip after the crippled uncle who had taught Billy to love nothing more than the silence of the woods. He was a large, strong and loud child, one that was bounced happily between the arms of a mother and father who were, unknown to all but themselves, beginning to feel less and less like husband and wife.

Diamond knew that he was changing. "After I'd signed the agreement," he says, "people began to keep me at a distance. They didn't know how to talk to me, I guess, and I took it as resentment.... The Crees were outcasts. My own name was dirt with other Indians. I was finished. I was shunned by Indian leaders across Canada. I don't know what happened. I guess I offended a lot of people. I pushed a lot of people to the limit, pushed them to the wall to get them to push back, to get them to do something—anything. It got so I hated being the grand chief."

He felt he was losing touch—with people, with his children, with Elizabeth. When James O'Reilly's young law partner, Bill Grodinsky, was seriously injured in a plane crash at Quebec City, Grand Chief Billy Diamond plunged into a depression over the frailty of life. The support he could not give even his own family he was able to offer freely to Grodinsky, and during the young lawyer's difficult recovery the two men formed an intimate and lasting bond of friendship. They talked of the preciousness of life and health, but he could not transfer the lessons of Grodinsky's accident into his own life: every time the double vision struck, Diamond was reminded of his mortality, but he could not stop, would not stop. There was no time for anything but his job, and a marriage, like a goose camp, became something quickly patched together every time shelter was required, then abandoned on whim.

Everyone was busy. Johnny Jolly had been setting up the Income Security Program for the Cree hunters and trappers, and the scheme soon reached a point where 40 percent of the Cree workforce were counted as full-time trappers, and a further 20 percent were doing it part-time. In 1981 there were more Cree trappers in the bush than there had been in 1971. The trappers had even formed their own association, pooling their resources to buy in bulk and—in a wonderful irony that passed by none of them—three hundred years after the fur trade began along the eastern coast of James Bay, they managed to cut out the Hudson's Bay Company as the trapper's main supplier by establishing the Cree Distribution Centre in Val d'Or.

The trappers' Income Security Program, however, was a rare success for those days. The Crees and Inuit had signed the final agreement with the firm belief that government funding would be forthcoming for the programs the officials had said were their due. But nothing had happened.

The problem was one of implementation. Though the Crees had believed the agreement was the equivalent of a set of rules and regulations of behaviour for the government, in practice they were being treated no differently than before the signing. Anthropologist Brian Craik—by now so fluent in Cree he was asked by the Rupert House band to represent them at meetings with Hydro-Québec—remembers being told by the provincial corporation that a bulldozing operation the Crees were complaining about was essentially none of their business. "If we see any bones," the official said, "we'll give you a call." This, after a signed promise to search out and, where possible, relocate the Indian grave sites.

To make matters worse, nothing in the legislation spelled out exactly when funds would be given for precisely what purpose. The Crees and Inuit had expected that a special body would be established by Ottawa and the province of Quebec to oversee implementation, but none was ever established. Instead, Quebec had offered a Secrétariat des Activités Gouvernementales en Milieu Amerindien et Inuit (SAGMAI), which operated in a distant, dictatorial manner toward the Natives. The Crees soon came to blame SAGMAI for everything and, searching for a human face to put on the nameless bureaucracy, they singled out SAGMAI's director, Eric Gordeau.

But SAGMAI could not be blamed for everything. It was the federal government that had set out to bring proper sewers to a number of the Cree villages in the early 1970s and then abandoned the project, thinking the province would complete it. But nothing was ever done. The ditches turned into stagnant water catches to the rear of the houses.

In Rupert House in the summer of 1980 there were eighty new frame houses, with more being built, all equipped with the proper pipes for running water. Unfortunately, they were not hooked up, since there were no sewers to carry away the waste. Outhouses had to be built as well, and while this was a solution of sorts for the long winter, in spring the excrement also thawed, sending giant smears down into the trenches Ottawa had dug for the province to fill in with sewer pipes and forming vast, pungent pools behind the residences. In hot weather, villages like Rupert House and Paint Hills smelled like open cesspools. Flies bred in the water and swarmed out of the ditches and over the people. Yet nothing the Cree leaders could say would turn the interests of Ottawa or Quebec City from the issue at hand, the one thing that obsessed both governments and made all other concerns irrelevant, at least for the time being: the Quebec referendum.

Four years after his stunning defeat of Bourassa, René Lévesque had another shock in mind for the rest of Canada. The people of Quebec were being asked to vote "yes" to a referendum that would permit the Parti Québécois to seek out sovereignty-association with Canada, the phrasing not quite as disturbing as "separation" but the intention very much the same. Pierre Trudeau was now back as prime minister after a reconsidered retirement and the fall of Joe Clark's Conservative government. For him and his opponent Lévesque, the referendum issue became the battle of their lives.

The Crees, lacking French and with more historical ties to Britain than Quebec, were quietly working for the "No" side. They feared that the popular Lévesque would carry the day, and so were afraid to speak out. "We could vote yes and we could vote no," Billy

Diamond fudged at a press conference in Montreal early in February 1980. What the Crees wanted, he said, were "written assurances" from the Parti Québécois that the James Bay Agreement would be fully honoured if the separatist party won the vote. He said nothing, however, of talks he had had with certain federalists. The pressure was on him to make a grand gesture such as the one made by Charlie Watt when he ordered Quebec bureaucrats out of the Inuit territory until the vote was over. The Crees did hold secret discussions within their own organization about the possibility of themselves separating from Quebec if the Parti Québécois won, but Grand Chief Billy Diamond refused to commit himself publicly on the issue.

Oddly enough, it was in James Bay that the Lévesque "yes" campaign first began to falter. Lévesque had travelled north to the LG3 site outside Chisasibi, convinced that it was the perfect setting for a resounding rally. Here, after all, was the symbol of the New Quebec. Hydroelectricity was supposed to be what powered the pride of the new, confident Quebeckers.

Or so the academics and politicians believed. The workers brought in for the rally, however, had far more pressing concerns on their minds than whether or not Quebec would mint its own currency, control immigration, seek new and unknown international ties. What they wanted, they angrily told the tiny, chain-smoking premier, were more beer rations and mixed dormitory privileges. The rally quickly disintegrated into a shouting match, with Lévesque angrily lecturing the workers about attaching more importance to their beer than their futures. It was the beginning of a growing rift between the intellectual pro-independence side and the average Quebecker, and the average citizens, of course, far outnumbered the committed intellectuals.

In May 1980, the "no" side carried the day by a 60–40 margin. The Crees were delighted, and believed that now that this all-consuming debate had been dealt with, they would be able to get the implementation of the legislation back on track. But they were wrong.

The Crees had always counted on Jean Chrétien, who had led the charge against separatism for Trudeau, to listen to them. But Chrétien was far too busy for the Crees now that he held the new, important position of minister of justice and attorney general in the returned Trudeau Cabinet. The new minister of Indian affairs, John Munro, was privately sympathetic but seemed to have little voice in a Cabinet that was far more wrapped up in healing a country at large than applying quick bandages to a small group of forgotten Indians in the Far North.

But then Tommy Wapachee died.

In the spring of 1980, the grand chief closed up his trailer in Val d'Or and took Elizabeth and the four children back to Rupert House for the goose hunt. It had been a long, hard winter along the coast, and the spring runoff had filled the sewage ditches in villages like Rupert to the point where it appeared, as you looked down from a plane, that the houses were joined by narrow canals of green slime.

Nothing had yet been done about the sewers. With no running water, the women were forced to carry buckets down to a central well tap, fill them up and carry them home. But the stagnant water was also finding its way into the river and polluting the area around the intake pipes. Bad water was being carried in unwashed pails back to the houses, mixed with formula and fed to babies. Every young mother in the village was complaining of the same problem: the babies had diarrhea and it seemed nothing they did would stop the children from losing weight.

Elizabeth Diamond was worried. It had been eight years since she had lost little Joanne to vomiting and diarrhea. And every time she changed Philip she couldn't help thinking of that tragic summer and fall. But it couldn't possibly be the same. Joanne had been a small, sickly baby from the start. Philip was huge: a thick, active child with ballooning cheeks and a shock of black hair that fit his head in almost precisely the same way that old Malcolm's greying mat fit his. Philip could not possibly be compared to Joanne. He was taking his medicine and holding it down. He would be all right.

In one of the inland villages, Nemaska, almost all the newborns were ill. Their stools were green and liquid, and they were throwing up after every meal. Instead of gaining weight, they were losing. Nancy Wapachee was even more worried about the situation than Elizabeth Diamond over in Rupert House. Her Tommy had not had three months to put on weight and gain strength in Val d'Or, as Philip Diamond had. Tommy had been sick since his birth in April, and in the first week of June, Nancy and her husband, James, had flown with their newborn to Val d'Or to see if the doctors at the hospital could tell them what was wrong.

Tommy Wapachee was taken to the emergency ward and examined, then discharged as not being sick enough to keep in the hospital. Nancy Wapachee took Tommy back into her arms and carried him out of emergency, but as soon as she got outside she told her husband there was no way she was going to take the baby back to a village where there was not even so much as a basic nursing station.

The Wapachees arranged for Tommy to be looked after in a temporary home, but could not afford to stay on themselves in Val d'Or. The foster home would get him to the hospital if he worsened, and though Nancy Wapachee cried as she stepped into a taxi for the quick trip out to the airport, she was certain she was doing the right thing.

She never saw her son again. After weeks of showing no improvement, Tommy Wapachee died on August 10, 1980, while en route from the foster home to the Val d'Or hospital. He was four months old. He had been away from his parents for half his life.

Billy Diamond was in his office when word came that a Cree baby had died of the same symptoms that were showing up in every village where the open sewers remained. In May an infant in Rupert had died of the symptoms, but Tommy Wapachee's case was the first where medical experts had been involved both before and immediately after the death. The cause of death was undeniable: severe dehydration brought on by vomiting and diarrhea. Gastro-enteritis, the child killer of the Third World.

A quick check of the two villages most affected—Rupert House and Nemaska—produced a tally of 117 children suffering from the same diarrhea, many of them on medication for the problem. It was said that three other babies had previously died in Nemaska of the same sickness. The parents were contacted and they said only that their babies had died and no one had ever offered the slightest explanation.

This was hardly unusual. The bodies of dead children were often taken away by police for autopsies and the parents would go a month or more without knowing what had happened. Babies would be returned in pieces, often wrapped in green garbage bags. Dead babies had even been brought back for burial in nothing more than a cardboard milk carton, the package dropped off at the door without an autopsy report, a death certificate or the slightest explanation.

On August 13, the Grand Council of the Crees sent off urgent telegrams to Lévesque, Trudeau and the minister of health and welfare, Monique Bégin. Then the grand chief, Billy Diamond, flew to Quebec City and called a press conference, where he laid the blame for what he was calling an "epidemic" on the jurisdictional fight between Quebec and Ottawa, one in which the Crees were being "caught in the middle."

Though the 1975 agreement had clearly spelled out that control of health care was to be turned over to an independent Cree health board, it had not worked out as the legislators had envisioned. The Cree Health Board had inadequate facilities and few nurses. Housing built under regular Indian Affairs programs was so dismal that compensation funds were shifted from other projects to housing merely to cut drafts, finish sewers and pipe in water. Health and Welfare Canada, which had responsibility for Native health, had let the few available facilities fall badly below standard. Rupert House had only two nurses, a doctor who came in once a month and a dentist, who appeared once every three months or so. For five years responsibility for Indian health had been in the process of being transferred from Ottawa to Quebec City, and if it had taken that long to get that far, the prospect of the Crees getting full control and proper funding seemed remote indeed. In the meantime, Billy Diamond told the press, three babies, including Tommy Wapachee, had died of the dreaded gastro-enteritis.

In fact, he had no idea of the numbers. Nor had it been officially established that Tommy Wapachee had died of the Third World scourge. Accuracy, however, was less a concern at this moment than expediency for reasons that were personal but went unstated that day. Staring out at the microphones, his vision doubling and then focussing for a moment, Billy Diamond did not see newsmen scribbling and taping, but only the image of his own son, Philip, who was becoming sicker as the summer went on, his diapers soaked with green slime, his food rising as soon as he swallowed, his weight falling, his attitude listless and his eyes glazed.

Billy Diamond, who had shown a sense of the dramatic from birth, who knew how to seize a spotlight and make it personal, discovered that he could not tell the reporters that his own son had the same symptoms as Tommy Wapachee. Back in Rupert House, Elizabeth was becoming hysterical with fear that Philip was fading away from her as surely as Joanne had left eight years earlier. And he was afraid if he voiced it, the fear would become fact.

The response from Quebec was quick: a team of doctors would be dispatched to the two villages and an immediate investigation launched. Officials promised a full report. The doctors came and returned to the city, leaving behind more of the same medication that several of the parents were already giving to their sick babies. A report was filed to the provincial department of social affairs, but the department refused to let the Cree Health Board see its full contents, sending instead a brief précis by telegraph. While mentioning the outbreak of infantile diarrhea, nothing was said of an epidemic. And though the doctors had specifically recommended that a nursing station be established at Nemaska, again nothing was actually done to remedy the situation.

Billy Diamond flew to Montreal, where he called a second press conference. "Things have come to a head," he told the gathering. "We're thinking of taking the ultimate step—legal proceedings to shut down the whole project." But it seemed that whatever the threat, neither Quebec nor Ottawa was inclined to act. The political climate had rarely been more sensitive.

The tension over Philip's worsening condition made the faltering marriage worse. As grand chief in the middle of a health crisis, Billy Diamond was never home. He blamed himself for causing the open sewers, sitting night after night in the Val d'Or trailer, trying to come to some understanding of what had gone wrong and what could be done to make things right again.

In Quebec City, a senior official had accused him to his face of "fixing a death." They said Billy Diamond was using dead babies to further his own political ends. And he wondered if perhaps they were right ... maybe he had gone so mad with this notion of a Cree nation that he would sacrifice his own child if it meant a few more government dollars. Maybe Nelson Small Legs, Jr., had been right: kill yourself fast and get it over with or let the government do it to you slowly. Had Billy Diamond become Joseph Brant and not even noticed?

Some nights, alone in Val d'Or and drinking, he would kneel down in the centre of the floor, lean back and scream as loud as he could at the ceiling, blaming God for this mess and demanding that He get out of his life and his family's life forever. God seemed to be toying with him. He knew Elizabeth, now back in Rupert House, had been going to the Pentecostal Church and he knew, because she told him, that she had been praying for Philip. She said she was praying for Billy, too. She thought the devil had been taking possession of her husband, destroying him. But it wasn't any devil, it was God Himself, the grand chief became convinced, a cruel white

God who wanted to ensure that Indians knew their place and stayed there. Billy's reaction to Elizabeth's prayer was to drive a fist through the wall of the trailer.

In an attempt to patch up the marriage, Elizabeth got Billy to agree to take her camping. Philip had improved and his grandparents, Hilda and Malcolm, insisted he would be fine with them, giving Billy and Elizabeth time with themselves and the older children. They went to Sault Ste. Marie, saw where *Arrow to the Moon* had been staged, and were camping on Lake Superior when word came that Malcolm and Hilda had flown to Val d'Or with a very sick Philip.

But as in Tommy Wapachee's case doctors in the emergency ward said Philip was not ill enough to be admitted. What he needed, they said, was lots of milk to drink. But Philip could not keep the milk down. Two days later they took him back to the hospital and this time were given pills, but the pills would not stay down either. On July 19, 1980, Philip Winston Diamond, aged eight months, was finally admitted. He was passing thirty liquid stools a day and losing weight quickly. They put him on an intravenous food supply, but eleven days later decided to transfer him by jet to Sainte-Justine Hospital in Montreal, without his parents. And there a syringe analysis found the dreaded *e. coli* bacteria in his system—proof that the infant was suffering from gastro-enteritis, not just the runs.

But soon there were more complications. Philip developed chicken-pox and broke out in open sores, then was struck by meningitis. On October 19 the Montreal hospital called with word that Billy and Elizabeth should come quickly. Philip was suffering seizures.

Elizabeth was crying when they got into Montreal, and crying still when they came to Room 3616 where nurses were moving in and out as if something terrible had either happened or was about to happen. They would not let the parents enter the baby's room until a doctor first warned them: "What you are going to see in there is not a pretty sight."

"We couldn't even recognize him as ours," remembers Billy Diamond. "He was bandaged from a spinal tap. He was swollen up like a red balloon. They had him hooked up to monitors that beeped every time his heart stopped. Elizabeth couldn't handle it. The doctor came and took me aside. He said they were worried because they couldn't seem to get any reaction out of him. He was alive, but there was no spark. 'I want you to get as close as you can to him,' the doctor told me. 'Right up to his face, and I want you to say something in Cree to him. Speak to him as his father. See if we can get some reaction from him.' "

For a long moment, the grand chief of the James Bay Crees could only stare at the son he could not even recognize. *Speak to him as his father*, the doctor had said. If the child were well, would he even know his father's voice? What would he say? He edged closer, leaning down until his face was so close to Philip's that the baby's quick, shallow breaths could be felt on his own skin. He could feel the heat of his own child, a burning so intense it seemed like the last desperate flicker of a fire. But still he didn't know what to say.

Then he spoke in Cree, whispering, "Philip! . . . Don't die . . . . You can't die, Philip. You've got a future . . . . Don't let it go!"

You've got a future . . . . It struck him as strange as soon as he said it. He hadn't thought about saying this—it just came out. But it was what he'd wanted to say. It was what he wanted. Philip must not miss what was happening.

He spoke now, still in Cree, louder: *"You've got a future!"*

The baby's eye blinked. The doctor noticed and he pushed in closer, telling Billy to speak again.

"You've got a future, Philip. Don't let it go."

The eye moved again. Nothing but a slight flicker. The baby's parents were discouraged, but the doctors argued that there was still hope. Billy was afraid to hope.

Before Billy and Elizabeth had left for Montreal, the baby's grandmother, Hilda, had asked if they would have Philip baptized as a favour to her. This would already have been done in the village church if the baby had not been so ill, and Hilda, by insisting it be done in the hospital instead, had confirmed what the young parents were themselves afraid to say aloud: Philip would never see Rupert House again.

James O'Reilly knew a young Anglican priest, who came to the hospital soon after a telephone call explained the situation. Billy asked Bob Epstein, who had made the trip with them, to come in out of the waiting room and serve as the child's godfather. Together they gathered around the dying baby—an Anglican priest, a Pentecostal, a non-believer and a Jew—and they prayed together for a miracle none expected to happen.

"It was the most powerful emotion I have ever experienced," remembers Epstein. "The priest did the baptism and every so often the buzzer would go off and a nurse would run and shake the baby until he started up again. There was no one in that room who wasn't crying. The priest, the nurses, me—every one of us, standing there crying because we all thought he was dying."

Billy Diamond was more comfortable with the tears than the prayers. How could he, who had been screaming his heart out at this God he despised only a few days earlier, bow his own head in prayer? He didn't know what else to do. He stared down and simply pretended to pray along, and after a while he began to remember the old prayers from the residential school. The words came back without his having to think. His mind was now free to roam, but instead of drifting off to meetings and strategy and government roadblocks, it refused to leave the room, and he sat there for the longest time with his head bowed, praying aloud and weeping openly.

"The next day," says Epstein, "I swear Philip was better."

Three months later, on January 19, 1981, Philip was discharged from Sainte-Justine after 121 days of hospital care worth $48,363. The sores were gone, the swelling down, his stools solid—Philip was going to be all right. But there was no celebration. Just before they left the hospital with Philip, Billy and Elizabeth Diamond were taken into a private office and told the disturbing news that in all probability, Philip would never walk. He would likely never talk. Certainly he would be retarded. And he would likely have the hideous seizures for as long as he lived, which might not be very long at all.

They took Philip home to Rupert House, where Malcolm Diamond held the squirming baby and predicted it would not be long before his grandson performed the traditional Cree Walking Out ceremony. He could see Philip dressed as a hunter and holding a wooden gun as he walked by himself into the tent where the elders would give him their blessings, and Malcolm said he planned to be there himself to see Philip formally accepted into the Rupert band.

Billy Diamond got up and left the room, tears in his eyes. He could not tell Malcolm that the baby in his arms would never walk, no matter how much the old man imagined. Philip was not squirming because he was anxious to get up and walk; he was twisting to get away from whatever tried to hold him, sensing in human hands the relentless clasp of the leather straps that had kept him still in his crib while he was fed intravenously. The child's entire left side was paralyzed, and though Elizabeth had been given instructions on how to knead the tiny muscles and stretch the tissue until it pulled back, she could not walk for him. Sometimes a leg would move on its own, or the arm, but the parents were not fooling themselves. It would take more than sheer reflex, far more than the wild imagination of an old man for Philip to walk.

But Billy Diamond had finally reached a decision that Philip would not pass by unnoticed. Perhaps he would never walk and could never talk, but his story would be told. Philip had been luckier than Tommy Wapachee. And perhaps he could accomplish what no other Cree had managed: perhaps Philip Diamond could ensure that there would be no more Tommy Wapachees when the next summer came and the sewers again filled up with the green slime.

The Crees decided to approach the CTV Network, and arrangements were made to meet with Henry Champ, a reporter with *W5*, the network's flagship public affairs show. Diamond, along with several of his village chiefs and the Cree legal advisors, went to Toronto where they met with Champ. Diamond told the story of Tommy Wapachee and the story of his own son, and he told the television reporter of how it had happened and why it was so necessary to make sure something like this never happened again.

Henry Champ listened, and CTV began researching the story. But very shortly they were back with a single question: "Where's the smoking gun? You've got to have a smoking gun."

It didn't seem like much of a story to CTV.

CHAPTER FOURTEEN

"PRACTICALLY MILLIONAIRES"

"Ka-ronk!"
"Ka-ronk!"
"Ka-ronk!"
On a brittle spring dawn in 1981, the grand chief of the James Bay Cree knelt on a bed of sweet, soft balsam and brought his curled right hand to his mouth. *"Ka-ronk!"* he called. To his left, hidden behind a sculpted snowbank frozen solid with splashed water, Malcolm Diamond leaned against the ice wall, curled his hand in precisely the same way and sent out the same call. *"Ka-ronk!"* To the left, behind a third snow blind, Malcolm's nineteen-year-old grandson, Bert, leaned back and sent out a third call. *"Ka-ronk!"* Three generations of Diamonds waiting for the spring geese to circle over the mouth of the Broadback as Malcolm had waited and called with his own father sixty years earlier—waiting as Billy Diamond now believed he would never wait with his own son.

Philip was now in his eighteenth month and showing no signs of being able to walk. The paralysis was beginning to work out of his left side, but only because Elizabeth spent two or three hours every day massaging the muscles along that side, working the soft tissue in and out until her own hands would cramp.

"Ka-ronk!"
Hilda had made sure the men had bannock when they set out in

the dark. And in Billy Diamond's blind a small tin kettle was bouncing a handful of tea bags over a small fire of dried spruce twigs. It was a scene that marked the spring of every year he had ever known: Malcolm making sure fat from the first goose was offered to the fire, then tying the bones high in a spruce behind the camp so the wind could whistle through them and call in even more of the great, graceful birds, Malcolm giddy with the hunt.

Everything seemed the same. The decoys strung about the small saucer of open water that always formed at this spot. The stubble of larch and spruce signalling the near shore. His white cotton cap low over his eyes, white poplin coat loose over his hunting jacket, twelve-gauge pump shotgun smooth and oiled and comfortable over his lap, loaded and waiting. In the far blind, Bert was singing "O Canada!" in Cree, and it struck Billy as funny. O Canada, indeed.

He had been in this blind on another spring day ten years earlier when word first went out over the radio that Robert Bourassa had a mighty plan for these waters. It seemed like such a short time, such a long time. And if he was angry when he first heard back then, he was far angrier right now.

"*Ka-ronk!*"

Bert's call—urgent this time, not speculative. Billy Diamond listened and he could hear the faint barking babble of the geese far to the south, and he crouched, waiting, calling plaintively. "*Ka-ronk! Ka-ronk!*"

The geese came into view, a check mark in dot-to-dot at first, then a chevron formed of elegant geese with whispering wings and flashing white undersides. But he did not think of them as birds. He was imagining that the slow circle above him was made up of the faces of all those who had begun to haunt him. And when he rose, blasting, it was not a Canada goose that buckled high and collapsed in the air, tumbling down toward the saucer of open water. It was Eric Gordeau, the head of SAGMAI, the Quebec bureaucrat whose reaction to the sick baby crisis was to say: "The Cree are very rich people now. They can take care of themselves. They're all practically millionaires, you know."

Practically millionaires . . . . They were still fighting over the funding. In Quebec City they had accused the Crees of "fixing" Tommy Wapachee's death. At Indian Affairs in Ottawa it was said that Tommy Wapachee had been a victim of "crib death." The ice was beginning to break up in the river. Soon there would be the thaw, soon again the diarrhea.

The guns were now silent, the geese who had turned on the first shot were now far to the north, heading high out over the saltwater bay. The geese who for a moment had been the government officials lay crippled on the ice, the light snow covering growing pink with the spreading blood.

The grand chief of the James Bay Cree stood in his blind and raised his rifle over his head. He faced south and he screamed into the barrens: "Do you hear me out there?"

"Do you hear me out there?"

"DOOOOO YOOOOUUU HEEEEARRRR MMEEEE OUT THERE?"

Late that night, Billy Diamond sat up late into the night with a bottle of Glenfiddich scotch and the pickings of a fresh-roasted goose. He sat on a broken-backed kitchen chair beneath a faded world map and a faded crayon sign Lorraine had made at school and her father had carried out to this cabin and tacked on to the wall: "Home Sweet Home."

The sign blessed one of the few tangibles of the James Bay Agreement. Charles Stewart MacLean's private hunting lodge on Nuskanis Island had been transferred over to the Crees for the price of $1 and the right of MacLean's daughter to visit should she ever so desire. But she had never bothered, and the broken-down lodge had been given to the Diamond family for their spring and fall goose hunts, to Billy for what he had done for the Crees and to Malcolm for all the years he had put in here as head guide for the Kentucky businessman. Now Malcolm Diamond was not only sitting in his former boss's chair, but eating geese that had fallen from what Charles MacLean had believed was his territorial air space. In Malcolm's opinion, it gave the meals of this island a special sweetness.

Billy Diamond sat leaning over the faded oilcloth on the table, speaking softly over the hiss of a Coleman lantern. "I don't know what to do," he said. "Maybe a march on Ottawa would get some attention. Maybe if every single Cree went down: seven thousand men, women and children standing out on the lawn of Parliament Hill demanding to see Pierre Trudeau would make people listen." He smiled, lifting the tailings of another drink. "And maybe while we're there they can load up a DC-3 and bomb Rupert and Nemaska and Paint Hills with a payload of Javex." But the smile quickly faded.

He knew what he was up against. By Cree count, twenty-seven young Indians were being treated for tuberculosis, yet the director of the federal medical services in Quebec City was saying there was only one case of tuberculosis in the entire Cree area. And they were still saying that Billy Diamond had fixed Tommy Wapachee's death to suit his own greedy purposes. There were even those in Indian Affairs who joked about the "dead kids" as if there were doubt that the children even suffered from the runs.

"Some people within the department thought it was not a fair way to deal," acknowledges John Tait, now deputy-minister to the solicitor general but then a key official in Indian Affairs. "But not me. Billy Diamond is a very honourable guy. I'd tell my colleagues, 'Look, he's tough, and if you ever make a mistake, he'll nail you—but he's honourable.'" Certain medical experts were also sympathetic, such as Dr Frank Hicks, an assistant deputy-minister in Health and Welfare, who said simply that "the poor health is linked to poverty, social disintegration, overcrowding, bad housing, bad sanitation and unsafe drinking water." And Dr Elizabeth Robinson of Montreal had gone to Mistassini and confirmed that tuberculosis was a growing concern there. But the Taits and Hicks and Robinsons were in the minority.

Quebec did not seem concerned about the crisis. When John Ciaccia raised questions in the National Assembly, "the government tried to downplay it." And Ciaccia, now an Opposition member, was in no position to force the government to pay attention. "These are things that never should have happened," says Ciaccia. "You don't need a James Bay Agreement to tell you that you have to take care of health matters."

But in the opinion of Eric Gordeau of SAGMAI in Quebec City, the whole thing was "just politics—the Crees are politicians and the name calling is just part of their strategy to gain the best deal for their people." As far as Gordeau was concerned, the health problems encountered by these "millionaires" were their own, and if not the Crees' then Ottawa's. Quebec could not be held responsible.

At the same time Ottawa had little intention of accepting a buck being passed from this troublesome province. When an Opposition member of Parliament demanded to know what was being done about the sewer problem, he was told by Dr Lyall Black of Health and Welfare's medical services branch: "That's the chief's responsibility."

The federal officials' callous responses could be traced to an internal memorandum dated December 12, 1980. Entitled "Some Thoughts on Negotiations and Agreements between the Government of Canada and the Native Peoples," the paper was written by Romeo Boulanger, the associate director-general of Indian Affairs' Quebec Region, and it was a damning indictment of the James Bay Agreement. In Boulanger's opinion, the federal government had been rushed into the agreement without ensuring that sufficient funds were guaranteed at the outset. What Ottawa was fast discovering, the memo contended, was that the very agreement other Natives were sneering at as being a "sell-out" could, in fact, entail costs that would soon be "astronomical and beyond the means" of Ottawa. Though negotiations had taken two years and the final agreement was thicker than a family Bible, Boulanger's contention was that the whole experience had been "rush, rush, rush." Whereas great attention had been paid to the lands and regional government, specific sections—health, above all—had been left to be detailed after the signing. "Now," said Boulanger, "looking at it from a distance, something went wrong."

At the time, Billy Diamond had no sense that this was the prevailing attitude in Ottawa. All he knew was what Boulanger had concluded: *Something went wrong.* The Crees were desperate. They had tried to shake up Quebec by moving $7 million of their land claims money out of the province and into an Ottawa bank. They had launched a suit against Quebec for $264 million for not providing the services that had been promised in the agreement. They had launched a separate court action against the federal government, claiming $300 million in damages from Ottawa, saying that Ottawa had abrogated its constitutional responsibilities by transferring health services to Quebec. And they had made the unprecedented move of establishing a permanent political presence in Ottawa in the form of Gary George, a Potawatomi Indian from the Kettle and Stoney Point reserve in southwestern Ontario.

George had training and experience in journalism, but little knowledge of the inner workings of Parliament Hill. "Billy hired me and said, 'I want you to go to Ottawa and set up a lobby,'" remembers George. "At that time, I didn't even know what a lobby was." Nor did Diamond exactly, but he did know that no one was listening to the Crees shouting from James Bay. They would have to go to Ottawa, and George's first assignment was to make sure they got to see the right politicians.

At the end of March, the Crees and Inuit appeared before the House of Commons Standing Committee on Indian Affairs and

Northern Development. So compelling was the testimony of Billy Diamond and Charlie Watt that the committee took the unprecedented step of drafting a special statement of concern, which was then presented to Indian Affairs Minister John Munro. In the opinion of the standing committee, both Quebec and Ottawa had failed to live up to their promises under the agreement.

Indian Affairs, however, had little interest in reviewing the situation in James Bay. The sick and dying babies had been a tragedy, officials agreed, but the fault lay with the Department of Health and Welfare, not Indian Affairs. At a meeting convened by John Munro, Munro's deputy-minister, Paul Tellier, put this argument to the Crees and Diamond erupted in anger, accusing both Munro and Tellier of trying to cover up the story so blame would not fall where it was most deserved.

"What do I do, John," Diamond asked Munro, "crucify you here in this office, or do I do it outside?"

"What's that supposed to mean?"

"I only have to walk across the street to the National Press Gallery, you know."

But the Crees did not go to the media, not yet. Outside Munro's office, James O'Reilly took Diamond aside and suggested he not blow up so easily.

"What got into you in there?" O'Reilly asked. "You were vicious to Munro."

"There are dead children. Somebody's got to take responsibility for what happened."

Diamond then decided to gamble on Jean Chrétien. In addition to his position as minister of justice and attorney general, Chrétien had a second, undefined portfolio that had been tagged on for prestige. He was minister of state for social development, and Diamond wondered if somewhere under this vague label there might be found an opening for the Crees.

When it proved impossible to arrange a meeting through Chrétien's office, Gary George tracked down the minister where he was appearing before a parliamentary committee on justice matters. Together with Diamond and Bob Epstein, he gained entry to the proceedings. Diamond picked out a prominent chair directly in Chrétien's sightline and sat with folded arms, staring ferociously at the politician until the former Indian affairs minister could not help but notice. Finally, Chrétien got up and walked back to the big face glowering from the back row. "Billy," he said, "you want to see me—here I am."

They agreed to a formal meeting in Chrétien's office. Diamond would bring along Charlie Watt, to represent the Inuit, and Epstein, who had documented the crisis and the lack of government action. "We had the meeting," says Epstein, "but Chrétien made no commitments. We walked out and I said to Billy, 'What a lousy meeting,' but he said, 'No, it was a very good meeting.' And it was Chrétien who, as minister of state for social development, jointly announced with Munro that there would be a full review undertaken."

"I had a weakness for Indian Affairs that I do not regret," Chrétien says of his interference. Munro came on side, as did his deputy, Tellier, and the review was assigned to precisely the person the Crees had hoped for: John Tait. Tait threw himself into the task, undertaking an exhaustive review of the agreement itself and trying to determine what, if anything, had gone wrong.

The grand chief of the James Bay Crees wanted to go home, but he was no longer sure where home was. Coming back to Ottawa had made him realize the essential failure of the agreement he believed would solve everything for the Crees. It was only paper. Legislation, yes, but legislation was not enough. It needed something more powerful backing it, and he had begun to think that the key might be in somehow getting his precious agreement locked into the new constitution Pierre Trudeau was promising for Canada. As part of the constitution, the Cree agreement would have the backing of the courts, and it could never be ignored.

But a fight like that would take years. Elizabeth had made it clear: there was a home in Rupert House for him if he cared to leave what he seemed to love more, the meetings and the paper and the celebrity. A large part of him did enjoy that, he knew this, and he also knew that another part wanted nothing more than to return to James Bay and the family. Yet whenever he thought about the family, he thought about Philip, and how Philip had lain in the Sainte-Justine hospital all those months with his hands and legs strapped to the bed. Even now, whenever Billy Diamond would try to hold his damaged son tightly and hug him, Philip would scream and twist furiously, desperate to escape from the grip of his own father.

What if there had been no James Bay Agreement? he would ask himself. Would the boy be well, hugging back?

John Tait, a tall, balding, serious bureaucrat from Montreal, had nothing in his background to recommend him for the full review intended "to determine if Canada has fulfilled, in spirit and letter, the obligations which it assumed pursuant to the James Bay and Northern Quebec Agreement." Tait had previously served in the Privy Council Office, the policy wing of overall government, and his specialty was legislation and corporate planning. As he himself admits, he "knew very little about Indian people."

The attitude Tait brought to the project was simple: the James Bay Agreement had started out in good faith and then "kind of fizzled." He was given *carte blanche* to examine every aspect of the agreement. "There was," he says, "pressure on the department to surpass itself in its ability to deal with the issue." And that pressure was now coming directly from the Crees. At the end of May 1981, Grand Chief Billy Diamond appeared on the cover of *Maclean's* magazine holding a rifle and staring out in fury over a large yellow headline, "Rumbles from the North." Inside, an eight-page spread, complete with full-colour photographs, told the story of Tommy Wapachee and Philip Diamond and the failure to implement the James Bay Agreement.

Before that summer was out, Grand Chief Billy Diamond had taken his complaint to Geneva, Switzerland, for the first United Nations Conference on Indigenous Peoples and Land, and among the exhibits tabled and examined was the *Maclean's* cover feature. From Geneva, Diamond and the other Cree leaders spread out across Europe, telling their story to anyone who would listen, knowing that whatever was said would be listened to back in Ottawa with rather more rapt attention than if they had remained voices fading out over the bay, lost in the wind.

Do you hear me out there?

The heat was on John Munro as well. A burly, chain-smoking politician who spoke with the metred caution of a man in the witness box, Munro had been stung by his change of political fortune. From the labour portfolio, where he seemed to speak for the little guy, he was now in a ministry where history advised putting the boots to the little guy. No politician before or since had managed what Chrétien had—emerging from the Indian affairs portfolio larger than they had entered—and Munro certainly seemed no exception to the Ottawa rule of thumb. "Indian affairs," he still believes, "will never be a winner."

John Munro flew up to James Bay on a whirlwind tour shortly after the Tait review had been announced. For a day and a half he walked through the muddy villages wearing white loafers and with the national media in tow. He stared into stagnant sewage ditches, checked out foul water supplies and listened to tales of diarrhea and tuberculosis. What he found, he told the press, were "some awfully bad situations." It was frustrating, he added, not to be able to change things overnight, as he would certainly like to, but the fact of the matter was there was no free money in his departmental envelope. "If the review of the agreement shows that we've breached the spirit or intent of the agreement," he promised, "I'll have to find the money somewhere."

But it was not just the poverty that shook Munro. It was the pitiful gap that so often stood between the promise and the realization. At Chisasibi, the new village built upstream to replace Fort George, he toured a new $3.5 million hospital, its beds empty, the floor shining, the surgery equipment in place, unused. Over rooms where the sick should have been undergoing treatment there were signs reading "Nobody is allowed in this room." No money had ever been allocated to run the hospital.

In Mistassini, a garage door was raised to reveal a sparkling yellow fire truck, in mint condition though it was, in fact, four years old. No money had ever been released for the operation of the truck, or for the training of firemen to ride it.

That night, back in Chibougamau, Munro and his assistant, Dan Brant, sat up long into the night drinking and talking with Billy Diamond. All were agreed that what they had seen was wrong and would have to be fixed, and quickly. But by noon the next day, with the minister on his way back to Ottawa, Diamond was pessimistic again. While his monstrous hangover might soon pass with God's mercy, the Cree headache would not be cured so easily.

Tait did not deliver his report to Munro until February 1982. It had taken him the better part of a year. The report had gone through eight full drafts, each openly discussed with the concerned parties, and though Tait had lived up to his reputation for using a single word where another bureaucrat might have written a full chapter, it still ran to 126 pages of cool, reasoned condemnation. What Tait found in his examination was an agreement that was "vague, ambiguous and open to widely varying interpretations." The federal government had gravely underestimated the costs of implementation. While he was convinced that Canada had not committed any legal breaches of the agreement, he was equally certain that "given Canada's special responsibilities for the Cree and Inuit of Northern Quebec . . . the matter does not end there." Over the first five years of the agreement, Tait calculated, Ottawa had spent $155 million on the Crees—four times the federal share of the original compensation package—and, clearly, this was still not enough. The two levels of government had, he believed, used the vagueness of the treaty as an opportunity to ignore the promises. Tait argued that this was where key words like "special responsibility" and "spirit" came into play, as the agreement was never intended as "a fixed and static legal document but rather a flexible agreement which would allow problems to be worked out through ongoing interaction."

"In a nutshell," James O'Reilly said at the time, "we feel that what happened was that the federal government did not realize what it was signing. We knew. When it started to come in, we knew, with the education provisions, with the health provisions, that the funding was to continue for housing and other matters—and that this was the best part of the agreement, that the Crees weren't supposed to have to use their own money for that and could instead use their money to build up a heritage fund and get into economic development."

The government now had the bad international publicity, the increasingly negative domestic press, the damning Tait report and, perhaps most troublesome of all, Billy Diamond himself to deal with. "I found him formidable," remembers John Tait. "The Crees hired *very* able lobbyists who were led by Billy, who is very canny, very able, very, very tough. The Crees are rough and hard on people—and they catch you out all the time. In dealing with them, I felt I had to be on top of my form or I'd be in difficulty. I have never seen anyone more skilled at lobbying. They are the masters."

Billy Diamond turned in one final virtuoso performance before the Standing Committee on Indian Affairs. He spoke of what had happened in the year since the committee had sent their message of concern to the minister, and he warned that the entire treaty was about to collapse unless the federal Cabinet took action. "I have no words to express my outrage," said Conservative member of Parliament Frank Oberle. James Bay, Oberle said, was becoming "another horror story of outright deceit and fraud perpetrated on our Native people."

It was a difficult time for the federal Cabinet. Restraint was the operational word of the day, and yet, at the end of February, John Tait's unfavourable review had been reworked into a Cabinet document stamped "secret" that outlined the high cost of the federal failure. The maximum new dollar requirement to set things right was set at $93 million, the minimum at $61.6 million. Significantly, John Munro, in making the presentation, said that Ottawa accepted the Cree and Inuit argument that the compensation money was their "heritage fund" to be used for the benefit of future generations, and this compensation was never intended to replace or supplement government programs and services.

At the end of June 1982, when the Cabinet met to discuss the issues of the day—soaring interest rates, rising inflation, increasing debt load—a quick decision was also made to pay out a further $61.4 million to the Cree and Inuit of Northern Quebec, slightly less than the minimum suggested in the secret Cabinet document. And Quebec would be spoken to. John Munro, of whom so little had been expected, had delivered.

It had been a debilitating battle. Billy Diamond was sick. John Munro was himself so exhausted that he fell asleep one evening after a gathering in his Parliament Hill office and let slip one of his ever-present cigarettes. It fell onto the back of a dry tamarack goose decoy the Crees had given him as they came to believe more and more that Munro genuinely cared, and the goose went up in flames, badly damaging the minister's office, though Munro himself was unharmed. The incident was a great joke around Ottawa for a while, though no one in Ottawa should have been surprised. The federal government had been given an object-lesson on how the Crees burn back if too much heat is applied.

Billy Diamond went back home to Rupert House, back to the cheers of the people and the chill in his own house. He had hardly found time to call. Philip was now two years old, going on three, and the news from the boy who would never walk or talk was heartening—even more heartening than the news that the Cabinet had finally come through. Somehow, on a quiet afternoon when Elizabeth was doing the laundry, Philip had found his feet. And now he couldn't be kept off them. And he was beginning to talk. He knew "Momma"—but he hardly knew his father at all.

CHAPTER FIFTEEN

PIERRE AND THE POPE

There had been no sickness at Rupert House that summer of 1982. The drinking water was now treated and tested regularly; more homes were being connected to the water supply; the sewers would soon be completed. One by one the families of Rupert were being moved out of their shacks and farther up the knoll into houses they had never before imagined: indoor plumbing, full basements, electrical outlets, deep insulation, glass in the windows where once plastic sheeting rippled in summer and snapped in winter.

They changed houses and they changed names, "Rupert House" being heard less and less and "Waskaganish" becoming far more common. They moved the needy families and the elderly first, and among those making the hike from the shores of the Rupert to the hill were an old man with salt-and-pepper hair and an old, white-haired woman with a slight limp. Malcolm and Hilda Diamond moved out of their weather-worn shack with the crooked plank flooring, faded oilcloth, washboard and buckets into a brand-new three-bedroom home with polished tile floors, electric stove and refrigerator, a washer, dryer and central heating from a state-of-the-art oil furnace. The children had chipped in to buy a new colour TV as a housewarming present. There was food in the freezer, oil in the tank, hot water at the turn of a tap. The only thing the children had failed to anticipate was the singular fact that Malcolm and Hilda Diamond hated it.

"It scared us," remembers Hilda. "The furnace would come on at night and my husband would jump up and wonder who was inside. The first night we were in it, we decided to sneak back to the old house to sleep. And then we got up early and walked back to the new house so they would think we had spent the night there."

But there were more problems than just the furnace kicking in. Malcolm lost his appetite and blamed it on the electric elements of the stove. Hilda also thought the food in the new house tasted different, so they began sneaking back during the day to use the wood stove, as well. Then Malcolm found he missed the outhouse. There was nothing happening in a gleaming ceramic bathroom with four walls, a tub and a stack of towels. He liked to sit and watch his village, ducking back behind the door when someone passed by too close. And so he began hurrying back to the old outhouse by the shore soon after his morning tea.

Eventually, the family noticed that an unmistakeable path had been worn between the rear of the new house and the old shack they had been planning to tear down. There was also, mysteriously, enough firewood split and stacked by the shack to last several winters. And food in the pantry, coals in the woodstove, new toilet paper in the old outhouse. Finally, Malcolm and Hilda admitted that they were using the new place only when they knew the children would be calling. Where they *lived* was where they had always been, down by the shore looking out over the bay, Hilda with her sagging clothesline, Malcolm with his woodpile and morning throne. The new home, it was decided, would be passed over to another family and the old couple, giggling like children, were moved back down the hill and back into the shack.

Billy Diamond understood. He knew the comfort of familiar surroundings. He felt it each time he came home to "Waskaganish" to see the children and began to realize that they might grow up with only the vaguest idea of who he was. Standing in the muddy street outside the house one day, he began to cry at nothing more than the sight of his youngest child trying to run and play with the rest. Perhaps Philip had looked like poor Joey, said Hilda Diamond, but he was as stubborn as her Billy had been. The paralysis along the left side was gone completely. He was walking and he was talking. Behind the other children his age, certainly, but Malcolm was still sure that sometime they would be holding a Walking Out ceremony for his favoured little grandson. Billy and Elizabeth had been starting to think that, just maybe, the old man's improbable dream had a chance of coming true.

But another unfinished dream was haunting the grand chief as deeply. The money the Cabinet had approved was already proving difficult for the Crees to claim. The economy was in such trouble that the talk out of Ottawa, when it was not the constitution, was all restraint and freezes and cutbacks. And Billy Diamond had become increasingly certain that there was a connection to be made between funding and law. The funding of the James Bay Agreement had to be guaranteed, and the best legal guarantee of anything, as Prime Minister Trudeau would say of other matters, was to have it enshrined in the constitution.

When he was home in Waskaganish, he tried to talk to Elizabeth about this exciting possibility, but she seemed to have no interest. She thought he was obsessed, driven mad by too many meetings and too much thinking. He took it as a further sign that they were drifting apart permanently, and that the obvious separation might as well move on to the next logical stage—divorce.

But Elizabeth was still hopeful, if silent, on the matter. For more than a year now, she had been clinging to a precious memory of the brief moment when she had looked up from her own tears in the Sainte-Justine hospital and seen her husband's lips moving in prayer for Philip. She had been further heartened the previous Christmas when Billy had gone through the entire holidays without a drink, but it had not lasted. She knew there were lost weekends and entire weeks when he was on a binge in Val d'Or. And she knew, too, that there was no chance she would ever see him answer an altar call at the Pentecostal Church and accept Christ into his life. While she had grown more and more religious since Philip's illness, her husband had, if anything, gone further the other way. Instead of accepting Christ into his life, he seemed intent on booting Christ out of town. In the minds of most of the congregation that surrounded her each Sunday and most evenings, Billy Diamond had become the church's worst enemy.

Since the early 1970s, the Pentecostals' fundamentalist movement had gained increasing control over several of the Cree villages along the east coast of James Bay. Roman Catholic missions such as the one in Waskaganish were becoming more removed than ever from the daily lives of the people. The Anglicans were losing members quickly to a church that lacked format and liturgy, that celebrated individual confession and personal experience in a manner not so far removed from campfire visits in other centuries.

John Whiskeychan had come home to Rupert House in 1971 as a

reformed alcoholic. After years of drinking and fighting in the northern Quebec copper-mining town of Chapais, the slow-moving, sad-faced Whiskeychan had been reborn as a Pentecostal, and he had become convinced that he could bring this fundamental Christian message back to his original village. It had been a long, uphill battle—at one point angry Crees had smashed into his house, beaten up his wife and threatened Whiskeychan with death if he stayed—but he refused to run. The Whiskeychans stayed, survived and John's ministry eventually prospered.

Everyone knew that a key convert for Whiskeychan had been Elizabeth Diamond, who left the Anglican church for the Pentecostal and brought many of her family and friends with her. She was the great chief's wife, and once word got out that Elizabeth had been reborn, the congregation increased weekly. If Elizabeth Diamond was going, others wanted to see why for themselves.

But the grand chief would have nothing to do with this strange church. He tore up the simple religious messages Elizabeth and others pasted over bumpers and onto refrigerator doors. He disdained the Jimmy Swaggart videos and the gospel tapes. He openly laughed at those who went trudging down the hill toward Whiskeychan's growing church each evening and twice on Sundays. "There are four religions in Rupert House," he bragged one evening when scotch had the run of his tongue. "Anglican, Roman Catholic, Pentecostal and Billy Diamond." No one doubted for a moment where Billy Diamond worshipped. Self-made men, after all, are eternally grateful to their creator.

One evening, in the middle of the service, the doors at the back of the Pentecostal church burst open and a very drunken Billy Diamond wobbled in, his face twisted in hatred. Elizabeth, praying in her seat near the front, never even turned, knowing exactly who it was by the sharp intake of breath around her. He stood for a long moment, scowling up at John Whiskeychan, who had been preaching, then yanked his coat off his back, threw it angrily down onto the floor and stormed out, slamming the door behind. Still, Elizabeth refused to turn.

Another time, unknown to either Whiskeychan or Elizabeth, Billy threatened Arthur Lemert, a white evangelist who had come into Waskaganish for a special service at the church. "I told him to get out," says Diamond. "I wanted to kill him. I told the ones who were with him, 'Get this white man out of here. This is an Indian reserve and we're going to kill him if he stays.'"

Lawrence Katapatuk tried to intervene. "Okay, Billy," he said. "But I'll go with you."

Billy, not thinking anyone would expect him to follow through with his threat, tried to backtrack. "Never mind!" he shouted at his friend. "Fuck it! Okay?" And he stormed out of the church and, once along on the road, burst into tears.

"I did everything I could to destroy John Whiskeychan," says Diamond. "I wanted to break him. I tried to chase him out of town. But he just wouldn't go."

The one who left was Billy Diamond himself. He caught a plane out of Waskaganish for Val d'Or. He went back to the lonely trailer on the outskirts and settled in, convinced that his marriage was done with, finished. He would go it alone. Without Elizabeth. Without her God. Without anyone but the only one who had always been there in the past, ever dependable, ever resourceful, ever successful: himself.

"The Crees," Billy Diamond decided as he sat in the kitchen of the Val d'Or trailer, "have to come out of the closet."

There would have to be a master plan. First, the James Bay Agreement had to be put into the Canadian constitution. It would have been better to have started on this earlier—Parliament had voted on Pierre Trudeau's new act on December 2, 1981, and the Queen herself had officiated at the proclamation earlier in the year—but Trudeau himself acknowledged that there was still much work to be done. After all, the entire province of Quebec had also been left out on the night of November 5, 1981, when, after the Quebec delegation had left the table and Premier René Lévesque had gone to bed, the others had struck the backroom deal that led, eventually, to repatriation. Lévesque, of course, was outraged. It was poorly handled, and even as the constitutional process moved ahead without Quebec, it was commonly held that one day something would have to be done to accommodate a Quebec that only two years earlier had voted down a move to leave Confederation.

It was not too late and it was not impossible. There was an egotistical prime minister who seemed to be becoming more and more concerned with how history would treat him, and surely, historically, it would look good to have a Native rights clause inserted into his greatest legacy. There was also a strong sense that certain premiers might soon be leaving, and surely they, too, would like to leave behind something to which they could point with pride. Finally, there was the premier who had been left out, René Lévesque of Quebec. He felt, as he would later write, a "burning resentment" against the others for the way he had been treated, and Diamond wondered if perhaps this bitterness might be turned to the Natives' advantage. Perhaps there was a way in which Lévesque could return to Ottawa unofficially to say what he'd dearly love to say officially. And perhaps when he was saying those things, he might help the Crees . . . .

The crucial difference between this sort of thinking and the thinking of most other Native leaders was that Billy Diamond's strategy involved the provinces directly, while the other strategies deliberately ignored that distrusted level of government. At one time there had been a draft section that was to become part of the final Constitution Act that had recognized and affirmed aboriginal and treaty rights, but it was pulled from the full draft in November 1981 at the request of several provinces. If the Natives' "trustee"—the federal government—could not come through for them, these leaders had come to believe that their best approach might be through the original trustee, the Queen and the British government. And to that end, various Native leaders had been lobbying in London, with little result except for some Fleet Street copy beneath a photograph of headdresses and peace pipes in Hyde Park.

"The lobbying was not handled correctly," says Joe Miskokomom, grand chief of the Union of Ontario Indians and a main player in London. "We didn't have the financing. There was no experience in an international forum. We couldn't put together a concerted effort by Indian people." Miskokomom had come across one Indian leader, however, who had impressed him during these difficult times. The Native leaders who were off to London had called a conference to find out more about negotiating, and Billy Diamond had come from Val d'Or to speak to them. Miskokomom had been moved by Diamond's words and liked his aggressiveness. But it was Diamond's flexibility that struck him as most intriguing. Most Native leaders were rigid in their opinions, not willing to listen to other sides. Diamond, on the other hand, was not only willing to listen, but willing to change as he went along, giving, then taking. Miskokomom could not forget the Cree chief who showed up and then vanished immediately.

While lobbying the House of Lords in London, Miskokomom had made contact with Lord Michael Morris, who seemed sympathetic to aboriginal rights, and, in 1981, was willing to travel to Canada to assess the land claims situation for himself. Miskokomom thought it would be best if he could see where a treaty had been signed and yet promises had continued to be broken, and so he asked Billy Diamond if he would lead the British Lord on a tour of James Bay.

The opportunity had intrigued Diamond and he had agreed. Lord Morris, he was told, was exactly as he sounded—a product of all the right schools, stuffy and enough of an elitist that he would sign "Lord Michael Morris" to his hotel bills—but he was also a man with a conscience. Diamond went to work immediately, arranging for Lord Morris to land in Val d'Or and look at that city before going up to James Bay to see life in the villages. He spread the word around Val d'Or that a British lord, of course, would be expecting the best, as befits his title.

"It was unbelievable," remembers Miskokomom. "They met him at the airport with a Rolls-Royce. They threw a dinner for him with the upper crust of the town at the best restaurant in town with the entire council sitting there with the most expensive wines and toasts and you name it—and sitting at the same table, smiling from ear to ear, was Billy Diamond.

"Next day we flew north to Mistassini and Lord Michael wants to know what's going on. Everyone in Val d'Or had told him there was nothing at all wrong with the relationship and then they'd driven him back to the airport in the Rolls-Royce. He lands in the Cree village and they grab his bags and throw them in the back of a half-ton. And there's Billy beside him, just grinning away.

"All the time Billy was talking to him about how the ones who would be hurt by this constitution were the Indians. He'd say it was only proper that Canada have its own constitution, but the Indians felt they had a special relationship with England and the Lord, therefore, had a responsibility."

At Waskaganish, Diamond put on a special meal that was to appear in sharp contrast to the Val d'Or extravaganza. Instead of a restaurant, they gathered in a cooking tent, with smoking geese dripping fat from the cooking hooks. There was tea instead of imported wines and the visitor's new brown Oxfords were caked with sewage-laden mud. "Lord Michael was flabbergasted," says Miskokomom. "All the propaganda he'd heard first from Canada House in London and then in Val d'Or, and now this. 'Somewhere,' he said, 'someone is not telling the truth.' "

The final stop was Paint Hills, the village where the water supply had been poisoned by sewage and bottled water had been flown in all summer long to the Indians. By the end of the day, the vain signature from the hotel bills—"Lord Michael Morris"—had been inscribed on an outhouse wall to commemorate the occasion. "A long-standing tradition," in the words of his guide, Grand Chief Billy Diamond.

"It was a great show," says Miskokomom. "Here you had a Lord coming from England completely filled with that propaganda from the Canadian government, and he ends up signing his name to a shithouse wall in an Indian village."

Lord Michael Morris returned to London as the great champion of the Indians in the continuing fight for the repatriation of the Canadian constitution. As Billy Diamond fully expected, the Lord had no success. There would have to be another way, and Billy Diamond had a notion he would be able to find it before it was too late for the Crees.

First, he would have to figure out how to cease being an outsider. Since so many other Native leaders had ridiculed the James Bay Agreement, Grand Chief Billy Diamond had avoided the national forum almost entirely, and if the Crees were going to come out of the closet, he was going to have to lead the way. "I was not in good standing," he says. "I had to come bearing gifts. I had to wave the white flag. I had to manoeuvre myself into a position."

In the spring of 1982 he attended, for the first time since 1974, a national meeting of the chiefs on the new Canadian constitution. "It was like going back in time," he says. "Nothing had happened. Nothing had changed. There was nothing for me to research, nothing for me to read. I felt time had stood still for eight years." He began appearing at constitutional conferences, speaking to universities, travelling about the country visiting with other Native leaders and trying to come up with new approaches to the problem of bringing their message to the attention of others.

He hadn't agreed with the thinking of the chiefs who had lobbied in Britain, and the visit of Lord Michael Morris had had little effect. Yet the Crees' other experiences on the international forum made him wonder if there might be another, as-yet-unexplored way of stepping outside of Canada to aim a prompting boot back at his country. Taking the dead babies crisis to Geneva, after all, had gained the Crees much-needed publicity in 1981. And after the *Maclean's* cover story, the *National Geographic* had featured the Crees at length. In West Germany the Crees of James Bay were the subject of books and photography exhibitions. Invariably, as soon as the subject left Canadian soil, the prevailing sympathy was on the side of the Crees and their fight to maintain a traditional style of life.

Diamond was well aware of the power of the church, and knew also that no church held power over people so much as the Catholic church. An earlier approach had been made by Cree consultant Gary George to the Roman Catholic Archbishop of Toronto, but it had gone nowhere. The idea simmered for several months until one day in Val d'Or, when George had come in to the Cree Regional offices for a meeting with Diamond and his executive assistant, Bob Epstein.

"I want to see the Pope," Diamond said.

Epstein burst out laughing. "You *what?*"

"The Pope. He's coming to Canada. He could say something."

"There's no hope," Epstein told him. "The Crees aren't even Catholic."

"So what? The Crees are Canadians. The Pope's coming to see Canadians, isn't he?"

"It's impossible. It can't be done."

"How would you get in? How does it work over there?"

Epstein and George explained what little they knew. They had gotten nowhere in Toronto, and Toronto was nothing compared to the Holy See and the Vatican. No one could demand an audience with the Pope. There were too many levels of command in between; the Pope was too well protected.

"If there's a bureaucracy," Diamond said, smiling, "there must be a back way in."

"How would *we* ever find out?" Epstein asked.

"If it's in Italy, it must have Italians. Do we have any Italians on staff?"

"One," Epstein laughed. "Guido Di Lenardo in Cree Housing."

"Get him over here."

Guido Di Lenardo was summoned, and a coincidence followed that would be considered forced if it appeared in a novel. But as it turned out, Guido Di Lenardo of the Cree Housing Authority did indeed have family connections to the Vatican—an uncle who, as good luck would have it, actually worked on the Pope's schedule. Gary George worked on Di Lenardo and eventually an exchange of letters was completed. The Crees were asked to meet with a designated *monsignor*—Gianpietro Cudin of Padova, Italy—to tell their entire story. Cudin then cut through the legendary Vatican red tape and the Crees of James Bay were duly informed that Pope John Paul II would be pleased to receive them once they arrived in Rome. A date was set in late November 1982.

Shortly before the Crees departed for Italy, the Assembly of First Nations—a new name for a recast National Indian Brotherhood—held its Christmas dinner at the Holiday Inn in Ottawa. The party was dominated by the latest gossip: the Crees were claiming they had lined up a meeting with the Pope. In the lobby, Minister of Indian Affairs John Munro caught up to Diamond and, Diamond claims, begged him not to go. But Diamond refused to discuss the issue. He then refused to attend the dinner, deciding instead to return to his room and decide what the Crees would do with this remarkable stroke of luck. Certainly, they already had John Munro's full attention. And the province of Quebec was paying rapt attention. Premier René Lévesque had been turned down when he sought to see the Pope as a "head of state"—yet here was the grand chief of the Crees being given a special audience.

The scheme that emerged from that hotel room was extraordinarily effective, if a bit unfair from John Munro's point of view. Diamond had Gary George—who stayed behind in Ottawa—call Canadian Press once the Crees were out over the Atlantic, well on their way to Rome. The wire service sent the message across the country: the Grand Council of the Crees of James Bay was in Rome to extend a formal invitation to Pope John Paul II to visit Native communities when he comes to Canada in 1984. The minister of Indian affairs, John Munro, had tried to thwart the meeting. The minister denied that he had done any such thing. "I was mad," Munro says. "I was very upset. I didn't mind him seeing the Pope. What I did mind was him going around telling everyone I'd objected. In fact, I actually thought it was a pretty good idea. But I was shocked he would say I'd tried to prevent him from going. I kept calling to get him to deny it."

When the Crees landed, there were urgent messages waiting for them to call Munro. Billy Diamond tore up the messages and called Gary George in Ottawa instead, telling him to forward all press calls to Diamond's hotel room in Rome. He would not speak with the minister of Indian affairs.

The night before the actual audience, Billy Diamond called home to Waskaganish and tried to patch up his broken marriage by long distance. He told Elizabeth he had been cutting down on his drinking. He wanted to know how Philip was doing. Lorraine. Ian. Sandy. He missed her, he said, surprising them both. Elizabeth seemed receptive, and when he said how much he'd like to go away and unwind once this was over, she suggested she could make her way down to Montreal, and they could spend a long weekend together and see if there was anything worth saving. He was delighted, and immediately booked a suite at the Four Seasons Hotel in Montreal.

At St Peter's Square the following day, the Crees were assigned a Swiss guard who took his job so seriously that he insisted on accompanying the grand chief on his nervous pee just before the actual meeting. The Crees were assigned to a chamber where they were instructed to wait. The Pope would stay one to two minutes and receive their gifts: a pair of snowshoes and a tamarack goose decoy. And that would be it.

Pope John Paul II came in a side door, accompanied by several cardinals, and when they had introduced themselves, he said to Billy, in English: "And how are you in Canada?"

"It's not working well," Diamond burst out, thinking the first minute had already passed. "We want you to speak on aboriginal rights when you come."

The Pope smiled. "You are the first citizens of this earth," he said. "I have read your material and I will speak."

Diamond pressed on, nervous that the cardinals were pressing in to move their charges on to the next room. "We want you to visit, as well."

"Yes," the Pope agreed. "I do want to see how you live."

The cardinals were getting edgy, but John Paul showed no sign of being in a hurry. He picked up the tamarack goose decoy the Crees had brought for him and admired it. He wanted to know everything about the decoy: how many days it took to make, how many Crees could do such work, if they were still used for hunting . . . . He lifted the decoy to his nose and breathed deep the rich fragrance.

"It is a special tree," Billy Diamond offered. "It grows only in the North."

"The same as in Poland," the Pope said, and smiled as if, through an ugly tree that grows only in swampland, Poles and Crees shared a world not understood by the rest, and because of this, he would do what he could to help others understand.

Billy Diamond flew home with rising hope. The visit with the Pope had been an enormous success: already the Canadian press was saying that a visit to a northern Native community would be added to the Papal itinerary. He was just as excited by another prospect, however: that of Elizabeth waiting back in Montreal.

But Elizabeth was not there. Although the plane from Europe was able to come in and land in a storm, she had not been able to get out of Waskaganish. He phoned and talked too much about what he had done with the Pope and how this was going to help with the overall negotiations, and it was several minutes before the chill on the line got through to him that this was hardly what she needed to hear. There was no time, unfortunately, to recapture the lost moment. The Assembly of First Nations was meeting in Ottawa and then again in Winnipeg, ironing out their strategy in preparation for the First Ministers' Conference that was slated for the spring of 1983, and Billy was needed. He had work to do on the plan. He would work on the marriage later.

In Winnipeg he ran into a furious John Munro. The meeting was intended to be a meeting about the draft amendment the federal government was proposing as a way to deal with the Native rights issue, but it nearly disintegrated into a fistfight when Munro came charging over to challenge Diamond on what had been said back in the Holiday Inn lobby in Ottawa prior to the Crees' leaving for Rome.

"You got beaten!" Diamond laughed, stabbing his finger into his own chest. "You got beaten by this Indian!"

Pierre Trudeau was not a person you could simply set up and trick. His concerns about inserting a clause on Native rights in his new constitution were tied directly to his overriding concern not to give in to Quebec on the dissenting province's demand for "special status." In Trudeau's logical mind, there was simply no discussion: how could you grant special rights to one ethnic group and not another? Was it not necessary, he would ask rhetorically, to first define aboriginal rights before taking the crucial step of enshrining something no one fully understood? Trudeau had been as consistent on this point in dealing with the Indians as he had been in dealing with the Québécois. In the 1960s, when Gordon Robertson, the clerk of the Privy Council, had suggested that the question of Indian policy be turned over to a royal commission for further inquiry, the late Jim Davey—a key strategist behind Trudeau's leadership victory—had come down fast and hard against such a notion. Davey's fear, and later Trudeau's, was that Natives might argue convincingly that they be regarded as "citizens plus," as certain groups had already proposed in writing. As Jim Davey reported in his memorandum: "I shudder to think that any royal commission might bring about such a similar document."

Native leaders knew that they were unlikely to gain "special status" from Trudeau, but at the same time they believed that he was on their side when it came to getting some small mention in the constitution. Most Native leaders accepted that their lack of clout in the negotiations could be blamed on themselves as much as on any arbitrary actions of Trudeau and the nine provincial premiers. The lack of cohesiveness on the Native side had led to endless confusion during the years of constitutional negotiation. Natives seemed incapable of stating together what it was they wanted in a constitution, and in the end they had simply been left out of the process.

Charlie Watt had been bitterly disappointed by the so-called "Kitchen Agreement" that had been struck by Jean Chrétien and the attorneys general of Ontario and Saskatchewan, Roy McMurtry and Roy Romanow, that had paved the way for the final patriation. He had been led to expect—as most Native leaders expected—a section on land claims and treaties, and full entrenchment of aboriginal rights if possible, but nothing at all was included. "That shook me," remembers Watt, and the Inuit leader went quickly to work on the problem.

Thanks to his connections, he was able to arrange a meeting with the prime minister at 24 Sussex Drive. Watt and another Inuit leader, John Amogoalik, met with Trudeau and his constitutional expert, Michael Kirby. Trudeau said there was little he could do: the provinces were against entrenchment of aboriginal rights and that was it. He might, however, be able to do something about the area north of the sixtieth parallel. Watt was adamant that this would not be acceptable; he needed time, he insisted, and begged the prime minister to give him enough leeway to contact the provinces that might support a change. Kirby was just as insistent that he sympathized with the Inuit position but worried that the opening would be used by other people for other purposes. "I don't give a fuck about other people," Watt said, rising to his feet.

Trudeau, calming Watt down, said he would have a week. But in the end, all that was inserted in the Constitution Act, 1982, was a clause that said, "The existing aboriginal and treaty rights of the aboriginal peoples of Canada are hereby recognized and confirmed." No one knew what it meant. As Roy Romanow later wrote: "This restatement, with its potentially unknown consequences, failed to quell the opposition of the aboriginal people."

The Native leaders, Charlie Watt and Billy Diamond included, wanted more. The spring 1983 First Ministers' Conference would be their first and best shot at it, and the preparations were frantic. The first element of the new strategy was to get René Lévesque to the table, and Billy Diamond and Max Gros-Louis—friends again after the bitter split between the Crees and the Indians of Quebec Association—met with Lévesque privately and spoke out publicly about the necessity of his coming.

"We challenged him," says Diamond. "We told everyone who would listen that Lévesque was going to go. We said he'd given us his word. He had to go. We talked him into holding parliamentary hearings on the Indian situation in Quebec and Lévesque even struck a special committee that included himself. That gave us our chance to challenge him. 'If it's true what you say, we *are* nations, and if it's true that you want to protect Native rights, then you *have* to go.' We had him."

"It was absolutely amazing," says Marsha Smoke of this time. "Lévesque was always there whenever Billy had to talk to him. He responded to Billy. They'd fought on the referendum, but deep down, they seemed to admire each other."

Diamond then went to work on David Ahenakew, the president of the Assembly of First Nations—a Saskatchewan Cree who uses the title "Doctor" from an honourary degree and sports a brush-cut so severe Diamond nicknamed him "our level-headed leader." Ahenakew was an easy convert. Diamond, with the help of Ahenakew's main advisor, Sol Sanderson, convinced Ahenakew that the tactics had to change completely, that the key to any success the Natives might have would be through their traditional enemy at these gatherings—the provinces. Diamond said the provinces could be played off against each other. Instead of British Columbia and Alberta forever joining to block the Native position, the two provinces should be arguing with each other. Ahenakew didn't think it possible, but Diamond was allowed to state the case and the AFN executive passed an agreement-in-principle to involve the provinces. As Diamond said, "You're going to have to deal with them sooner or later." Ahenakew bought the idea, and then proposed that Billy Diamond be made the AFN's chief negotiator, which met with approval.

Unknown to Ahenakew and other leaders in the AFN, however,

there was a shadow group formed that had taken to calling themselves the "BFN"—the "B-Team of the AFN," as Gordon Peters, then president of the Association of Iroquois and Allied Indians put it. Several of the secret "BFN" were also on the AFN, but they kept their activities well hidden from the other leaders like David Ahenakew. Diamond's role was to ensure open warfare didn't break out between the two camps, particularly if Ahenakew was to find out about the BFN. Diamond's friendship with Sanderson of the AFN and Peters of the BFN became crucial. He managed to be welcomed in both camps at once.

"Billy Diamond's contribution," says Neil Sterritt, one of the leaders from British Columbia, "was to bridge the hardliners and the softliners. Both parties respected Billy." The hardliners were a curious group. Their ultimate goal was to move Ahenakew aside and replace him, either with Diamond or else with the highly intelligent, if aloof, Georges Erasmus of the Northwest Territories. They also included two Ontario leaders, the frenetic Gordon Peters, and Gary Potts, a bright, angry young man from the Bear Island reserve in northern Ontario. Others came from Quebec, the Northwest Territories and Manitoba. Whatever organizations they represented were tapped for $5,000 contributions and they established a war chest apart from the AFN, and appointed the hyperactive Peters as coordinator.

The goal of the BFN at the 1983 First Ministers' Conference was to manipulate the AFN and, hopefully, the other key Native groups, so a united front could be presented in favour of specific constitutional change. Too often in the past the splintering had worked to the advantage of the politicians who had been able to say that the offers were on the table but the Natives had been unable to make up their minds. This time it would be different. The Inuit, thanks in large part to Charlie Watt and Zebedee Nungak, were agreeable, as were certain key leaders such as Smokey Bruyere, who later became president of the Native Council of Canada, a group representing non-status Indians, and Jim Sinclair, the tough-talking head of the Métis organization.

"We'd meet all day as the AFN," says Gordon Peters. "Then some of us would meet all that night as the BFN. When Ahenakew found out, he was furious. But he wouldn't meet with us when we invited him. So we stayed with it." It was Diamond's task to ensure that Ahenakew's anger over the existence of the BFN did not spoil the strategy, and with Sanderson's help, he succeeded in preventing a visible split.

The strategy settled on the Sunday night before the conference opened was to protect what had already been gained—the "existing" clause on treaties—and to force a second round of negotiations. The key negotiator, though he would not be seen as such, would be the grand chief of the James Bay Crees, Billy Diamond. He would stay "upstairs," away from the television cameras as much as possible, and this would leave him latitude to pound away at the provincial attorneys general and justice ministers. The Native coalition was also counting on Diamond to get to Pierre Trudeau. No one quite knew how, but when the time came, Billy Diamond would have to gain a hearing from the prime minister.

The conference was chaired by Mark MacGuigan, who was then minister of justice. Moments after the gavel came down, Grand Chief Billy Diamond asked to make a statement, to which MacGuigan objected, but the consensus at the table was that Diamond should be heard. What he was doing, as Jacques Beaudoin would have known were he alive to see it, was setting a *tone* for the discussions. He had a simple message: *Are the First Ministers ready to negotiate?* As predicted, it caught the politicians off guard. The premiers and their ministers looked around the table for dissent from the other Native groups, but none was forthcoming.

"It took them completely by surprise," remembers Diamond. "It made people move. We knew there would be no deal on the floor, and I said to Georges Erasmus, 'You put on a show out here, dance if you have to, but I'm going to be upstairs.'"

Upstairs the talk was with bureaucrats like John Tait, who was now with the Department of Justice. Diamond wanted his own people with him for this part of the negotiations. Ahenakew offered the usual AFN bureaucrats. Diamond insisted, instead, on the likes of Gordon Peters and Harold Cardinal and Joe Miskokomom. Roberta Jamieson would interpret the speeches, translating them from political vapourage into hard currency. For technical advice, he wanted James O'Reilly. Back-up would come from George Watt of British Columbia, Marilyn John, the sharp young leader from Newfoundland, Neil Sterritt and others who had been linking up with the secret BFN over the past several months.

The first day was a washout, with nothing said and nothing gained. Roberta Jamieson, once she had gone through the opening addresses and impromptu speeches, weighed the politicians' words and announced sadly that, in total, they added up to nothing.

"You're all Indians," Billy Diamond told the despairing group.

"And what do Indians do when you have a problem? You fall back and regroup—and attack again!"

They worked all through the night. By their reading of the climate, they felt that British Columbia, Alberta and Saskatchewan were all counted out. There would be no support there. But the day might still be won with the others, particularly with Nova Scotia's sympathetic minister of intergovernmental affairs, Edmund Morris, working on the senior ministers and New Brunswick's Richard Hatfield on certain of his fellow premiers.

There was also the wild card that Diamond and Max Gros-Louis had ingeniously helped to place at the table: Quebec Premier René Lévesque, observer. The night before the opening, Diamond had gone alone across the river to visit Lévesque in his Hull hotel suite. They met from before midnight until nearly two in the morning, a bottle of scotch on the table, a pad on Lévesque's lap, the premier taking notes on what he might say to prod the others into action. True to his word, Lévesque, the official observer, never lost an opportunity to push for the Native cause.

On the morning of the second day, Diamond approached David Crenna, who was a key negotiator for the federal side. "I knew he spoke for Pierre Trudeau," says Diamond. "I asked him to get rid of all the justice and Privy Council people. One on one we would work out a deal together. We had the clause before lunch .... I went down and sat with Ahenakew and Erasmus, who were sitting at the table. 'Gentlemen,' I said, 'we have a deal, but before you see it, it's good for the North, it's good for the South, it's good for the East, good for the West, good for treaty Indians, good for non-treaty Indians—no one gets left out.' "

Ahenakew stared at the clause for an inordinate amount of time, then looked up and grinned. "That's it!" he said. "By golly! We've got it!"

"We had a deal among ourselves," remembers Diamond. "Now we had to sell it to Trudeau. I waited until the break and then I pushed my way over. I told him we had a deal, and if the AFN agrees to it, then the other Native groups would as well. I told him it was in his court now."

Diamond asked Trudeau to let David Ahenakew speak and then immediately ask Billy if he had anything to add. "I'll summarize what David intended to say," Diamond said. Trudeau grinned, and proceeded to do precisely as asked. Ahenakew spoke, then Billy. And once the discussion had gone around the table, it was clear that the Constitution Act, 1982, had its very first amendments.

Section 35 of the constitution would be changed so that "treaty rights" would include rights that now exist by way of land claims agreements or that may be so acquired. There was no longer any uncertainty: the James Bay and Northern Quebec Agreement was now part of the Canadian constitution. It had taken enormous manipulation, tremendous negotiation and more than a little trickery, but Billy Diamond had accomplished precisely what he had set out to accomplish only a few months earlier—an amendment to his country's constitution that would protect the land claims of his own Crees and all other Native Canadians.

He could go home now. Perhaps there the double vision would go away for a while. Perhaps once he got back home the pins and needles feeling that ran through his arms and hands would subside. Perhaps he would be able to sleep again.

He had a plan and on paper it looked perfect. He would get rid of the trailer and take a small apartment in Val d'Or. He would work as he had seen so many of the members of Parliament work, coming in early Tuesday morning, leaving Thursday afternoon. He would *live* in Waskaganish. Elizabeth could come down with him when he had to work. They could go through therapy together. He would stop smoking entirely. Cut back on the drinking.

But it would take more than that. He would have to quit, he knew that. Not smoking or drinking. He would have to quit politics. He would step down as grand chief and go home permanently. The James Bay Agreement was now part of the constitution. The Cabinet had approved the funding. Soon the legislation would pass through to give the Crees full self-government, the dream of all the Native leaders he had been dealing with during this past year of tortuous negotiations. There was, after all, nothing left for Billy Diamond to do. He was thirty-four years old. He was sick. But it was not too late to start again.

In Waskaganish he found that Malcolm had anticipated this very move. The house that he and Hilda had abandoned was being readied for a new family and, just as Malcolm wished, that new family turned out to be Billy and Elizabeth Diamond and their four children, Lorraine, Ian, Sandy and Philip.

Philip was now the most famous citizen of Waskaganish, a rotund, smiling little devil who ambled about at will, welcome in all houses, knowing every person and dog by name. The doctors at Sainte-Justine in Montreal, where he still went every six months, did not know where they had gone wrong. A brain scan had failed to pick up the slightest damage, and, apart from the odd epileptic seizure and a slight lag behind the others of his age, he seemed like a normal kid. And Philip was going to be sent to school. Not pushed on the floatplane while his mother wept, but walked down the road to the school that had been built as a result of his father's agreement, the school where, when Ian's grade four class was given a test and asked to name the prime minister of Canada, eleven had put down the name "Billy Diamond." Only three had thought of "Pierre Trudeau."

"I thought I was leaving the Crees in very good shape," Diamond remembers. "I wanted Cree rights mentioned in a special way, entrenched in legislation so people would never have to worry again about having things like their fishing nets seized, and that was coming. People would have to realize a nation was there and that it would have to be respected. People from the South would know now that this was a special people, that a small unknown group of tribes was now a powerful nation. I felt their future was intact." In his own mind, it was only a matter of tying up the loose ends and then dropping out of sight. But, of course, it wasn't as easy as that.

In April, with the First Ministers' Conference now behind him, he was chairing a board meeting in Val d'Or when the double vision came back and would not vanish when he tried the old trick of rubbing his eyes. He looked at Bill Grodinsky and saw two of him, then two of everyone else in the room, and he couldn't shake it off. Frightened, he stood, closed his books and left the room, followed by his secretary, Patricia Lefebvre. He asked her to make an immediate appointment with the doctor.

At the end of a complete physical and a long series of tests, the best that could be determined was that he was suffering from extreme fatigue. The doctor's orders were to rest, and he headed off to MacLean Island for the goose hunt with Elizabeth, and there, slowly, the marriage began to be repaired. They stayed six weeks, and by the end of the rest he had determined to leave politics behind him, forever, just as soon as the opportunity presented itself.

PART FOUR

FIRE
ᐃᔥᑯᑌ

But any forecast of Indian civilization which looks for final results in one generation or two is doomed to disappointment. Final results may be attained, say, in four centuries by the merging of the Indian race with the whites, and all these four things—treaties, teachers, missionaries, and traders—with whatever benefits or injuries they bring in their train, aid in making an end.

> Duncan Campbell Scott,
> Indian Treaty Commissioner,
> *The Last of the Indian Treaties*,
> an account of the Canadian
> government's negotiations leading up
> to the signing of James Bay Treaty
> No. 9, 1905.

CHAPTER SIXTEEN

HOME

Billy Diamond was drunk. He had been drinking for five days solid, and though he kept telling himself and anyone else who would listen that this was the final big blowout of his life, he hardly sounded convincing as he fumbled with the cap of yet another bottle of expensive scotch. His good intentions to quit and return home had remained but a promise. He had not been in Waskaganish for over a month, and given his last visit, he didn't know how he would ever again be welcomed there. He was drunk and he was scared and he was barely aware of where he was or how he'd gotten there.

Where he was, was on the steel floor of the freight section of a DC-3, a plane so old and beaten it had been in the air years before Billy Diamond himself had come into the world. And yet the tired old freight plane was in far better shape than him, still throbbing confidently through a June night in 1983 as it might have flown through October mornings in the forties and January afternoons in the sixties—a battered, silver airplane three miles high over James Bay at two o'clock in the morning, with the northern lights rippling in orange and pink sheets above it.

How he'd got there was through a simple fishing trip. The grand chief of the James Bay Crees, some friends, some business partners, some political allies, just a simple fishing trip that would take them by jet to Val d'Or, by charter to the LG2 site of the James Bay

Project, and then by Beaver floatplane still farther north to the shores of Wawa Lake. Here, the Pepabano family had taken over an abandoned exploration camp from Hydro-Québec and were in the process of turning it into a fishing camp where they might one day lure rich Americans to the cold, trout-rich waters of Wawa. For Richard Pepabano it had been a trade-off and all part of the James Bay Agreement: the camp lay where his trapline had once run. The flooding had chased his beaver and this was a chance, a promising chance, for his family to remain in the bush for generations to come.

The grand chief's guests had grown delirious over the fish, their baitless lines barely breaking the surface of the swelling lake before rods would bend with enormous lake trout, some running close to twenty pounds. And when they tired of the lakers, they turned to the rivers, and speckled trout that rippled with the same colours as the northern lights.

But the grand chief himself had hardly bothered with the fishing. The floatplane had even made a special flight just to carry in the booze, and the cases of Chablis and Glenfiddich scotch and Canadian beer filled the tents on shore and the boats themselves: a drink before breakfast and lose count by lunch. At times, in the distance, the boat the grand chief was fishing in seemed only to hold a guide sitting alone by the outboard. The grand chief of the James Bay Crees was passed out on the floorboards.

It seemed he was having fun. Billy, loud and laughing from the boats; Billy, hilariously entertaining over the evening fish fries and endless drinks. At a shore lunch on the first day, he did a "sun dance," complete with Cree chanting, that coincided perfectly with the parting of the clouds and the first sun in days. In his underwear at four in the morning he stood by the shore, howling at the sliding colours in the remarkable sky and screaming for another bottle to be brought to the endless celebration. And when a freak snowstorm delayed the return of the floatplane for another day, he did not pull the sleeping bag a little higher and go back to sleep as others in the party did; no, the grand chief of the Crees of James Bay continued to party until most of the booze was gone. In the end, the pilot of the floatplane discovered he had one less trip out to make than had been necessary going in.

But it was no celebration. It was a wake, a personal wake for something that was dying inside. The actor was leaving the stage. The spotlight that had warmed Billy Diamond through a hundred press conferences and committee appearances and official signings and speeches now burned so it frightened him.

Only a year earlier, when the Quebec Nordiques of the National Hockey League had held a special "Cree Night," Grand Chief Billy Diamond had dropped the puck and been given as long a standing ovation as if he himself had scored the winning goal that put them into the playoffs against the Boston Bruins. Earlier in the day, he had even called a press conference and smoked a peace pipe with Marcel Aubut, the Nordiques' owner. Then he pretended to pray to the Great Spirit so that the team would have divine guidance during the march to the Stanley Cup, which never materialized. He could never do that now. He would feel like a fool.

"It had gotten so I really hated Billy Diamond inside," he says. "I didn't like the projection. I didn't like making the speeches anymore. It wasn't until the constitution came along that I began to realize this and tried to change. Up until then I'd always been "Billy Diamond, Super Politician"—but it was a role. I told them I wanted to work in the backrooms and I did, and I found out that I was a lot happier that way, happier with myself." Incidents that once he would have laughed at, he was now ashamed to admit had ever happened. Val d'Or had chosen the grand chief of the James Bay Crees as the "Citizen of the Year" and Billy Diamond had been tricked into coming to the dinner without first being informed of the honour. He had come drunk and, thinking the night was in someone else's honour, had been loud and obnoxious as he sat at the head table, throwing out insults at each lead-up speech, thinking he was the laugh of the gathering, only to discover that the joke was on him when his name was announced. He could barely make it to the podium, let alone manage a thank-you speech.

He had never hurt anyone. Drunk, he was beloved by those who gathered in his circle to listen to the endless stories of his dealings with Robert Bourassa, Pierre Trudeau and Pope John Paul II. But he had come to know it was phoney. His world was not the Vatican, but Waskaganish, his concern not the well-being of a constitution brought back from Britain, but the well-being of a young boy brought back from the dead.

It seemed like years since he had been home. He had been promising weekends and failing to show almost as consistently. The legislation, the constitution—there was always a ready excuse, but not one that would wash anymore with a four-year-old who kept grabbing the telephone out of his mother's hands and screaming into a distant ear: "Come home, Daddy! *Right now!*"

And now, high in the sky over a black bay, he was indeed heading home. The fishing trip was over, the wine gone, the whiskey a heel in the last bottle, the beer now a few empty cans that rolled irritatingly along the steel floor of the cargo hold of the DC-3. Finally the snow had let up and the floatplane had left the camp, but it had been too late to catch the scheduled flight down from the LG2 landing strip. Stan Deluce, the owner of Austin Airways and a longtime fishing and business partner of Diamond, had ordered up the cargo plane, which was heading back that way anyway. And now the freightless plane was heading back toward Val d'Or on a flight path that would take the grand chief of the James Bay Cree almost directly over the village at the mouth of the Rupert River, straight over the roof of the house where the four-year-old boy lay sleeping. Convinced he would not be welcome in his own house, the father was about to pass straight over his son without so much as a wave in the night. In Val d'Or there would be no one to welcome Billy Diamond—but he was getting well used to that. It was easier that way.

The actor was very nearly exorcized. The worst moment of the binge had passed only an hour earlier aboard the plane when the grand chief had staggered to the rear of the DC-3 and announced he was going to kick open the mail-drop chute to "piss on my people." A poor joke that he had not meant. And since then, he had sat staring out at the northern lights, quietly thinking. And then he had spoken to Deluce who had, in turn, gone forward to speak with his pilot, Serge Lavoie. Radio contact had been made with Waskaganish and yes, at two o'clock in the morning an empty cargo plane would attempt a gravel runway landing in the northern lights.

Down the DC-3 dropped, shimmying and rattling in a turn and dropping again until the wings bent and caught like those of a snow goose the moment it realizes the geese at the edge of the open water are tamarack decoys. Low over the bluff the big plane floated, passing once over the village to see who might have been roused for the landing. The lights of a half-ton were bouncing and stabbing out toward the runway; a kid on a bicycle was already there, pumping wildly past the storage shed with a strong flashlight held straight up in the air; more trucks were coming from the area of the new houses. The runway lights were not yet on—but they were on their way.

The DC-3 banked, turned, banked again and came back from the south, the lights of the arriving trucks unnecessary in the wash of a full moon that cut through the cloud. The plane skipped once, settled, and Billy Diamond, home at last, closed his eyes.

Elizabeth was in one of the trucks, scowling out through the headlights at her lost husband. She had been called and the call had wakened Philip, who insisted on coming out with her. When the grand chief of the James Bay Cree stepped off the plane, Philip Diamond came running out across the high beams of the truck, steam rising from his mouth as he screamed to everyone that his Daddy was home—as if they did not already know. Billy Diamond was hit by his four-year-old son as soon as he stepped out onto the gravel, Philip leaping for his father's neck and twisting as if it were a fight instead of a greeting. And in a way it was.

The marriage had been very nearly lost, irretrievably lost. The fact that Elizabeth had the grace to show up at the airstrip was some encouragement, but hardly forgiveness. Not after his last visit home.

The drinking that had been going on during the fishing trip had actually started on his birthday weeks earlier. He had come north to Waskaganish and was outraged when no one would join him in a birthday drink. Elizabeth had stopped drinking. His childhood friend, Lawrence Katapatuk, had stopped, men and women all over Waskaganish were giving up alcohol and turning instead to this fundamentalist religion that they claimed was saving their lives. *Crap*, their grand chief was calling it. *Utter crap*. This loving church of theirs had torn away his wife and stolen his friends. This understanding God had taken the village Billy Diamond had built and was making it over to suit His own purposes, which seemed to Grand Chief Billy Diamond both devious and destructive.

In Val d'Or and in a dozen hotel rooms, Billy Diamond had been trying to talk to this God who was tyrannizing them. He would sit up mumbling at the ceiling, convinced that he himself had gone completely mad and would be found in the morning, insane, never to return to the world of reason where the God Elizabeth and Lawrence described was no threat. Sometimes in these long nights he would hear languages howling in his head, but not know what was being said. Sometimes he would find himself screaming at this God who was twisting Cree minds as carelessly as Robert Bourassa had believed he could twist the James Bay rivers to suit his needs.

His imagination would race ahead of him. He had accused Elizabeth of trying to get rid of him so she could take up with another man, a white stranger who had come to work in the village and who was also around the church. Drinking alone on his miserable thirty-fourth birthday, he had suddenly erupted in anger, slamming his entire body into a hall wall near the bedroom.

"Get out of here!" he screamed at Elizabeth. "Get out of here—all of you—before I kill you!"

The young family was terrified. They had never seen their father act this way and they had no idea what they had done to offend him. He knew this but could not stop. He hit the wall again, shattering the plaster, screaming as Elizabeth hurried the children away. Billy booted the door shut behind them. But the rage did not leave him. He began walking around the house, methodically slamming his fist through doors and walls, systematically destroying the home that was a direct and immediate symbol of all that he had brought to James Bay. Had he become Joseph Brant and tricked his own people? Had he become Almighty Voice, the enemy ever pressing in on him until he was left alone with only his fury? Or was he Billy Diamond, some unfinished history that could go either way?

"I still don't know why," he says, looking back. "I was sulking, feeling sorry for myself. I was looking for praise for what I had done but I was also mad at what I had done. I thought the Crees had thrown away their culture and here I was in a white man's world. I fought the house." The scene went on for nearly five days: Billy holed up in the house, the family taking shelter with relatives, no one in the village having the courage to go and find out what had gone so dreadfully wrong with the man they had all looked up to for guidance. His older brother, Charlie, came over, but Billy threw him out of the house. He would not even talk to his parents. Annie and Gerti went over when the drinking was finished and, saying nothing, began cleaning up the house.

Finally, Elizabeth went herself, alone. When she entered, he was sitting at the kitchen table, brooding. She sat down on the couch. "Come and sit beside me," she said. He did and she took her husband's hands in her own. "If you believe in a God that is big and almighty," she told him, "He can heal you."

Billy said nothing. Elizabeth went on. "I also believe He answers prayers. Let's pray that He sends someone to come and speak to you."

Billy shook his head, tears falling. "I don't know how." But Elizabeth just held onto his hands and prayed alone. There was a knock at the door, and Lawrence Katapatuk's soft voice rose from the porch—"Billy? You there?"—that same soft, laughing voice that had been saying the same words all their lives.

Lawrence came up, sat down, and began weeping himself. "Don't push God away," he told his friend. "The spirit of God is speaking to you. I've come to tell you that you can totally surrender to Him. You've got to come to church, Billy, so more people can pray for your deliverance."

Lawrence put his arms around Billy. "I love you," he said, hugging tightly. "And I don't want to lose you as a brother and a friend." Billy could not answer. He was trying to follow Elizabeth in her prayer.

The drinking was over now, over forever he hoped. He had had his fishing trip, his last big blowout, and he was determined to quit. It would take a few months to sort everything out, but it would have to be done, could be done, and then he would announce his decision to quit politics as well.

But for now, with the self-government legislation still not through Parliament, with the constitutional talks scheduled to continue on aboriginal issues, with problems in the Cree Regional Authority and the Grand Council, he would have to keep the decision to himself—and to Elizabeth, who wasn't sure she believed him. She'd heard this talk before.

The double vision still came back every now and then, and the pins and needles sensation was still worrying; the doctor in Val d'Or had suggested further tests. The grand chief was overweight and overworked, never exercising except when he went off into the bush. Perhaps he was heading for a heart attack? He'd even been having chest pains. It *had* to be heart trouble. The thought so obsessed him that, back in Val d'Or he found himself driving one day with his hand over a heart that seemed to be pounding in desperation. He was certain the attack was either coming or had actually started, and he would be dead by nightfall. But instead of turning in at the hospital, he continued to drive until he turned the car into the parking lot of the local Pentecostal church. He parked and entered sheepishly, hoping no one would recognize the town's former "Citizen of the Year".

There were only six others in the church, and none of them turned from praying when Billy Diamond closed the door and tiptoed into a seat. The preacher—Arthur Lemert, the same man Diamond had earlier threatened to kill—was talking about healing, a long, rambling discussion about the restorative powers of faith and the evidence presented in the Bible about true believers being suddenly and miraculously cured—the very claims Billy Diamond loved to ridicule when they came out of the mouth of John Whiskeychan back in Waskaganish. But this time, instead of laughing, Diamond got down onto his knees and prayed for himself. "God," he mumbled into his hands, "I'm sick. I'm a sick man and I don't know what's wrong with me."

At the front of the church, the preacher asked who believed in the healing power of God to raise their hands, and the grand chief of the James Bay Crees pulled his left hand from over his mouth and slowly pushed it up. "It was like an electric shock had been sent through my entire body," he remembers. "It came through my hand. It was like my hand began to glow and I started to get very, very warm, right down to the very pit of my soul. Then I started to shake and tremble. But it wasn't from fear. I had no fear at all. I kept my eyes closed and just kept praying that this feeling would continue to fill me. . . . I sat there just basking in the glow of what was happening to me. It seemed like hours. And when I opened my eyes, the double vision was gone. The pain in my chest was gone. The feeling in my arms and hands was gone."

The following day, as scheduled, Billy Diamond checked into the Val d'Or hospital for three days of tests. At the end, the doctors told him that he seemed fine. According to the tests, nothing was wrong. He was probably working too hard and he could stand to lose some weight, but otherwise, he was in fine health.

He could not, however, cut back on the work. The Crees still needed to get their long-promised self-government legislation through Parliament. Fortunately, Billy Diamond and John Munro had patched up their disagreement. Since the last First Ministers' Conference, in fact, Diamond had come to regard Munro more as ally than enemy, and regretted all the pain he had caused the minister in the past. Munro was even assigned to feel Diamond out about a possible posting to the Canadian Senate for the Cree chief.

Trudeau, motivated by the constitutional experiences with Native people over the past few years, had said it would be appropriate if a Native leader were sent to the upper chamber of the Canadian Parliament, but the notion did not excite Diamond. He felt he was being approached so that he would publicly endorse the government's proposed self-government legislation, and he was convinced he would once again be ridiculed as a "bought Indian." He was thirty-five years old. If he went to the Senate he would be guaranteed forty years of high income, no election, no duties, and free travel—the "taskless thanks" as it is called in Ottawa—but it did not seem appropriate when there was still so much work to do. Not only legislative problems, but there was once again talk of building more dams along the east coast of James Bay. He could not consider the appointment, and, shortly after he made his decision, it was announced that Billy Diamond's old Inuit colleague from the 1975 agreement would become Senator Charlie Watt.

Robert Bourassa was running again for leader of the provincial Liberal party and a key plank in his platform was more development in James Bay: more dams, more electricity to sell to the United States. And it seemed to be working: Bourassa, so recently declared not only politically dead but extinct, was now considered the front runner.

In February 1984, Pierre Trudeau announced he would be stepping down as prime minister, and it struck Billy Diamond that it would be appropriate for him to consider stepping down about that time, as well. He met with the leader of the Opposition, Brian Mulroney, for nearly three hours and came out of the meeting both extremely impressed and convinced that Mulroney, whom he believed would soon be prime minister, would be the saviour of Canadian Natives. Mulroney seemed to understand perfectly the need for economic development; he understood the need for legislation; he understood the historical significance of the agreement; and, perhaps most important of all, he genuinely seemed to care. There was even some preliminary talk about the possibility of Billy Diamond going into the Prime Minister's Office in an advisory capacity for Native affairs.

It was a happy meeting that, several months later, would leave a bitter taste. Mulroney was indeed elected prime minister on September 4, 1984, and soon after that the Crees eagerly paid out $100 a ticket to buy an entire table at a Montreal fundraiser. They lobbied through a junior minister to stake out a good table and arrived, only to be told by the organizer, "Sir, we have a Native table." It was in another room. They could watch the speech from there. A complaint was made, a new table assigned and an apology offered by a frantic Mulroney aide, but already Diamond and the Crees were having a change of heart about the prime minister who had seemed to offer so much reason for hope.

The Crees did get their legislation before the Liberal government passed from the scene in 1984, but it did not come easily. The Crees of James Bay and a small neighbouring band, the Naskapi, were to get self-government under the same bill, C-46, the Cree-Naskapi (of Quebec) Act. By June, the bill had been delayed numerous times for no apparent reason other than that there always seemed to be more pressing business. The self-government legislation that had been promised in the James Bay and Northern Quebec Agreement nine years earlier could not seem to reach final reading and passage. The Crees grew increasingly suspicious.

Finally, in early June, Billy Diamond went to Ottawa to press the issue, and informed the Liberals that C-46 had better go through fast—otherwise they were going to have the Cree nation marching on Parliament. It was a gamble, but the Crees were desperate. The Liberal leadership convention was only days away, the House would soon be rising for the summer and, more disturbing, there was election talk in the air. If John Turner won the leadership, as expected, and the polls held promise, then Turner might decide to seek the dissolution of Parliament and go for a fresh mandate. And if that happened, then bills like C-46 would die on the order paper and perhaps not be raised again for years to come. Perhaps, under a new government, never.

On June 8, Billy Diamond, accompanied by the village chiefs, went to the public galleries, determined to sit and wait until the final vote was taken. Diamond had every reason to be confident. Working through the offices of the three party House leaders, he had helped engineer an all-party agreement that there would be unanimous consent given verbally on the floor of the Commons. The House would then instantly go into a committee-of-the-whole, instead of shuffling the bill off to the standing committee for further examination. With third reading and unanimous approval thus given, the bill would head off to the Senate, where fast passage was also assured. Others, however, had other ideas.

But it did not go as planned. The New Democratic member for Spadina, Dan Heap, accused the acting prime minister, Jean-Luc Pepin, of "lying" during a heated exchange about unemployment, and the House business was derailed while members voted to expel Heap. What the NDP was doing, charged government House Leader Yvon Pinard, was "jeopardizing the passage of the Cree and Naskapi Bill today." With the division bells ringing for a recorded vote and valuable time slipping away, the Crees began to worry. Heap was expelled, left slowly, and the NDP then began a long series of points of privilege.

Diamond panicked. The other chiefs were demanding to know what he was going to do and Diamond quickly dispatched Bob Epstein to call Ed Broadbent's office to see if the NDP leader could intervene. Epstein raced off to the telephone. And Diamond, with his chiefs staring at him, waiting, closed his eyes, knelt in the gallery chair as if it were a pew, and prayed. He didn't know what else to do.

Epstein had failed to get through to Broadbent. Diamond had no alternative but to head down to the lobby during the delayed lunch break and see what was happening in the large, cordoned-off area where the press scrums the politicians. Ignoring the security commissioners, he led his chiefs into the marble foyer and confronted, in turn, the two key figures involved in the House business of that day, Liberal Yvon Pinard and Conservative MP John McDermid, who would be speaking on the bill for the Conservatives. Whit Fraser, a CBC newsman with a strong sympathy for Native affairs, noticed the excited exchanges and had a CBC technician eavesdrop with a boom mike on Diamond's next confrontation, a testy attack on New Democrat Rod Murphy, who had been delaying matters with his points of order on an unrelated labour bill.

"You guys are screwing us!" Diamond shouted as the mike swung overhead. Fraser let them argue for a moment and then stepped in while Diamond was calling the NDP hypocrites for saying they were in favour of Indian rights while all along they had their own agenda for this crucial day.

It was brutal, all recorded on videotape, and certainly more than a bit unfair toward the innocent Murphy, but the message got through. The New Democrats quickly regrouped and headed back into the House, where they duly voted for the Cree-Naskapi self-government bill, just as had been the original plan. As the clerk read out the final tally of the vote, Jean-Luc Pepin looked up at Diamond and raised his fists in victory, with the Cree chief making the same sign back. Three weeks later the Cree-Naskapi Act was through the Senate and declared law, just before Parliament was prorogued and a general election called. And in August of that year—less than a month before John Turner's ill-considered election call would throw the Liberals out of office—the government signed a letter of understanding, providing for proper implementation and an agreed-upon funding formula. The Crees and Naskapis would have control of their own affairs, and they could work on long-term financial plans.

"The Crees were lucky to have had Billy Diamond there," says Doug Frith, who served during the summer as Prime Minister Turner's minister of Indian affairs. "If there had been no Billy Diamond, there would never have been a Cree-Naskapi Act."

With that legislation, the Cree nation officially became the first experiment in Native self-government in Canadian history. It was time, Billy Diamond decided, to go on home and savour the victory.

Billy Diamond came home to plot his exit from the role of grand chief. There was no more drinking. He was even joining Elizabeth in prayer and reading voraciously the religious pamphlets and books she was bringing back from John Whiskeychan's brand-new meeting hall. But he would not go. He could not go, he thought, to the one place where he had publicly sworn no Cree would ever see the face of Grand Chief Billy Diamond.

"You can't know God in your bedroom," Elizabeth laughed at him. "Come to church. You keep saying you're a Christian now—why don't you show it?"

He shook his head. "I'm afraid what people will think of me. I'm going to lose my position."

"I thought you wanted to lose it anyway."

Sunday mornings she would go to church alone while he stayed in the bedroom, reading from the Bible and at times debating aloud and furiously the necessity of going public with his religion. But he could come to no resolution, and finally the question was answered one Sunday evening when he happened to ask Elizabeth if she was heading back to the church for the evening service and she stood at the door, silently waiting.

"It was the longest walk you ever imagined," he says. "I heard voices in my head, laughing, people yelling, 'You've gone beyond help now, Diamond.' I was sure I could see faces in every window. I knew everybody would be talking. I figured I'd be the laughing stock of the community." He took the first available seat in the back row and stared straight ahead, ignoring the gawkers, pretending not to hear the whispers. The last time he had been here he had come to run John Whiskeychan out of town and now here he was letting John Whiskeychan tell him what to do, when to pray, what to think. He began sweating. His shirt soaked through and then his jacket. He tore off his jacket, but it did no good. When he moved in the chair, the bottoms of his thighs caught with small wet sounds, embarrassing him. He tried to stand, but his knees were shaking too badly to support himself.

John Whiskeychan issued the altar call and many of the congregation began to move to the front, swaying, praying aloud, calling out names. Billy Diamond silently wrote his own prayer:

"Lord, whatever you do with me, don't embarrass me in front of these people." He could not go up.

The crucial moment was yet to come. A few weeks later, with Grand Chief Billy Diamond now a church regular, the Reverend Garnet Gunter came into the village for an evangelical meeting, and the Pentecostals of Waskaganish were understandably excited. The huge evangelist—"The Big One," as they called the 270-pound Ontario preacher—had come to the village before, and his massive size and huge, rumbling voice had always been a major draw at the church, converting more Crees with a single altar call than the quiet, uncharismatic John Whiskeychan might manage in a year. It was to be a special service, and the request was put to the newest convert: would Billy Diamond speak before The Big One? He was nervous but he agreed. Billy Diamond had spoken in front of hundreds of audiences, usually strangers. Why would he not be able to speak in front of family and friends? He scanned through the Bible and settled on Matthew, Chapter 10, the story of the assembling and sending out of the twelve disciples of Christ. Straightforward, easy and, he believed, apt. He would have nothing to say about Billy Diamond, and nothing to add about what God had done for Billy Diamond.

But Billy Diamond would never know what it was he said the day The Big One came to Waskaganish. He spoke, obviously, and the squeeze of Elizabeth's hand when he returned to his seat meant that it had gone well enough. They were standing up, applauding, and he still didn't know what he had said. Some, including Elizabeth, were crying. But all he could do was sit grinning like a fool, without the slightest sense of what had caused this strange reaction among the congregation. Then he realized he was crying. And later, when Elizabeth wanted to know when he had memorized all the scriptural references, he would still not know what he had said.

The Reverend Garnet Gunter rolled out onto the stage, choked up himself. "I can't preach after *that*!" he bellowed. "There's nothing to add. I'm making an altar call right here and *now*!" The Big One then fixed on Billy Diamond. He began to walk toward Billy Diamond, who was still wondering what it was he had said to cause this scene. But the evangelist's microphone cord would not stretch all the way down the aisle to the position where Billy had planted himself. It caught, and The Big One stopped, pointing toward the grand chief, the evangelist's thick finger shaking: "Get up!"

Billy closed his eyes, praying: "Oh Lord no, not here!"

"Get up!" The Big One shouted.

Billy Diamond rose, every eye in the congregation turning to him. He took several steps forward and his knees buckled. He fell forward, unconscious.

"We got within fifteen feet of each other and the spirit of the Lord *struck* that boy!" Reverend Garnet Gunter remembers. "The power of God *struck* that boy and he lay prostrate! The chiefs' chief was lying there on the floor and he was *healed* right there!

"I prophesized over him for twenty minutes. He was spaced out with God, I tell you! I stood over him and I prophesized for twenty minutes over that boy. 'God is going to give you the brains of a goose!' I said. 'So you will know when to go north and when to go south. God will cause you to speak the right words at the right time!'

"My thought, you see, was the wisdom of the goose. I've raised goose and I've raised ducks—and the goose is the smartest bird on earth. It shouldn't be 'silly as a goose,' but 'smart as a goose.' I said, 'You will sit among the highest echelons and you will speak the right word.' He was healed. He was called to the ministry."

But Grand Chief Billy Diamond, lying on the floor of the church beneath the bellowing of The Big One, did not hear a word of what was said. "It was total silence to me," he remembers. "Nothing but silence. And then I heard someone speaking another language, a language I'd never heard before. I listened, it was so sweet and flowing. And then I thought I heard a translation of what was being said, and I listened and listened to that."

When he emerged from the trance, he was haunted by what he had been told, but could not place the words in any context. For nearly six months he searched through the Bible, and finally became convinced that the message of the trance came from the beginning of Chapter 43 in Isaiah:

> But now thus saith the Lord that created thee, O Jacob, and he that formed thee, O Israel, Fear not: for I have redeemed thee, I have called thee by name; thou art mine.
> When thou passest through the waters, I will be with thee; and through the rivers, they shall not overflow thee: when thou walkest through the fire, thou shalt not be burned; neither shall the flame kindle upon thee.

Convinced that he had been called into another service, Grand Chief Billy Diamond attended the 1984 Annual General Meeting of the Grand Council of the Crees of Quebec and told the gathering that he had accepted Christ into his life. He did not intend to run again for office, and though he was still nominated, he refused to allow his name to stand. He was finished.

"I think I have accomplished what I wanted to do," he told the Montreal *Gazette*. "I wanted to change laws so the Cree Indians could practise their aboriginal rights, including hunting, trapping and fishing.

"I feel the age of confrontation is now basically over and now it's down to nation building."

CHAPTER SEVENTEEN

THE LIVING FLAME

During the fall goose hunt of 1984, Malcolm Diamond was busy. He bought extra shells at the Hudson's Bay Company store and gave them to the better marksmen in the village, asking the hunters if they would keep him and Hilda in mind if the geese were fat and thick this fall, which they were. The geese the men shot he cleaned, smoking half in the cooking tent, freezing half for storage. He hauled pulp and birch in from the bush, cut them into sixteen-inch blocks with his chainsaw and split and piled the wood until his children laughed aloud at him, saying he had already cut and stacked enough to last two winters. Good, he said, and went out to work on a third.

On the night of October 20, a bitterly cold night with *chuentenshu* sweeping down out of the north and the plastic windows purring steadily in the wind, Malcolm and Hilda went to bed early and put the light out immediately. Sometime before midnight he heard a snap in his chest that was neither the wind nor the window, and he lay there wincing and sucking quick shallow breaths until just before first light, when he finally asked Hilda if she would mind moving to the spare bed. Why? she wanted to know. "Because," he whispered, purchasing air for each phrase, "the pain is killing me every time you move."

Billy Diamond was in Val d'Or when the telephone rang. A

school board meeting had dragged on into its fourth day, but was finally over and he would be going home as soon as a seat could be found on a plane heading up the coast. It was Elizabeth, calling from Waskaganish. "You better come home quickly," she said. "Your Dad has had a heart attack and they're going to fly him out." The former grand chief—now merely chairman of the Cree school board—flew straight home by charter, arriving at ten in the morning, but he was still too late. The air ambulance had already taken the old man to Moose Factory. Albert was aboard. He'd said he would call. And the call came quickly.

Doctors at Moose Factory believed part of Malcolm's heart had collapsed. They wanted to take him another five hundred miles south to Kingston, but they couldn't find a plane. Billy called Stan Deluce, his old friend from Austin Airways, and an hour later a Citation Jet was in Moose Factory, complete with oxygen hook-up. Albert called again in the evening from Kingston, and this time the news was good: Malcolm was talking. They had him hooked up to more machinery than Albert could describe, but the old man was talking right through the mask, yelling at Albert to tell Hilda not to worry.

But Hilda was very worried. She hadn't told the children that he had said goodbye to her before Gerti could come running over to take him to the nursing station. "The next time you see me I'll be in a coffin," he'd said, and tried to smile as if it were a tease.

John Whiskeychan phoned. They were holding a special service for a woman who had been buried that day, a friend of the Diamonds, and the Pentecostal pastor wanted to know if Billy would come and close the service. It seemed like a good idea. Hilda wanted to go as well, and on towards midnight they were still in the church, listening to Billy read from Psalm 46: "God is our refuge and strength, a very present help in trouble. Therefore will not we fear, though the earth be removed . . . ."

The phone was ringing when they came back into the house. It was Albert and he was crying: "Dad's gone," he said. "He seemed perfect. He was sitting there talking and then he told me he was tired and wanted to be left alone for a few minutes. He told me to go and grab a sandwich, so I did. And when I got back he was dead."

Billy could not tell his mother. Four months ago she and Malcolm had gathered with their family in this house to celebrate their fiftieth wedding anniversary, and now it was over with a phone call. He had taken on the prime minister and the premier, he'd been to see the Pope, he'd spoken at the United Nations in Geneva, but he hadn't the courage to tell Hilda Diamond that Malcolm Diamond was dead. John Whiskeychan told her instead, and Hilda nodded as if she'd known all along. She sat up through the night, afraid to go to the familiar bed where Malcolm had lain so long the mattress had taken his form along one side.

Philip came in the following day, bursting through the doors, shouting and running as he always did, then popping out of his grandmother's arms, twisting down and speeding into the bedroom, then coming out with a puzzled look on his face.

"Where's grandpa?"

No one could say.

"*Where's grandpa?*"

Billy Diamond picked Philip up and carried the five-year-old back into the bedroom. He sat the boy on the bed and told him, and then the father and the son who would never walk or talk wrapped their arms around each other and lay on the bed sobbing until both fell asleep on the spot where Malcolm had felt the strange snap in his chest.

Later in the afternoon, with Philip, his brothers and sister off with relatives, Billy and Elizabeth went back to their own home to try to get some rest before another long night of sitting up with Hilda. Elizabeth was worried about Billy. Since he had come out of his father's bedroom leaving a sleeping son behind, he had been weeping constantly. She told him to be strong for his mother, but he could barely handle speaking to her. She suggested he lie down on his own bed and try to get some sleep.

"I fell asleep," he remembers, "a deep, good, sweet sleep. I remember thinking, 'I hope I don't wake up. Maybe this whole thing is one big nightmare.' And then I felt someone touch me on the side. It felt really good. I thought someone was telling me, 'Get up! Wake up! Arise and eat!' " He woke up and Elizabeth came back in to see how he was doing. Was he hungry? she asked. No, he said, but someone had been telling him to get up and eat. Someone had been there in the room with him.

"If it's God speaking to you," Elizabeth said, "God's word will confirm it in the Bible." He reached for the Bible on the night table and began flicking through the pages, a trembling finger settling on I Kings, Chapter 19:

> But he himself went a day's journey into the wilderness, and came and sat down under a juniper tree: and he requested for himself that he might die; and said, It is enough; now, O

Lord, take away my life; for I am not better than my fathers.

And as he lay and slept under a juniper tree, behold, then an angel touched him, and said unto him, Arise and eat.

And he looked, and, behold, there was a cake baken on the coals, and a cruse of water at his head. And he did eat and drink, and laid him down again.

And the angel of the Lord came again the second time, and touched him, and said, Arise and eat; because the journey is too great for thee."

They went to the Sunday morning service before heading back to Hilda's home and during the altar call Billy Diamond found himself moving trance-like to the front of the church, where he experienced a sensation that soon startled the other worshippers around him.

"I could literally feel the hand of God come down on me," he says. "I'm a big man, but it totally surrounded me. I felt this sweet glow and then, down, down in the bottom of my soul, I heard a voice. Very quiet at first, like the formation of another language. And then I heard it come up inside of me. I wanted so desperately to say those words, but I was worried, I was afraid—was it a real language I was hearing or just gibberish? Another *voice*? Come on—you're going to look pretty dumb."

But he could not stop himself. "It just came out," he remembers. "I don't know how long I stood there. I felt I was speaking a language only God could understand. It was endless, infinite, and when I stopped I couldn't see anyone. Nothing. I staggered to my chair and sat down. *I was no longer the same.* I felt someone had taken my heart and cut it out and dropped it into a deep well like a stone. I could hear the sound. That was where the sound began, the language. I felt I could move *mountains*. I had enormous strength. I could comfort anyone—*anyone*."

Holding Elizabeth's hand and still shouting in tongues, he was led back to his own home where they sat him in a living-room armchair. Still he was speaking in that unknown language. But he had also stopped crying. He got up from the chair and began dancing around the living room, his big body floating knowingly among tables and chairs, his mouth emptied of the unknown tongues and filling instead with unfamiliar laughter.

Around and around he danced and laughed, the floor bouncing with his weight while Elizabeth stood leaning against the wall, holding her stomach and giggling hysterically at the sight of the grand chief of the Crees come home. There were still tears, but now they were celebrating life, rather than cursing it.

The next day a funeral was held for Malcolm Diamond in the white clapboard Anglican mission by the water. A fresh grave waited in the far eastern corner of the small cemetery filled with the simple white wooden crosses of the Crees and the elaborate headstone of their former Hudson's Bay Company factor, James Watt.

Billy Diamond gave the eulogy in Cree and English, and Charlie Diamond, who could understand only the Cree, wept at the story of his father's life and what he had wanted for this village. Bob Epstein, who could understand only the English, thought it the most powerful speech he had ever heard, and wept as well for a man he barely knew and to whom he had never been able to speak. Billy Diamond, who said the words, couldn't remember later what he'd said. But he did remember going home and going into his bedroom and getting down on his knees. He had one simple question: "Can You show me where my Dad is?" He fell asleep on the bed, and fell into a deep dream. He could see a bright, bright place, and Malcolm was standing there, Malcolm with his grinning face and salt-and-pepper hair, and he could hear Malcolm Diamond's voice as clear as if he stood beside the bed: "This is where I am, son. I'll keep an eye on you. And I'll wait for you here."

Christmas came and went. It was the fourth sober Christmas Billy and Elizabeth had spent together, but it differed in that once he had proved he could get through a holiday without a drink, he did not look for a drink to celebrate. There was no longer the urge. Nor did he smoke anymore. He had stopped just before Malcolm's death, and when he didn't take it back up again during that time, he knew he would never smoke again.

But more than that had changed. Friends who used to call no longer bothered. The word was out that the chief had changed, and not everyone approved of the change. Billy Diamond, after all, had stood for years as the last line of defence against this overbearing village church. Billy was the Cree with the highest profile. He was the most vocal enemy of the church's techniques. He had sworn aloud that he would never be found in that place even if, eventually, the entire village joined up. He would stand alone, if need be, the one Cree who saw through it all. And now he was the most visible member of the congregation, not only preaching but speaking in tongues. Some were saying that God Himself had spoken to Billy Diamond, and for others, that was more than they could take.

"The church divided this community quite a bit," says Albert Diamond, who has not joined the Pentecostal faith. "Billy hated it. They had to have a service every night and some said the more money you give, the more blessings you'll have. People were borrowing money from their relatives to put into the church. You can't deny the good. You could see some of the guys who used to be into the booze, guys who'd beat up their wives and kids, now they weren't drinking and smoking. But it's still a bit fanatical. Now they're at church every night—still neglecting their children."

Political foes who had known and negotiated with Billy Diamond when he was grand chief believed they saw a pattern in Diamond's behaviour, whether he was sitting down at a table with government bureaucrats or moving to the front of a village church filled with fellow Crees. "Power," says one who was a minister in the Trudeau government. "That's all it is about—pure, unadulterated power. That is all Billy Diamond has ever been interested in. That, and money."

"It is shamanism," says a Roman Catholic priest who has worked in northern Quebec for thirty years. "It's crazy to have a religion based on *not* drinking. It's shamanism. Shamanism requires a taboo. This one has two: not smoking, not drinking. There's a superior being, with the people subject to this superior being. One person is chosen to be accepted by this Great Spirit and then passes on what is said."

Such brutal assessment—dismissed entirely by the Pentecostals, who say the missionary priests of the Bay are now flockless and bitter—may help explain a remarkable series of incidents that occurred in the village of Waskaganish in the first week of January 1985. They were experiences that many of the faithful have come to see as a direct sign from God that the prayers of the Crees have been heard, and now answered.

A winter picnic was planned to be held outside the village. The participants were all members of the Pentecostal church, some recent converts like Billy Diamond, others, like his childhood friend Lawrence Katapatuk and Elizabeth Diamond, longstanding and faithful members. It was a pleasant gathering, nearly two dozen snowmobiles going out to a gully where the kids could slide in the sun and a fire could be built for cooking. Later they were to meet in the school gymnasium for a volleyball game. But first Billy Diamond went home to take a quick nap.

He lay down and entered what the dubious priest would call self-induced hypnosis and Billy Diamond would argue was totally beyond his own control. "I lay down," he says," but I was *not* asleep, I know that. Philip came into the room and said, 'Dad, are you going to go to the school?' but I couldn't answer. Elizabeth came in, 'Honey, are you going over?' But I couldn't answer.

"I was lying there but I wasn't seeing her, I was seeing the inside of the church. I could see the panelling, I could recognize everything. I saw myself and I was standing at the front facing the people. They were all there. John Whiskeychan was in his front row seat. Everyone was where they should be. I could see the people praying, lifting their hands.

"And then a flame came down through the ceiling. It came down and it landed on top of my hands. It didn't burn me. I felt this glow go through my body. It was marvellous. But the flame stayed on my hands. It was transparent, it changed colour: red, blue, yellow—*it was alive*! It danced on my hands and I handed the flame over to Johnny Whiskeychan and it danced on his hands. It danced all through the rows, all the way to the back of the church." He wanted to stay with the flame, to retrieve it and hold it again and watch it roll and rise and return again to his own hands, but there was a voice speaking. It was the same voice that had spoken before when he lay there alone, unable to sleep or awaken, helpless. The voice said he would find "a gift" in the Book of Acts, Chapter 9.

And then he was up. There was no more flame. No church. No voice. Just him, alone. Elizabeth and Philip had gone ahead to the school gym without him. He dressed, but found he could not leave to join them. He had to find out where those Biblical references were coming from. He was still haunted by his first experience with the Isaiah passage—"Fear not: for I have redeemed thee, I have called thee by name; thou art mine"—and he had been unable to come up with any explanation that satisfied. He had never studied the Bible, yet every time he preached in church they had been saying how well he knew Scripture. And the voices in his head had referred him time and time again to pages where the words he believed he had heard were sitting, waiting. He had always had a remarkable memory for dates and events, but surely these passages couldn't be the morning chapel readings from residential school bubbling up thirty years later? Or had he been subliminally affected those long nights in the bush by the "Voice of Power"—R. W. Schambach's radio program out of West Virginia?

He wanted to understand how this could happen, but no explanation could satisfy. He turned, as he believed he had been instructed, to the Book of Acts, Chapter 9, and was hardly surprised to find there the story of Saul's conversion on the road to Damascus. But there was more. Saul had gone blind until healed by Ananias, who had received a vision, and Ananias had been astonished that his God would have anything to do with one who had as evil a reputation as Saul. The reborn Saul, Ananias was told, was now a "chosen vessel." And when Saul preached, "all that heard him were amazed." Through Saul's work, a man named Aeneas, who had been kept in bed eight years with palsy, was compeltely healed, and a woman named Dorcas who had already died was brought back to life.

Billy Diamond, sitting alone in his house over a cup of coffee, read and reread this section, then flicked through the Bible absent-mindedly until his finger settled on Ezekiel, Chapter 20:

> Moreover, the word of the Lord came unto me, saying,
> "Son of Man, set thy face toward the south, and drop thy word toward the south, and prophesy against the forest of the south field;
> And say to the forest of the south, Hear the word of the Lord; Thus saith the Lord God; Behold, I will kindle a fire in thee, and it shall devour every green tree in thee, and every dry tree: the flaming flame shall not be quenched, and all faces from the south to the north shall be burned therein.
> And all flesh shall see that I the Lord have kindled it: it shall not be quenched.

The flaming flame . . . the story of Saul . . . the healings . . . it all began to knit together in a remarkable and, to some, bewildering manner in the weeks that followed. When Robert and Winnie Moar brought their young grandson back to Waskaganish from a Montreal hospital they came with the doctors' assurance that the child would never see. His eyes had become severely infected, and while medication would clear the pus, too much damage had already been done. There was no chance. The Moars brought their daughter and son-in-law and the sick child to church, his damaged eyes wrapped in bandages, and when Billy Diamond reached for him, both parents were convinced the "flaming flame" was on Diamond's hands and passed through them into the bandaged eyes as Billy Diamond held the boy's head and prayed aloud. When the prayers were done, they removed the bandages right in the church, and the child could see. With no other explanations available, the Moars remain convinced the cure was a miracle caused by the prayers of the man who had been their chief and was now their spiritual leader.

When Russell Saunders, a white from Nova Scotia who now lives and works in Waskaganish, became ill with cancer, his condition deteriorated so quickly that scheduled surgery was cancelled. "They had me on a breathing machine," Saunders says. "On Sunday they said my condition was so grave they couldn't operate. I had a neoplasm on my left lung. But I'd been in close contact with Billy and I knew that Sunday that he was holding a special prayer service for me, even though I was down in Halifax. I lay in bed and prayed, too, thinking of him. I felt better by Sunday night. On Wednesday the doctors came back in and they wanted to take more X-rays, thinking maybe they could go in and whip her out now. So they took them. Nothing there. Completely healed. I was fit as a fiddle.... I am absolutely convinced that the prayers of Billy Diamond cured me. I have no question about it. None. I'm a strong believer."

Billy Diamond did not know what to make of this remarkable new power that others—the Moars and Russell Saunders first and foremost—believed had been handed down by God Himself. He fought talking about it, fought even thinking about it. He treated the incidents like a huge joke at first: when the outboard on his boat failed out in the bay with a high wind licking, he placed his hands on the engine cowling, prayed, pulled the starter rope and the engine that a moment earlier had been dead coughed once, caught, and brought him and a laughing Elizabeth back to the Waskaganish shore.

But late at night, when the family was asleep and there was only the former grand chief and the coffee pot still going, he would sit at the table in his house and stare at his hands as he once would scrutinize final agreements, and later he would pore over the Bible, searching for something that everyone else had missed.

If these hands did indeed have power, how, he wondered, should they be put to work?

That there was work to be done was obvious even to someone who had deliberately set out to run away and hide. The Conservatives had started out with great promise, naming the popular David Crombie as minister of Indian affairs, but Crombie, who had run against Brian Mulroney for the leadership of the party, did not have the prime minister's ear. He could not deliver.

The First Ministers' Conferences on aboriginal issues and the constitution were still on, but the gatherings quickly dashed any hopes that aboriginal rights would ever be entrenched during the lifetime of those Native leaders who had begun the constitutional process with such great expectations. Although a First Ministers' gathering in Ottawa in the spring of 1985 came extraordinarily close to ending in an agreement on aboriginal rights, the solution put forward by the government appeared to "entrench" two opposing forces at the same time. Natives would have a right to self-government, but this right would, in the words of Assembly of First Nations spokesman Gary Potts, "be given with one hand and taken away with the other." Self-government would be fine, but it was to be subject to approval by an act of Parliament and acts of the legislatures of the affected province. In other words, more power than ever to the provinces, no real power to the Natives.

Still, the notion had the backing of the politicians and it won the immediate approval of two important Native organizations, one representing the Métis and another non-status Indians. It also very nearly gained the approval of the Inuit Committee on National Issues, which elected to consult Inuit people on the matter before deciding. Only the Assembly of First Nations rejected it, and there was some sense that within the AFN there was disagreement over whether to accept or reject. The hardliners strongly suspected that AFN president David Ahenakew was, in fact, very much in favour of accepting the government proposal.

When Prime Minister Mulroney closed the meeting with a request that Native leaders go off and consider the offer for sixty days and reconvene again in June, the former BFN group went into a panic.

"We were so afraid," says Gordon Peters, a key player during those weeks. "We were worried about the fear factor. Some of our own people were even saying, 'Maybe that's all we can get—let's go for it.' We wanted Ahenakew out of there."

For this battle, the BFN forces went after Billy Diamond—no longer grand chief now that Ted Moses was speaking for the Crees of Quebec—and Diamond agreed to come out of "retirement." But this time, Diamond kept entirely in the background, operating within both camps, BFN and AFN, and more as a manipulator than an open negotiator. There were good reasons why he could not be out front. His distaste for Brian Mulroney he could not hide. After beginning with such promise, the Conservative government was adamantly refusing to follow through on the block funding agreed to by former Indian Affairs Minister Doug Frith in his 1984 statement of understanding. What had started as a promising friendship between two leaders was now filled with bad blood.

"It was clear that there was a backlash against Billy," says Peters. But there was also something else: "It would have been very easy for the ones who wanted us to take the deal to say that Billy had sold out, that he had taken the Crees down the road and look how the Crees had benefited. We didn't want that."

Diamond and Georges Erasmus travelled across the country speaking privately to key leaders to turn them against the Mulroney proposal while Peters set up a telephone lobbying operation in his Toronto office. Other crucial leaders came on board—Zebedee Nungak and John Amagoalik of the Inuit, Louis "Smokey" Bruyere of the Native Council of Canada—and when they gathered again in Ottawa in June, as requested, the meeting was considered a failure before it was even opened. Thanks to Diamond and Erasmus and Peters and Potts, all four Native groups were now solidly against the offer that only sixty days earlier had seemed not only likely but probable.

The BFN group then turned its attentions to removing Ahenakew from office and replacing him with Georges Erasmus, something that was accomplished after what Peters calls "the worst year of mud-slinging and personal attacking that I have ever seen." But it was done. Erasmus became national chief and Billy Diamond, who had tried to stay out of the attack on Ahenakew, vanished back into the northern bush. He said he was gone from the national political scene for good, and for the most part he kept his word. Diamond appeared but briefly before the final scheduled constitutional conference in March 1987. The Crees held a pre-conference conference in Ottawa and offered a simple message: don't trust the premiers, don't trust the prime minister. They brought in observers from the United Nations Human Rights Commission and even from the African National Congress. Billy Diamond spoke briefly about the lack of government commitment, spent about ten uncomfortable minutes at a Cree reception, and left for Waskaganish even before Brian Mulroney's gavel fell to open the doomed, final scheduled gathering between the Canadian Natives and the politicians.

The Crees weren't the only Native group to be bitterly disappointed by the Conservative government. Even five years after it happened,

Billy Diamond could not understand how the magical three-hour meeting that he had with a compatible Brian Mulroney, leader of the Opposition, could have turned into such a long and sour relationship with Brian Mulroney, leader of the government.

David Crombie, Mulroney's minister of Indian affairs, had certainly started out with the right intentions. He had assigned Conservative backbencher Frank Oberle (later to become minister of science and technology) to head up a task force that would review and renovate past treaties, but Oberle's report was ignored by Cabinet and never acted upon. Crombie had even appointed his former chief of staff, Murray Coolican, a man with impeccable credentials among Natives, to a nongovernment task force on the government's comprehensive claims policy. Coolican's report, *Living Treaties: Lasting Agreements*, had strongly urged the Conservative government to take the high road and quit thinking of land claims agreements as if they were treaties like the ones Duncan Campbell Scott negotiated—little more than real estate transactions. Coolican argued for aboriginal rights to be affirmed rather than extinguished, and he strongly backed the notion of self-government, which was then being practised in precisely one Canadian location: James Bay. Soon, however, Crombie was gone, moved in a Cabinet shuffle to the position of secretary of state. His successor, Bill McKnight, announced a new government policy in December 1986 that followed some of the direction laid out by Coolican, but which took education, health and self-government off the table in the current negotiations over comprehensive claims. Relationships had deteriorated all round between the Natives and this new government. The constitutional process was collapsing. And Native leaders had never recovered from the insult of "The Buffalo Jump of the 1980s."

That phrase—referring to the place where Plains Indians would stampede buffalo over a cliff for slaughter—was used in a 1985 memorandum to Cabinet concerning the task force on government spending that had been set up under Deputy Prime Minister Eric Nielsen. Nielsen, long viewed as Government Enemy Number One by Canadian Natives, had recommended shifting specialty services for Indians from Indian Affairs to whatever department handled the same services for other Canadians. He also wanted to make more use of federal-provincial agreements that would allow the provinces to deliver such programs as health. And he wanted fixed ceilings on block grants. After a furious outcry from Natives and a repudiation by the prime minister himself, the crisis was defused. But the damage had been done and could not readily be repaired.

Fixed ceilings on block grants were a direct slap at the agreement that had been signed in 1984 between then minister of Indian affairs Doug Frith and the Crees and Naskapis. Funding in this case was to take place along a base system, which would have taken into account locally derived revenues and allowed for necessary adjustments. The Conservatives, however, argued that Frith had had no authority to sign such an agreement. Only the Treasury Board could authorize such a financial transaction, they said, and the government refused to provide the disputed funding until the Crees agreed to sign off on the document, which the Crees refused to do.

The Crees' contention that they were being short-changed by Ottawa's reneging on a signed deal was given much-appreciated backing in 1986, when Auditor General Kenneth Dye tabled his annual report. In Dye's opinion, Ottawa had simply elected to ignore the 1975 James Bay and Northern Quebec Agreement. By the Indian Affairs department's own estimates, the cost of implementing the outstanding obligations of the agreement amounted to $190 million. Dye charged that Ottawa had used a convenient loophole in the agreement—"subject to the extent of financial participation possible"—to avoid funding such matters as adequate housing, community centres, hospitals, fire services, sanitation, access roads and electrical supply. "It is essential," Dye argued in his report, "that one department be responsible for co-ordinating implementation of agreements." Indian Affairs, he determined, had not been able to "exert enough influence over other federal departments and agencies to ensure they will fulfill their obligations under the agreements."

It was a damning report. Under Section 10 of the agreement, the minister of Indian affairs was obliged to submit an annual report on the implementation of the provisions, yet Dye was able to determine that this had happened only once in the eleven years since the final agreement had been signed. There was, therefore, no reporting mechanism that would enable Parliament to monitor its deal.

A week after the auditor general's report came down, the officials of the Department of Indian Affairs were slated to testify before a three-man Cree-Naskapi commission that had been set up under the 1984 Cree-Naskapi Act. The commission—which included the former chief of Fort George, Robert Kanatewat—had been established to oversee the first self-government deal and report to Parliament. The new minister of Indian affairs, Bill McKnight, refused to appear, and when the commission could not subpœna him, he sent instead his assistant deputy-minister, Richard Van Loon, who read a statement contending that Ottawa was indeed living up to its obligations under the agreement. Further, he argued, the government was not going to recognize a funding deal signed by a former minister, Frith, "as a fully-binding undertaking."

Five months later, in March 1987, the Cree-Naskapi Commission reported: "In the course of Canadian history, a notion persists that governments make promises to induce Natives to surrender their lands and other rights and then routinely break these promises, frequently hiding behind legal technicalities. Regrettably, the evidence supporting this notion is extensive." The report went on to focus on the fiscal problems of the Crees that had arisen from the government's failure to abide by the agreement signed by Frith. According to legal opinions sought by the commission, "the Government of Canada [was] legally bound by the Statement." The commission strongly urged that the federal subsidy be immediately adjusted to make up the shortfall.

The government responded by dismissing the commission as a creation of the Crees, despite the fact that it was chaired by Quebec Justice Réjean F. Paul, vice-president of the Law Reform Commission of Canada and former chief prosecutor of the Commission of Inquiry into Organized Crime.

The government wanted to renegotiate. A federal negotiator, Toronto's Andrew Croll, was appointed, and the Crees were asked to send their representative. At Billy Diamond's suggestion, in the fall of 1987 they approached René Lévesque and the retired premier of Quebec agreed to serve. He seemed delighted with the opportunity to stir the Quebec-Ottawa pot one final time. When Indian Affairs heard of the scheme, the department moved to veto the idea. And soon afterwards, Lévesque's fatal heart attack rendered the possibility academic.

Grand Chief Ted Moses refused to meet with Croll. And Moses' successor in 1987, Matthew Cooncome, continued the standoff. "The Crees are a nation," Cooncome said. "I am the prime minister of the Crees. When I meet, I meet with the prime minister or his ministers. I don't meet with people like Andrew Croll." The government, however, would not back down, and eventually Cooncome did meet with both Croll and his minister, but the meeting went poorly. The call went out to the Crees' master negotiator, Billy Diamond. Early in 1988, he did take up the task briefly, but soon walked away in disgust.

"It was set up so we would never win," he says. "Obviously, the Cabinet had already made its decision." A few months later, it seemed he was right: the federal Cabinet arbitrarily decided to forward a $14 million "settlement" to the Crees. It was interpreted as an election gambit, an attempt to clear up one more minor Quebec irritant before going into a general election. The July 1988 "settlement" was to serve as a basis for future dealings with the Crees, and was indexed to consider such matters as population growth and inflation in the coming decade. During this time, the government agreed to come to terms with the 1984 Statement of Understanding that the federal bureaucrats had said was inoperative. It was an unusual settlement that the Crees believe is going to cost Ottawa between $250 and $300 million over the coming decade.

Billy Diamond's brief sojourn back at the negotiating table assured him that he had little taste left for meetings. His heart wasn't in it; he had completely lost faith in the small print, in the promises. No longer was there a sympathetic and credible John Ciaccia sitting across the table. No longer was there a federal government in a hurry. No longer did he himself have much faith in the political process.

Nevertheless, there could be little doubt that, a decade after it had been signed, the James Bay and Northern Quebec Agreement was now regarded as a landmark settlement. Many Native leaders who had once laughed at the Crees for selling out now thought there would never again be such a deal, with so many openings for the Natives to improve their lot and take charge of their own political affairs and finances. Jean Chrétien, who had started the modern land claims process, felt that no matter what the continuing squabbling, the agreement stood as "a hell of a good precedent that might be improved upon. What was so important about it was that it established the principle of more-than-a-one-time settlement, that the benefits would continue to flow, that this was not a one-time $5-beads deal. We have a mortgage here, and if they have been screwed by inadvertence, then they can have another kick at the cat sometime."

They had been screwed. The Crees had government documents like the Tait Report and the Auditor General's Report to back up their claims, but they never seemed to provide enough weight to force the issue. And so it was that the Crees turned, once again, to the international stage to plead their case. Their first step was to invite Dr Erica-Irene Daes, chairman of the United Nations Sub-Commission on the Prevention of Discrimination and the Protection of Minorities, to the 1987 First Ministers Conference in Ottawa.

Her presence did not go unnoticed. Daes, a kindly, grandmotherly woman who nevertheless fought in the Greek underground as a fifteen-year-old student, was hugely impressed in a meeting with Billy Diamond, and she went quickly to work for the Cree cause. She went on to become an invaluable Cree ally at the United Nations when former Grand Chief Ted Moses and Cree advisor Bob Epstein launched a long-term lobby in Geneva, Switzerland, for a full—and potentially embarrassing, for Canada—study of aboriginal treaties to be undertaken by the United Nations Human Rights Commission.

At the United Nations headquarters in New York City a year earlier, the Crees had managed to gain, for the northern Quebec Indians, full Non-Government Organization (NGO) observer status at the United Nations—roughly the same recognition enjoyed by such groups as Amnesty International—which allows for entry into United Nations gatherings and associations throughout the world. The move was a strike against Canada's Department of External Affairs, which had lobbied to prevent the Crees from obtaining such status. Unfortunately, External Affairs was up against not only the Crees and their sympathizers in the international community, but a key player who operated behind the scenes in necessary secrecy: the Canadian ambassador to the United Nations, Stephen Lewis. "Some people in Ottawa," Lewis said with a mischievous smile shortly after he returned to Canada in 1988, "were very, very unhappy about this."

The Crees also used their Papal connection to great advantage one more time, when Grand Chief Ted Moses fired off a letter to Monsignor Gianpietro Cudin on January 22, 1987:

> I am writing to you on behalf of my people because of the impending visit by the Prime Minister of Canada, Brian Mulroney, to His Holiness the Pope in Rome. His visit with the Pontiff includes a private session with him and we do not wish in any way to interfere or influence the meeting.
>
> However, as we tried to explain in much detail during our visit to Rome and as the Pope saw himself during his visit to Canada, the problems of the Native peoples of Canada are far from being resolved.

> In every category of social, health, educational and economic criteria, the Native people in Canada are underprivileged and in a most difficult situation. Third World conditions exist for many tribes and groups in our country.
>
> In such cases as ours, where an agreement such as the James Bay and Northern Quebec Agreement has been entered into with the Government, we have found major problems in having the Government respect its commitments and obligations under the Agreement and provide to us that which was agreed to.
>
> Government can be a most insensitive and dispassionate adversary and under the present Government in Canada led by Mr. Mulroney, we are faced with this situation.
>
> We had hoped that His Holiness would remember our presentation to him and would be informed that the situation with respect to our relations with the Federal Government has not changed. Further, the situation for other Native groups in Canada has also not improved.
>
> I understand that through your good offices, it may be possible to His Holiness to make reference to the situation....

It was possible. When the prime minister met with the Pope, the issue was raised, much to the consternation of certain Canadian officials. And three weeks before the 1987 First Ministers' Conference, in which no agreement on aboriginal rights was reached, the Pope granted a thirty-minute audience to Canadian Native leaders in which he once more gave his unqualified blessing to the aboriginal right to self-government. Six months later, when Pope John Paul finished his 1987 tour of the United States, he made a stop in Fort Simpson, Northwest Territories, where he had been unable to land during his tour three years earlier because of fog. With a rainbow hooped across the horizon behind him, he declared that Natives had "a right to a just and equitable measure of self-governing, along with a land base and adequate resources necessary for developing a viable economy." And he called for a new round of constitutional talks to entrench a "new covenant to ensure your basic aboriginal rights."

Indian Affairs Minister Bill McKnight says that "as a political strategist," he admires the Indians for taking their message to the world. But his assistant deputy-minister, Richard Van Loon, contends that the strategy has been only "marginally effective." The international mutterings of Canadian Natives have gone all but unheard in their own country, where the public has little interest and the politicians little time.

Van Loon's assessment is harsh but correct, and Billy Diamond knows this. When the James Bay Crees—the first self-government in Canada—wrote and asked if they could join the line of interested citizens and groups making presentations to the joint committee on the constitutional amendments in the summer of 1987, they were turned down flat. "What you have to understand," says Brian Craik, who worked in Indian Affairs at a senior level for many years and is now an Ottawa consultant, "is that this particular government hates the James Bay Crees. And the reason is twofold: one, because the Crees have demonstrated the inadequacy of Indian Affairs policies; and two, because they've only too often been able to force politicians to make decisions about their affairs."

Billy Diamond came to understand this, and though it took him more than a decade, he eventually learned that the battle against the government did not end with signatures on paper or even legislation. Even so, he did not consider that all had been lost. What the Crees had was the embryo of a nation. The scattered bands along the eastern coast of James Bay had always shared myth and language and way of life, but sometime between that day in 1971 when Robert Bourassa announced his "Project of the Century" and a time in the 1980s that has no specific date, these scattered Crees had—in the words of Montreal anthropologist Richard Salisbury—taken a handful of "home villages" and turned them into a "homeland."

The fight itself had been the victory, not the paper that supposedly represented their success. When the dream of Billy Diamond filters down into the mouth of the new grand chief, Matthew Cooncome, this is how it comes out: "We are a nation of hunters and trappers. We want to participate fully in the development of our nation as we see fit. Then, and only then, will there be true self-government—that moment when we can be totally economically independent of the federal government, independent socially, independent economically, independent politically. Our ultimate aim is to be independent completely, to move to a situation where we no longer rely on government handouts, whether they call them welfare or grants. But a nation alone."

Billy Diamond had always known this in his heart, but if he had listened to Malcolm Diamond more he would have known that Malcolm understood the key without even speaking the language.

THE LIVING FLAME

What was it Malcolm had said? Yes: they were sitting around at a meeting of the Board of Compensation, worrying about some payment and how it should be done and what would happen to it. The words came back:

"It's only money. It's a tool, like any other."

Malcolm Diamond had known all along. And Billy Diamond, with the fire dancing on the end of his hands, had been holding the secret without even recognizing that it meant more than mere paper, more than mere words. The white man's control over the Natives had never been muskets, never been transportation, never been legislation, never been language.

It had been money.

And Billy Diamond now knew that he had the hands to work with this tool that Malcolm had held out—a tool no one had noticed, until now.

CHAPTER EIGHTEEN

IACOCCA OF THE NORTH

September 22, 1986, was a crisp fall day on the campus of the University of Western Ontario: oak leaves spinning gently in the rumour of fall winds to come, the sun dancing off the students' leather university jackets, and men and women filing into a crowded lecture hall. A typical academic event, with one significant difference: the lecture these students and graduates were flocking to hear this afternoon—and the one to be delivered in the evening to distinguished alumnæ of the prestigious School of Business Administration—was to come from a man who had less formal education than any of those who came to listen and take notes.

Billy Diamond stood at the podium in his best suit and tie, staring down at lecture notes that had been dictated off the top of his head and then carefully prepared for presentation by one of the most exclusive law firms in the country. He looked up from his evening talk, out over a room thick with chartered accountants, company vice-presidents and chief executive officers, and paused, beaming. "One seriously wonders," he said through a widening grin, "if five years ago, an invitation of this sort would have been offered to me."

In the Gucci briefcase he had leaned against the wall before speaking, he had tucked the latest issue of *Canadian Business* magazine, with a cover feature on "The Successors: Canada's

Emerging Business Leaders." "They're smart, tough, talented and dedicated," the cover teased. "We searched the nation to find the men and women who are shaping our economic future. Meet twenty-nine of the new breed." And in full, gleaming colour inside, the smiling face now at the podium was leaning out of the cockpit of a bright orange Twin Otter. "Billy Diamond," the title announced. "Building an airline for himself and a new sense of prosperity for his people."

Diamond looked up from his prepared text and laughed. Here he was, addressing the cream of the crop in present and future Canadian business leaders. Three months earlier, *Newsweek International* had been on newsstands around the world—he even had a copy in Japanese—telling readers about this Cree nation builder from the northern Quebec bush who had a vision of Indians working "their way into the mainstream of the Canadian economy" and how he was himself trying to build "the Crees' ladder to prosperity." Without a single qualifying phrase, the magazine accepted Diamond's claim that "my greatest contribution is to have taken these villages, turned them around and developed a nation."

Billy Diamond had reason to laugh. They were reading about him in Japan, Germany, Australia. Princess Anne had found time during her summer visit to discuss his vision of economic prosperity for the British Crown's neglected subjects. He was a star on evangelical television. It was getting ridiculous.

"We're just a bunch of rich Indians with our own airline!" he shouted out over the room, and though they laughed, they could not know how absurd that notion would have seemed not so many years before.

On December 13, 1974, Billy Diamond, the young chief of Rupert House, sat scribbling in his diary. They had talked about putting some money into the estate of the late Jacques Beaudoin if they ever won anything from the government. They had talked about funding a "Cree Way" project that would look into the feasibility of teaching traditional Cree customs, language and history in the schools of James Bay. And the young chief had written at the bottom of his page that the executive should "look into" the possibility of leasing a small aircraft, a single Beaver, for the use of the Crees. And on the last line he had written down the regional carriers known—but not much admired—by the Crees: La Sarre, Fecteau, Air Brazeau, all

Quebec carriers, and then a single northern Ontario carrier called Austin, which operated out of a base in Timmins.

But it was not until five years later, long after the agreement had been signed and the Crees had set up their offices in Val d'Or, that Billy Diamond, the first grand chief of the Crees of Quebec, and Stan Deluce, the owner of Austin Airways Ltd., held their crucial meeting. The coast was being opened up to more licences—it had to be, with all the activity connected with the James Bay Project—and Deluce was keen on expansion. He had come to Val d'Or to solicit support from the Crees for the Austin application, but was not prepared for what the brash young chief was proposing in return.

"No," Diamond said at that 1979 meeting. "We will not give you support. That is, we're thinking of setting up our own airline."

It was the same message he'd given to other small carriers that had also come knocking. The difference here was that Deluce did not react as the other management had. He didn't treat the idea as a joke, dismissing Diamond as a dreamer. He wanted to know more about their plans.

"If you think we could do business together," Diamond told him. "I'm ready to talk joint venture."

Deluce was flabbergasted. Joint venture? With Indians? It wasn't done. But the young chief was dead serious.

"I have the market," Diamond went on. "I have the resources. I have the political savvy. But, unfortunately, I don't know a damn thing about airplanes."

Deluce listened and said he'd get back to Diamond, and when he did, it was to outline a scheme that would permit the Crees a limited role in the proposal as a minority shareholder.

"This has still got to fly with the Quebec government," Diamond countered. "And no way they're going to want control residing in Ontario. It's got to be majority shareholder position for the Crees or nothing."

Deluce was hesitant. "Look," Diamond added, "I'll own the company, but you'll run it. And during the time you run it, you'll train our people."

It was the young chief's good fortune to be talking to an adventurer, a former Timmins bush pilot with a voice like a broken muffler, an air force man who, using his service money, had parlayed his way into a multimillion-dollar transportation empire run entirely by himself and his seven sons. The idea struck Deluce as audacious enough that it just might work. And even if it didn't work, it might be fun to watch the pot stir once word got about that the Indian kid who used to pick up a spare dollar unloading the floatplanes at the Rupert House dock was now going to own the airline. Deluce returned to Timmins and turned the idea over to his son, Bill, the family's financial advisor.

"Our initial impression was very positive," remembers Bill Deluce. "The Crees were well-advised financially and legally, and the chemistry seemed very good. Usually, if any partner comes off the street cold, there's a natural hesitancy, but we felt good about this idea right from the start."

A proposal was eventually worked out. A new carrier, Air Creebec, would be established by having the Crees form a partnership with Austin and a smaller Quebec company, Heli Voyageur Ltée, with the Crees owning 40 percent and the other companies 30 percent each. Later, Heli Voyageur would be bought out and the Crees would assume proper majority control with a 51 percent interest, and Austin would control 49 percent.

For Austin the deal had one obvious advantage: consolidation. The Timmins-based operation already had operating licences along the Ontario side of James Bay, but the new arrangement would allow them to zero in on Cree country, from Great Whale down south to Val d'Or. For several years, Austin had operated freight runs along the eastern coast, but now they would have the opportunity to expand into a passenger operation as well. With new federally funded landing strips going into each Cree village, there would be regular, year-round runs. And now that James Bay was being developed, there would be more opportunities in the future. It was a chance the Deluces didn't want to miss out on.

His Austin operation had previously sought such an arrangement, but without success. The Quebec government had no time for Ontario carriers. An Austin proposal that went before the Canadian Transport Commission in February 1979 had been strongly opposed by Quebec, which argued successfully that provincial interests should be given first opportunity.

Since then, the Deluces had been seeking a way to both satisfy the provincial demands and obtain the commercial licence they wanted from Ottawa. Quebec had insisted on provincial involvement, but would the deal struck with Grand Chief Billy Diamond be enough to placate bureaucrats who might be more than a trifle aghast at the thought of Indians—even if they were Quebec Indians—operating an airline?

They did not expect to have an easy time of it, and they did not get one. The strategy was to have the embryonic Air Creebec take over a foundering regional operation, Quebec Aviation, for some $320,000, acquire its permits, and then bring in Austin Airways aircraft to operate under the Air Creebec banner. A simple business deal that would benefit everyone: Austin, the Crees, the troubled company.

Other Quebec operations were not supportive. La Sarre Air Services decided to oppose the Cree application and hired an exceptional young lawyer, Bernard Roy—who later became principal secretary to Prime Minister Brian Mulroney—to see if it was possible to block the transaction legally. Even more intimidating, the government of Quebec took the unusual step of passing an order-in-council that nixed the deal entirely.

Order-in-council number 3213–79, passed on November 28, 1979, stated that allowing Quebec Aviation to transfer its assets and permits to Air Creebec would "make Quebec lose the advantages" of the transport commission's earlier decision to allow the province to give preference to Quebec-based operations. The provincial minister of transport was therefore authorized to pay as much as $700,000—more than twice the amount the Crees were expecting to pay—to buy out Quebec Aviation. He was then to arrange for approved Québécois interests to take over the assets and permits. In other words, the sale to the Crees was forbidden. The best the Crees could hope for under the terms of the order-in-council was "eventual participation." It did not, however, sound much like the majority shareholder position they expected to hold in Air Creebec.

The Crees retaliated. They announced that Cree village airstrips would be closed to any consortium the province might strike a deal with, and went back to court. They also went to Ottawa to lobby the minister of transport, Don Mazankowski. It was a difficult time for Mazankowski. The new Conservative government under Joe Clark had been floundering all fall, and in mid-December had fallen over a botched House of Commons confidence motion against its first budget. Mazankowski was far too busy, it seemed, with other things to worry about a bunch of Indians in northern Quebec who thought they could fly. The Crees accepted that going to Mazankowski was going to lead nowhere.

Early in February, word came to them that Premier René Lévesque wanted a meeting. They gathered at Loew's Concorde Hotel, the site of so many past political meetings. The grand chief arrived with his advisors—John Mark, James O'Reilly, Bill Grodinsky—and Lévesque came along with his provincial transport minister, Lucien Lessard, and assorted officials.

Uncomfortable with all the briefcases and notes that were coming out onto the table, Lévesque turned to Diamond and said, "Look, do you think we can have the meeting privately—just the two of us and my minister of transport?" Diamond agreed, and the three went off to another room.

"Lévesque had three points to make," remembers Diamond. "First, the Crees must withdraw their application to take over the Quebec operation. Second, the Crees shouldn't be in the aviation business. Third, the Crees should take no partners from Ontario in anything.

"I dug in. I told him that never in the history of Canada has there been such an order-in-council passed as the one he'd hit the Crees with. I told him it was racism in its highest form. And I told him if this deal wasn't available to the Crees, then we'd just look elsewhere. But he had no right to be down on the Deluces. I told them the Deluces were honest and that the Crees trusted them.

"Lévesque cut me off and we got into an awfully heated debate. He told me, 'Billy, if you get into aviation, we will destroy you. We'll drive you into the ground even if we have to use government planes to do it.' I told him, 'I'm not scared. You can try. But I love competition.'

"And then I got him really upset. I told him that in any revolution, any successful revolution, the first thing they take over is the communications system and the transportation system, and we are taking over the transportation system."

The meeting ended angrily, and the Crees left, telling the Quebec officials they would see them in court.

In mid-February, just days before the Joe Clark government would be thrown out of office in an election they should have avoided, Transport Minister Don Mazankowski stunned the Crees with an unexpected announcement. The earlier Canadian Transportation Commission decision that gave Quebec such a strong say was overturned. The precious permit was taken away from the Quebec carrier and turned over to Austin. The understanding was that Austin would then pass the permit over to Air Creebec once the new carrier was established. Mazankowski, the politician they had given up on, had come through in the end. Mazankowski had acted on the belief that the government of

Canada had an obligation to live up to the economic development promises—however vague they might have been—of the 1975 James Bay and Northern Quebec Agreement. The Crees wouldn't even have to be bothered buying the permits through a takeover of Quebec Aviation.

Word of the Mazankowski action reached the Crees in court, as O'Reilly was beginning to argue the case against the formidable Bernard Roy. O'Reilly heard the details and asked for a delay in the hearings, which was immediately granted. Sitting and listening to the news, Roy threw his arms up in the air and turned to a colleague.

"*C'est politique!*" he said, shaking his head. It had been—right from the beginning.

On July 5, 1982, Air Creebec made its maiden flight under its bold orange, black and yellow colours. Billy Diamond sat in the Val d'Or terminal with his arms folded and his eyes closed, smiling as the announcement came over the public address system: "Air Creebec Flight 101 to Great Whale River, with stops in Matagami, Rupert House, Eastmain, Wimindji and Fort George is now ready for boarding. No smoking beyond the doors, please . . . ."

It was a sweet moment for Billy Diamond: "I was flying."

Air Creebec was an instant success. The partnership began with a single painted-over Twin Otter and soon added swift Cessnas and large, reliable Hawker Siddeley 748s. They built a brand-new $1.5-million hangar and ordered a new Dash 8 from de Havilland, an investment that more than doubled itself even before delivery was made. Within five years, the value of the airline had more than tripled. And in 1988, when the Crees assumed 100 percent control of the company from the agreeable Deluces, the airline was doing $8 million worth of business a year, more than half of it in passengers, and much of that, ironically, ferrying workers in and out of the James Bay hydroelectric projects.

"Billy Diamond had a vision," says Jim Morrison, the general manager of Air Creebec until 1988, when he moved to a larger operation. "He had a vision of his own airline. Not just for himself, but for all the Crees. And he pulled it off."

Morrison came to Air Creebec to be the hands-on manager of the operation, representing the Deluce side of the investment. An established pilot with polished connections—his father, Angus

Morrison, was president of the Air Transport Association of Canada for many years—the younger Morrison was often accused of being the actual head of Air Creebec.

"There are problems within the non-Native public," admits Morrison. "They just refuse to believe that Billy Diamond is active in this company. But I've been around airlines all my life, and I'm starting to believe that he now knows more than the experts." And like the other airline experts, the president of Air Creebec wanted more. Inspired by the remarkable growth of Wardair—Max Ward began in the bush and ended up owning a major international carrier—Diamond plotted the takeover first of Nordair and then of Quebecair. His strategy covered all facets but one: the public's conception that Indians could not run major economic enterprises.

When Nordair fell into financial difficulty in 1983 after prolonged labour problems, word went out that the large Quebec carrier would be put up for sale. Billy Diamond was immediately interested. Once again, he tagged the Deluces as the ideal partner, partly because an association with them in this venture would allow the Crees to take full command of Air Creebec. The Deluces were themselves rapidly expanding as a full partner in Air Ontario, and if they were also full partners in Air Creebec, the Quebec government would turn down their takeover proposal without ceremony. Air Creebec was duly restructured to give the Crees full majority control, and readied to take aim at Nordair.

The Quebec government was, once again, less than amused. At one bitter meeting held earlier with provincial Transport Minister Lessard, it had even been said that *"Les Cris ne sont pas québécois,"* which had made Diamond blow up, challenging the government minister to prove that he was more a citizen of Quebec than Diamond, and then storming out of the meeting.

The Crees turned their strategy on Ottawa. The Nordair shares were owned by Air Canada, which meant that Air Canada's single shareholder, the government, would have to decide in Cabinet just who would take over the airline. Cabinet was to meet May 30, 1984, to decide on the merits of the various bids, and the Crees made sure they were in Ottawa to present their side of it.

They met with John Munro, who was still minister of Indian affairs but who was then running full out for the leadership of the Liberal party. He was hoping the Crees might help him and he seemed most accommodating when they gathered in Munro's office.

But he said there was no chance the Crees would ever get Nordair. Diamond wanted to know why. Munro was evasive, worried. He said he had been so busy lately he hadn't paid much attention to the debate over the sale, which was Transport's concern, not Indian Affairs'. Diamond argued that the Cabinet was basing its decision on all the wrong reasons. Munro said he had no time to find out what the reasons were. He had this early morning meeting and then he had the Cabinet meeting. It was too late. Besides, he had to go to the washroom.

Munro excused himself and left the room. Diamond then plucked the confidential "Memorandum to Cabinet" off Munro's desk, flipped through it with a pocket pen, and walked out of the office as well. He pushed open the washroom door, checked for Munro's shoes and shoved the document in under the partial screen. "Here you go, John," Diamond said. "Read the underlined parts while you're sitting down."

The Cabinet document discussed two bona fide bids. One came from Delplax, which represented the Deluce holdings and the Cree Regional Authority. The other came from Innocan Investments and 132793 Canada Inc., which was basically a group of six hundred Nordair employees who were seeking to buy out their own company. The Cabinet memorandum presented by Transport Minister Lloyd Axworthy was clearly on the side of the Innocan bid. The Delplax plan was straightforward: a new company, NEWCO, would be incorporated, with the Crees holding 51 percent of the shares and an offer would be made at $16.47 a share for a total of $31,102,162.11. Innocan, on the other hand, offered $16 a share, or $29,714,608. Through a number of other projections and interest variables, however, the Innocan offer could rise even beyond the Delplax plan, though it could also end up being lower. Axworthy's memorandum concluded that "the two offers are very close to each other in net value." What was indisputable was that the Cree-Deluce offer included more "up-front" cash.

It came down, then, to a political decision. Cabinet was asked to consider the importance of employee involvement—something the Delplax offer also promised—but also the distinct possibility of provincial hostility to a takeover by the Crees and their Ontario partners. The decision was, according to the confidential document, does Cabinet please Ontario or does Cabinet please Quebec?

But there was more. The document noted that the Cree company had complained that its initial sealed offer had been leaked to Innocan, but the claim had been dismissed by Air Canada officials.

And yet, a page later, the Cabinet memorandum conceded that the Innocan offer "was slightly modified on May 29"—the day before the Air Canada board of directors recommended Cabinet move immediately to accept Innocan's proposal. If Air Canada did not leak the information to Innocan, then it had to have been Transport Canada itself.

It was precisely this underlined section that John Munro sat reading on the toilet that morning. He came out and returned to his office and announced that he had time to hear Diamond out. The Crees' NEWCO offer was the best commercial deal, Diamond argued. Probably, Munro conceded. But the Cree offer was right for another reason, Diamond pressed. Under the terms of the James Bay and Northern Quebec Agreement, the Crees were assured of special consideration if something like this ever came along. Munro agreed. He said he would do what he could.

"Billy briefed me extremely well," Munro remembers. "I had a hell of a fight in Cabinet. I was really quite upset with my Cabinet colleagues. I got some backing and we got it held up for a while. We fought it pretty damned hard." But Munro could not find enough allies. The decision eventually brought down by Cabinet was the one Billy Diamond had been expecting. The Crees would not be allowed to buy Nordair.

"The decision had already been made," says Diamond. "We knew that we had the best commercial deal, but we also knew the political situation. They were about to go into an election, and let's face it, there are not that many Cree votes in the North. I guess my money was not green enough."

"We tried to raise hell, but what was the use?" says Bill Grodinsky, the Crees' lawyer who worked on the deal. "Innocan got the company and then sold it back to the individual shareholders and eventually it all ended back at Canadian Pacific under Canadian Airlines. So it was a failure.... The selling of Nordair was supposed to create more competition under deregulation. But it didn't happen. The Crees would have helped make that happen."

Two years later the Crees got another chance. In 1986, the Quebec government—once again under Bourassa—sought to divest itself of Quebecair Ltd. And Billy Diamond, the president of the by now highly successful Air Creebec, announced with a smile that if the Crees were allowed to buy the troubled firm, it would "keep the airline operating as a Quebec company." The transaction would also have catapulted Air Creebec into the big leagues, for Quebecair had the potential for $100 million in annual sales, and with some nine hundred employees, was almost as large as Nordair. Ironically, Quebecair also owned 34.5 percent of Nordair, which meant that a portion of what the Cabinet had denied the Crees would end up with them anyway.

Canadian Pacific, which indicated that it had no interest in buying the actual airline, was keen instead on picking up the Nordair shares, which would then give CP almost complete control of Nordair. A standing share offer had already been tabled by CP.

On the surface, it seemed obvious that the deal should go through. Air Creebec and the Cree Board of Compensation—the Crees' investment fund—would buy the airline and Canadian Pacific would buy the Nordair shares and everyone would be happy. A meeting was arranged between the Cree representatives and Quebec government officials, but it did not go well. They could not get even the basic information out of the government. And though they had been told that five conditions would have to be met, the five suddenly became fifteen. The Crees knew they were out of the running.

Two years later, when Air Creebec sought to become part of a grand plan by Air Canada to set up a regional feeder system to be known as Air Alliance, Billy Diamond was shut out again, for reasons that were never fully explained. In his mind, however, no explanation was needed.

"I call it sophisticated white-collar apartheid," Diamond told his University of Western Ontario audience in 1986.

Even so, he vowed to keep on trying to increase the airline's holdings. "If you see an emptiness," he says, "if you don't make a move toward it, you're not going to be successful. A lot of people see a void and just step back and avoid it."

But there is a bitterness inside that does sometimes pour out. On a late winter night in Val d'Or, he says, "Over the years I have become convinced there is a conspiracy in Canada to keep Indians out of business. They tie everything up with conditions. They make no venture capital available. If there is some money to make available, the idea seems to be to tie the Indians up with feasibility studies and then, once the feasibility studies are finished, add on new conditions, whatever it takes to keep the realization just out of reach.

"They do it convinced they are saving the Indian from himself. They think they are doing the right thing, but they do it also because they simply *cannot stand the idea of a successful Indian.*"

And few things give Diamond more pleasure than reminding whites. At a Hallowe'en party that was held during a Toronto convention of the Air Transport Association, Diamond was challenged by Rhys Eyton, the chairman of Canadair, to explain why he hadn't bothered to change from his business suit to a costume, as the invitations stipulated. "But I did," Diamond shot back. "I came as a white man!"

It took five years and four attempts before the Crees of James Bay were finally permitted to expand their air operation. They had been blocked, they believed, by the federal government, by the Quebec government and by Air Canada itself. But on December 6, 1988, little Air Creebec dramatically increased its corporate clout with an imaginative takeover of the northern assets of Air Ontario.

The large regional carrier—a profitable $80-million-a-year airline 75 percent owned by Air Canada and 25 percent by the Deluce family—had been trying to manage the entire operation out of its London, Ontario, base, and had come to the conclusion that a northern service was not compatible with a slick, highly scheduled southern operation. In April the Deluces had contacted Diamond at his goose camp by radio and he had come out of the bush for a hasty meeting. Would the Crees be interested?

Indeed they would, but Diamond had a few ideas of his own to add. First, he wanted the Crees to take complete control of Air Creebec, and the Deluces were immediately agreeable that the Crees could buy out the remaining partnership for $1.3 million. That done, Diamond then turned to his other, more surprising, suggestion. The Crees would be able to raise the capital necessary to buy out the northern assets of Air Ontario—a money agreement was eventually signed with Central Capital Corporation—but he wanted to make it a special deal, one that would involve Indians who, so far, had been all but locked out of mainstream business.

He was thinking of the Crees and Ojibways of northern Ontario, the very natives who back in 1905 had signed Duncan Campbell Scott's treaties and had given up everything they had for $8 a year in scrip. "Most of us went to school in northern Ontario," Diamond said, "and we'd like to return something." Contact was made with Bentley Cheechoo of Thunder Bay, the grand chief of the poverty-stricken 22,000-member Nishnawbe Aski Nation, but a formal agreement proved impossible under the takeover timetable and, in January 1989, Air Creebec assumed full control of the northern Ontario operation. For $19.4 million, Diamond's airline would assume ownership of six Hawker Siddeley 748 turboprop aircraft, two fifteen-passenger Beechcraft airplanes, hangars, equipment and routes servicing twenty-three communities from Timmins west to Manitoba and north to the coast of Hudson Bay. Some 200 jobs would be salvaged.

It was, Billy Diamond said, "The biggest commercial deal and business venture done by any native group in the country." It had come together in the same week in which Air Creebec suffered its first crash—a cargo plane went down near Waskaganish without injuries—and enjoyed its finest moment: a brand-new $8.5 million de Havilland Dash 8 began thrice-daily service between Val d'Or and Montreal under the bright orange, black and yellow colours of the little Cree airline. Billy Diamond went home and slept for two days.

A week later and he was back at another new project—Arctic char farming. Fish eggs would be purchased through a New Brunswick company, fertilized and raised in tubs brought to Waskaganish over the winter roads and fifty new jobs would be created. In 1992, the Crees would begin shipping char south—by Air Creebec transport, of course.

"My philosophy is simple," says Diamond. "If you're going to get things done, you're not going to get it done by sitting in a fancy office. You're going to have to shake things up in Ottawa and Quebec City—wherever you have to go. You have to knock down the walls.

"That's what you're up against: a wall of prejudice. *'Indians can't handle money.' 'Indians are failures.'* You're always put in a position where you have to prove yourself. You not only have to deal with the people you're up against, you have to back everything up with facts.

"And later on, even if you've knocked down the prejudice, even if you've come up with all the facts, you still have to prove yourself. *'Indians aren't educated.' 'Indians aren't smart.'* You had to become a lawyer, a financial expert, an accountant. We had to learn to speak the language of the engineer, the planner, the biologist, the lawyer.

"The only thing I didn't have to become was an anthropologist. I didn't have to dig up the bones of my people—I knew the bones of my people already."

The consultants—from James O'Reilly, the legal brain, to the scientists studying mercury pollution—have long been the subject of sore debate both within the Cree community and among those with whom the Crees must deal. Viewed by some Crees and a great many government bureaucrats as holding Svengalian control over the Cree leaders, the consultants and lobbyists and scientific experts have become as much a part of the Cree bureaucracy as the Crees themselves. And while their contribution is difficult to measure, their cost is not. In the 1976–77 fiscal year, consultants' and legal fees amounted to $850,000, approximately 30 percent of the total Cree budget. This was a time of organizational difficulty and fine detail work on the legislation that would follow the agreement, so the high costs were not considered to be cause for alarm at the time.

In the years since, however, the heavy expenses have continued. In a confidential study conducted in 1987 for the Crees by Joanne St Lewis, it was calculated that the consultants billed the Crees nearly $1.5 million for the fiscal year 1986–87. So complicated were the fees listed under "federal negotiations" that St Lewis could only conclude: "It is difficult to ascertain the services performed in some instances, or the existence of duplication since the tendency is to perform services in a group format."

St Lewis also expressed concern that the lobby process involved no Crees in an ongoing way, but was left almost entirely in the hands of whites, though Bob Epstein had expressed eagerness to train young Crees in this work. Her report outraged the consultants who gained access to it. They point to the fact that negotiated settlements alone have brought the Crees more than $0.5 billion, not to mention inestimable value in education and health services. "The annual worth of these monies as investments," says one, "makes the consultant payments miniscule. Joanne St Lewis never brought in even one cent."

"I have no hesitancy," Billy Diamond told the University of Western Ontario business students, "in hiring the best lawyers, accountants, consultants and marketing people available to meet specific needs when my people cannot do so and to use outside advice in those areas where it is needed. The president of General Motors has no reticence in doing so, and neither do I."

The total number of "outsiders" employed by the Crees comes to roughly 470, if secretaries and pilots are added to the long list of lawyers, teachers, accountants, health professionals, engineers and band employees. "The Crees are out of the bush only twenty years," says Brian Craik, who has worked for the Crees in many capacities. "Why pick on the fact that they have not yet fired all their consultants?"

Billy Diamond has himself become a consultant of sorts, advising but not billing other Indian groups with problems in negotiating with federal and provincial officials. And, in a reversal of the accepted manner of consultant, he has numerous times left more money behind than was there when he arrived.

The involvement began in the mid-1970s when Diamond was approached by Gary Potts, who would become a close ally in the constitutional battles but who was then a young chief from Bear Island in northern Ontario trying to block a huge resort development. Potts' idea was to accomplish this through a massive land claim—going all the way back to 1877—that, it was hoped, would put a freeze on a huge tract of land that would include the development and assorted logging operations. He turned to Diamond for both technical advice and, if possible, financial help. Diamond came through with visits to Bear Island and strategy advice, and the Crees arranged a $50,000 loan for Potts' small band to begin a court case, which did not meet with much success. "The only request he made was that we keep it entirely confidential," says Potts. "We were floundering at the time. Without that help we would have sunk—it was that crucial."

Diamond's deepest involvement, however, came with another Cree band located in the Peace River district of northern Alberta, the Lubicons. The Lubicon Cree—who would later become an international *cause célèbre* through their attempts to bring about a boycott of the 1988 Calgary Winter Olympics—had somehow been missed entirely around the turn of the century when Treaty 8 was signed by other northern tribes. They had never surrendered their land rights. Not that anyone much cared, so isolated was the small band from any other group—but there had been no treaty for them.

In 1940, the Lubicons had been offered a small, sixty-five-kilometre reserve which they would have moved onto had Ottawa ever followed through on the offer. But the Lubicons were ignored until 1979, when oil companies began exploring in their territory and it was discovered that the boreal forest trapping grounds of the Lubicon Lake Crees were rich in oil and gas deposits.

The oil explorations had a devastating effect on the Lubicons. A commission undertaken by former Justice Minister E. Davie Fulton had determined that the average family's annual trapping income had fallen from $5,000 to around $400. Instead of moose, the Crees were reduced to stalking squirrel. The World Council of Churches was warning that, unless action was taken by the federal government and the government of Alberta, there could be "genocidal consequences." But neither Ottawa nor Alberta would budge.

Early in 1980, when the Lubicon first began panicking about the oil drilling, they contacted Diamond, who was then grand chief of the James Bay Crees and they suggested he might be able to offer some advice to this isolated band as they came against the full force of government and development. Diamond flew into Little Buffalo Lake to meet with the Lubicon leaders and encourage them to fight. He stayed three days with the Lubicon chief, Bernard Ominayak. The Crees, he said, would guarantee a loan of $400,000, and a second one would follow for $300,000. On the way home he stopped in Montreal and went to O'Reilly's office with a message: "Have I got a court case for you!" O'Reilly signed on as the Lubicon legal counsel.

"I was so glad," says Lubicon chief Bernard Ominayak. "He seemed to have a better knowledge of what people were up against. He had an instant appreciation of the problem."

Lubicon advisor Fred Lennarson is even more to the point: "Nobody even knew about Lubicon Lake back then. And Lubicon wouldn't be here right now if it wasn't for Billy Diamond."

In the fall of 1988—shortly after the Dene Indians and Métis of the Mackenzie Valley reached an agreement in principle to settle their long-outstanding land claim for $500 million, ownership of 180,000 square kilometres of land and a chance for self-government—the Lubicon Indians also moved toward an agreement. Following a highly publicized roadblock during which lawyer James O'Reilly was arrested and the band declared itself "a sovereign nation," Alberta Premier Don Getty and Chief Bernard Ominayak met and agreed to begin the transfer of 246.5 square kilometres to the Lubicon. Though the talks stumbled again shortly afterwards, the two negotiations—the Dene and the Lubicon—did show that finally, thirteen years after the James Bay agreement, the government was once again prepared to strike formal deals with Canada's aboriginal peoples.

The Cree message of support, as delivered by Ted Moses, was simple: We would sign again if we had to, but you should know from our experience that the government "will most certainly make every effort to cheat you." So they should watch accordingly.

"Great obstacles make great leaders," says Diamond. "When the James Bay Project was announced, people said, 'Billy, you're crazy to fight it. You can't fight a province. You can't fight a federal government. You're going to fail.' I used to tell them, 'No failure is as bad as the failure to try.' . . . That obstacle wasn't going to make me a loser. You must be willing to risk failure. Leadership requires that you have strong personal convictions, that you can convert people to your cause, that you can challenge people to do their best, and that you know when to cut the cord and let them lead on their own.

"You pay a price for not being content with the average. But what you have to remember is that the most important thing in your life is the people—not fiscal responsibility, not debit-credit ledgers, not annual reports, but people. It's people that matter. People must be more important to you than possessions.

"You know what leadership really is? Leadership is stretching your creativity. It isn't in the title. If you let your imagination work you can do great things. That's it—you just have to let your imagination work . . . ."

CHAPTER NINETEEN

CREE-YAMAHA

Billy Diamond rolled along the shore, a fleshy, hanging wave of a man moving easily against the wind, his green slicker snapping as he pushed through the overturned canoes and lost ground slightly in the loose gravel along the banks of the Rupert. He laughed and shouted into the sudden blow that had come up out of the north—the *chuentenshu* Malcolm Diamond would have welcomed during the winter hunt but feared during this, the last spring fish. Yet whatever he had to say it was not heard by those heading out into the saltwater bay in Billy Diamond's most prized scheme to bring "sustainable growth" to his own village.

"Economic development is not money alone," he said over breakfast on that late spring day in 1986. "Economic development is taking your own creativity and translating it into projects the people can use. Economic development is taking the old traditional knowledge of the Crees and making it modern and viable. Indians can make canoes. They were doing it long before Columbus came."

Out on the black chop of the river, a gleaming white and turquoise freighter canoe—a fibreglass version of the symbol of the Hudson's Bay Company's James Bay fur trade—shrugged once with a surge of power, rose high and then slowly leaned into a perfect, quickening plane. It was the first canoe in more than three hundred years that could not be called, as they have always been called, a Hudson's Bay boat. It was a challenger moulded in a new shop on the sand hill beyond, a canoe financed through a curious partnership that included an eager Japanese multinational, a reluctant Canadian government and an Indian band that was once so pathetically destitute that relatives of Lawrence Katapatuk, who was now waving from the luxurious Cree-Japanese vessel, lost all thirteen of their children to starvation.

When Billy Diamond returned to the village after his 1984 retirement from politics, he had thrown his enormous energies into the local council in an effort to see if the Cree success with Air Creebec could somehow be translated to the local level. He was convinced now that economic development—not agreements-in-principle, not legislation, perhaps not even the constitution—was the true key to entrenching Native rights. And in his opinion, the Crees had to begin taking control of their own economy.

He had returned to his own village and discovered, much to his surprise, that his plan had detractors as formidable as any premier, any bureaucrat. The toughest sell turned out to be the Crees themselves. "We were indoctrinated to think that we couldn't do anything," Diamond said as he showed off the first products of this joint venture, "that we were failures. The church told us that, the Bay store told us, Indian Affairs told us."

And out on the ruffled waters of the Rupert River, the direct challenge to this psychology of failure was now hurtling further away from shore as the man who dreamed it up yelled again. But neither Lawrence Katapatuk nor the southern journalist nor the other white from the south who were sitting in the bow of the canoe could hear Diamond's shouting over the singing of a forty-horsepower Mercury outboard at full throttle. And as for the one in the boat with the ear best suited to picking through the wind—full-time trapper Charlie Diamond—he could never understand a word of what his young brother said when he spoke softly, let alone shouted, in the language of the whites. Charlie Diamond did not even turn. Lawrence Katapatuk waved back and grinned, having long ago learned to worry only when his lifelong friend goes suddenly quiet. Anyway, no one needed to hear to know that Diamond was calling out yet another warning, afraid of even the slightest scratch appearing on the gleaming vessel that had come to symbolize the future of the Swampy Cree of James Bay.

Moving in that fluid gait that is peculiar to big, athletic men who have grown accustomed to paths clearing in front of them, Billy

Diamond continued to laugh and wave from the shore. It was only when his realized dream turned again and headed directly out into the bay, a perfect rainbow folding from the spray, that Billy Diamond realized the shoreline had run out. And finally he stopped, a very large man determined never to shrink out of sight.

The move to build canoes again began, oddly enough, with a scheme to sell snowmobiles. Billy Diamond's arrival back in the village had coincided with the creation of a financial arm for the band that would be known as the Waskaganish Enterprises Development Corporation of Northern Quebec. And WEDCO, as it was called, was looking for a suitable project into which they might sink some of the band's money.

It was a moment of *déjà vu* for Billy Diamond. A dozen years earlier, in the months before the court case, he had been instrumental in setting up a village development cooperative, which, unfortunately, had turned into a total disaster. Indian Affairs had approved of the Rupert House initiative in 1972, but had believed it was their own responsibility to control the development. With Indian Affairs taking charge, the new enterprise first built a sawmill, which had to be moved when it was discovered the structure had the wrong orientation to the river and could not draw in either water or logs. It was re-erected several miles away in a dry gravel pit. In winter, the sawmill was buried in snow; in spring awash in muck; and soon it was bankrupt and abandoned. This time, Billy Diamond vowed, no one would be telling the Crees what to do.

Snowmobiles seemed a natural. There was no proper dealership in the village, although the Hudson's Bay Company store carried certain models and would order others, so most families were buying from dealerships in distant Val d'Or. Repairs were a major problem. The band had approached the largest dealer, Quebec-based Bombardier Ltd., makers of the popular skidoo, but had been turned down flat. The only other manufacturer anyone could think of was Yamaha. Unfortunately, no one knew anything about the company apart from the fact that it was very big—$4 billion in annual sales—and very, very foreign.

"Let's talk to them about *more* than a dealership," Diamond suggested at the first council meeting he attended.

"What do you mean—*more*?"

"Something big."

"Like what?"

Billy Diamond said the first thing that came into his mind. "The canoe factory," he shouted. "We'll open it up again—modernize it."

"How?"

He winged it: "We'll get rid of the wood."

One of the councillors burst out laughing. "But how would they float then?"

In June 1985, a letter arrived in the North York office of Masafumi ("Mark") Aoba, the president of the Toronto-based Yamaha Motor Canada Ltd. It was from an address he had never heard of, from a man he had never heard of, and suggested a possibility he had never thought of, but he found the idea of meeting with a Cree chief irresistible. At the very least, it would make for a great anecdote when he got back to Japan, where Indians were still romantic figures locked in time and old movies, masters of the barren wilderness.

But Aoba was also fascinated by the sentiments expressed in Billy Diamond's letter. When this Cree he had never heard of wrote of the band corporation and what it could mean to the well-being of all the Waskaganish Cree, the words sounded uncannily like Japanese corporate philosophy. Aoba had never heard a Canadian businessman speak this way, and he had long since come to the conclusion that it was not part of the Canadian corporate landscape. This man he had to see for himself.

They met in the boardroom at 480 Gordon Baker Road, complete with tea, translators and a lot of awkward silences. The Japanese brought out one of their new outboards to impress the Crees and Diamond immediately told them it was no good. He then showed them why—having an engineer take apart the engine housing to illustrate how a Cree hunter hundreds of miles back in the bush would have difficulties managing emergency repairs that would normally be done at a nearby marina—and the Japanese, rather than taking offence, were much impressed, taking notes as he picked apart their treasured product. They talked about outboards and snowmobiles and the possibility of a franchise, which the Yamaha officials thought very possible indeed.

But then they talked boats. Diamond told the story of the Hudson's Bay boats. He calculated there were seventeen thousand of them in the region owned by Cree and Inuit hunters, and he complained that, though they cost $4,000 each, they were lasting only two or three years. The Japanese took notes carefully. And then Diamond turned to other accounts of the boats, stories about entire Cree families being wiped out on the unpredictable waters of James Bay and the tricky rapids of the thundering rivers. He told of people he had known who had been swamped and drowned. And while the Japanese took no notes during this exchange, Mark Aoba would later concede that it was this, more than anything, that convinced Yamaha to become involved in the first North American joint-venture in its history.

"What we are looking for," Diamond told the meeting, "is a technology transfer. We have the know-how. We know the waters. But you know how to build boats."

Indeed Yamaha did: twenty thousand a year, from tiny sailboats to thirty-metre coastal fishing vessels, boats all over the world but never even considered on James Bay. Aoba said he would take Diamond's suggestion to head office in Japan.

"I was so impressed with his personality," Aoba says, "by the way he thinks about his people and their development." Head office was also impressed, and a decision was made to look into the possibilities.

In August, Kent Minami from the Toronto offices of Yamaha, and a high-level company engineer from Japan, Isao Toyama, arrived in northern Quebec to study the situation. The trek began awkwardly in Val d'Or—"Like a dummy I took them out for Chinese food," says Diamond—but soon they were in Waskaganish for several weeks of intensive research and preliminary design.

Toyama stayed and worked constantly on the concept, with Minami moving back and forth between the Toronto office and the distant Cree village, each time becoming more certain that the Cree and Japanese were not as different as he had at first assumed.

"There were so many similarities," he says. "First of all in physical structure, the face is so much the same. The Cree are very shy. Japanese are also shy. And they are both very proud. But there was one other thing, and that was they had a tradition that was the same as ours. When we visit anyone we always bring a souvenir, it is our custom, but it is one we find in Western countries never—until we went up there."

The experience of the engineer, Toyama, illustrates perfectly the speed at which friendship developed. A quiet workaholic who kept to himself and his drafting board when he first went to Waskaganish, by the end of his time in the village he was instructing Elizabeth Diamond on how to make Sukiyaki sauce for wild goose.

When Toyama left, he asked for, and received, an Indian name—"Gadstad," which means "expert"—and on his return to Japan immediately had his treasured business cards reprinted with the Cree name added. He also took back to Japan the finished designs for two boats.

Toyama had gone out in the old-style Hudson's Bay boats and seen how they performed in the high waves of the bay and the violent twists of the river rapids. He had watched as Cree hunters poled their crafts through eddies, sat in the bow as Cree hunters stood with their throttles full open and skipped across the crests of a light chop. He wanted more protection from splash on the bow, more height against backwash on the stern. He wanted weight for strength and extra width for stability. Back in Japan, he oversaw the building of the two prototypes—one twenty-three feet long, the other twenty-five—and the finished products were then shipped from the Iwati plant to Vancouver by sea and on to Moosonee by freight train, arriving November 3.

Two days later, on a bitterly cold, grey morning, Kent Minami, who had flown up from Toronto, oversaw the official launching of the Yamaha boats in the freezing waters of James Bay. It was a ceremony unrecorded by film, attended only by two Japanese, two Crees, Russell Saunders of WEDCO and two Ontario Provincial Police officers who were adamant that no one even go out beyond the harbour in such weather. In the distance the swells were white with fury. The north wind was hammering in from the bay and snow was threatening. Only a fool would go out beyond the docks in such weather, the police said, but the Japanese and Crees said they were going out much farther—a hundred miles straight across the bay, travelling in boats that had never been tested before. The police warned them again, saying that it was not only foolish but dangerous, yet the men loading the boats refused to listen.

"We made a commitment," says Minami. "We told them we would bring a boat before the winter. We promised we would deliver."

With the Japanese trussed in full survival suits and the Crees standing, as usual, in faded rainsuits over light clothes, they set out into the maw of the storm, into waves heavy enough that one boat would lose sight of the other on the swells, into a storm that lashed and blew with stinging snow and eventually into darkness so black they could not even make out a star for guidance.

"We trusted the Cree," remembers Minami. "I couldn't see a thing."

Four hours later—half the normal time in good weather—the two boats skimmed into the light of flashlights held along the shore of the village. The Crees were amazed that the boats had dared the crossing and they were even more astonished when they ran their lights over the men bounding over the bows of the big, turquoise boats and realized their clothes and jackets were perfectly dry. The Japanese boats had been in the village less than thirty seconds, but everyone knew the idea had been a remarkable success.

However, it was still just an idea—and one that needed financial backing. The consulting firm of Raymond, Chabot, Martin, Paré and Cie was hired to do a feasibility study, which concluded what everyone already knew. There was indeed a market out there. By word of mouth after the bay crossing, orders for twenty-five of the remarkable boats had already been received. All that was needed now was a factory.

Using existing facilities in the village, the feasibility study had concluded, the venture could be launched for a mere $200,000. Yamaha Motor Canada would be in for 30 percent, the Crees for 60 percent, and Yamaha Japan for the remaining 10 percent. The Crees, however, would somehow have to come up with $120,000 of their own.

No one expected that they would have the slightest difficulty. This, after all, was precisely what government officials had always held up as the future for Native businessmen: dealing in the mainstream, setting up their own companies, marketing, enjoying the profits from their own enterprise. There had even been a specific government fund designed for precisely this sort of a deal. The Native Economic Development Program had been announced with great fanfare, and the minister of Indian affairs had said that $345 million had been set aside to encourage job creation and Native enterprise. The Crees had shown the enterprise. The boats meant jobs. There was even a partner from private industry that had the know-how.

There was just one problem: the Crees couldn't pry the money out of the fund. They applied, waited; called, were put off; wrote, waited. Encouraging words, but no money. WEDCO could, of course, have applied to get the money from the Cree Regional Authority, but the government's promise to help with Native economic development became a matter of principle, so they continued to press and continued to be dissappointed. They knew their boat factory was, as Mark Aoba called it, "a very unique project," but it seemed to arouse no interest in Ottawa.

"It is strange," Diamond said at the time, "that even after the visit of [Japanese Prime Minister Yasuhiro] Nakasone and all the talk about the possibility of Japanese-Canadian joint ventures, now that the Crees have done it, the government has shown very, very little interest."

Eventually, the Japanese and Crees decided to go ahead anyway and let the government catch up later if it was still interested. Deliberately to embarrass the uninterested politicians, the Crees used a political connection to arrange an elaborate ceremony on Parliament Hill on March 18, 1986. It was to be the formal signing of the joint-venture contract—representing a financial deal smaller than a house mortgage—yet one that would be witnessed by two hundred strategically invited guests, including the Japanese ambassador. The minister of Indian affairs, David Crombie, was also invited, and he came, representing the government that had showed no interest in becoming a partner.

At the same time, the Crees went public with their charming business story. It was splashed across the front page of the Ottawa *Citizen* and written up prominently in the business pages of the Toronto *Star*. Mark Aoba told the *Star* that he viewed the joint venture as his company's way "to contribute to the Canadian society." It did not pass by readers that the Canadian government had been given the opportunity to *contribute* as well but had elected not to—a decision that was then rapidly reversed in Ottawa.

Cree-Yamaha set up in an old government building high on the hill sloping down toward the Rupert River. Fibreglass supplies, moulds, machinery and equipment were brought in, workers were hired and the Crees were taught by the Japanese how to make the boats they had helped design for James Bay.

Less than a year after the first Japanese-built boats had arrived at the Moosonee dock, the first Waskaganish-built craft rolled off the assembly line and was hauled down the dirt road for a test run. An official launch was scheduled, and not only would Yamaha officials come from Toronto to witness the occasion, but the senior executives from Japan were insisting on coming as well.

Twenty years after the Hudson's Bay Company had closed down the factory on the river, the Crees were once again making boats. The difference was that, this time, they owned the factory.

Four hours after his final wave from shore, Billy Diamond's precious canoe was still at full throttle—only now more out of desperation than pride. A late spring storm had come down James Bay, through the Charlton Island narrows, and was blowing with a fury village elders would later say they had not seen since childhood. What started out as a simple fishing trip was verging on disaster, and the evidence was both on the floor of the canoe where the snow was rising and on the faces of the Cree where the tension was mounting. The last big blow out of the north had taken five Cree lives in the boat that this untested, hybrid prototype was hoping to replace.

For hour after hour the canoe pounded through the swells, each rise giving sight to distant islands, each spine-rattling fall giving cause for prayer. In the stern, Charlie Diamond—in a single shirt, a worn and useless rain slick and no gloves—held steady to the throttle, certain that if he only continued to run the crests of the smaller swells on a cross angle, the shore would eventually present itself. This storm was no particular surprise to him, though not because he had heard of its coming on the radio. The storm had come because, just as the canoe skimmed out onto Rupert Bay, the white journalist pointed to a rising bare rock to the west as if it were something they might never have seen before, and no Cree hunter would ever point to that particular bad luck rock without inviting *chuentenshu* to test him mightily.

The whites, in assessing the situation, could only reason that they had lost. Lawrence Katapatuk—thinking himself that it might indeed be over as a renegade wave whipped the boat sideways as a breaker lunged—could only point into the falling crest as the canoe slipped under and away and shout: "He almost got us there!" *He*, the sea. Not that *he*, Lawrence, had lost anything at all, but that *he*, the sea, a full equal in this gaunt world and every bit as alive, had simply won the day.

Just when it seemed that all had been lost, tiny Obejiwan Island came mercifully within sight. Lawrence Katapatuk had previously come to this parking-lot-sized island to shoot the blue goose that comes in to feed in the shallow marsh on the leeward side, and he shouted that there was a sheltered shore on the far side. But it was only a brief cause for cheer, for the canoe plummeted again in the swells and the hope of land was blocked by a rising wall of angry water. The wind began to howl, now louder than the outboard, now drowned out itself by the machine-gun bursts of sleet against tarpaulins and useless rain suits.

There was no passageway to the leeward side of Obejiwan Island. The shallows and the shelter were denied by large rounded rocks that rose from the shallows and exploded the breakers moving in from the northwest. In one harrowing moment the Mercury clipped one of these granite guards and popped the stern clear out of the wash, but the sheer pin held and the propeller balked but once before kicking back in. Powerless, the canoe would have been helpless against the pounding, doomed. There was no alternative. "We're going to have to head straight out into it!" Lawrence Katapatuk shouted toward the bow. "Once we're beyond the rocks, we'll turn back and come in with the wind!"

It was now that the years of watching the Malcolm Diamonds nurse a canoe filled with supplies and wife and children and new babies up through the rapids paid off. Lawrence took the throttle, sorting through the less savage swells, riding a tacking pattern that had the canoe surfing rather than ploughing; Charlie stood forward with his knees rammed against the prow, thrusting with a pole to test for rocks that would announce themselves but once, forever.

Out into the heart of the storm they headed, both men standing while the canoe pitched wildly and the wind cut in random lunges, out into the heart of the storm and suddenly, remarkably, around in an instant 180-degree whip that lifted the canoe magically onto the back of a massive swell. The sea picked the canoe up so high the propeller became a siren screaming in mid-air when it pitched the vessel from that wave onto another. A push of the pole and the canoe rose again onto another, and then another, and suddenly the wind was not only to the backs of those who were in the canoe but was cut again by a stubborn stand of black spruce and poplar, and the canoe planed once again through a moderate chop toward a welcome beach.

For three days this storm attacked out of the north, pounding Obejiwan Island with snow and wind and freezing rain. Meanwhile, the Japanese executives from Yamaha landed for the official launch and there was no boat to show them. *Morningside* called, Peter Gzowski asked about the canoe, and Billy Diamond only laughed and managed to avoid talking about the missing canoe and talked instead about how Canada's Native populations will gain control over their destinies once they have created, as the Crees are doing, their own economies. "Sustainable development" was what he called it. A simple concept, but so difficult at times to explain that Diamond has had to have an anthropologist friend come up with Cree translations for "debentures" and "compounding interest."

Billy Diamond did not even begin to think about rescue until well into the third day, at which point the Yamaha executives had gone back to Toronto and Japan and the storm had died down enough for a search party to assemble on the shore of the Rupert River. But by then it would not be necessary. Just as other hunters were loading the search boats, the Cree–Yamaha twenty-five-footer slipped into view where the estuary widens, Charlie Diamond standing with the throttle as gently in his hands as he had held it three days earlier when the boat had left for the test run.

The Cree–Yamaha canoe returned to Waskaganish and would never again need to be tested. The terrible spring storm and Obejiwan Island would, in time, become part of the sales pitch. The lost party came back warm and dry from two nights in a tent constructed of cut poles and the canoe tarpaulins, heated by driftwood in a convenient oil drum that Lawrence Katapatuk had stashed years earlier in the island bush. They were not even hungry, having dined that morning on fresh whitefish taken in the gill nets that Charlie Diamond set when the evening tide was out. What the modern boat had managed on the water, the traditional ways had managed on the land. A perfect example of the link Billy Diamond has said is the secret to Native development.

"Worried?" Billy Diamond said as he came laughing and shouting down the sand hill onto the gravel shore. "Why would I be?—you are with *Cree* hunters."

Charlie Diamond, not understanding what had been said, pulled together his pack, lifted his rifle onto his shoulder, and headed up the hill to the house where his growing children and first grandchildren were watching American sitcoms on the television, also laughing at words he did not understand.

But he did know that it did not matter, not now. Just as the Shouting Chief had predicted, changes beyond imagining had come to this forgotten land—come fast, frightening, at times exhilarating, often disturbing. But he knew that while his children were watching colour television in the heated living room, eating from the refrigerator, cooking in the microwave and dancing to the stereo, he could go into the basement and oil his beaver traps for the coming winter. And not as a hobby, but as a way of life.

And he knew, too, that what Malcolm Diamond feared most—that future generations would not live off his magical garden that he tried, but failed, to tell the premier about—was now a diminishing fear. Already, one of Charlie Diamond's children had decided to join his father on the trapline.

"The key to making this work for Cree society," Billy Diamond believes, "is to keep that dollar circulating." For three centuries James Bay had existed on basic trade alone, a single exchange for bare subsistence. In time, flour and powder was replaced by money from Indian Affairs, but this currency worked more like an Indian rubber ball than like Malcolm Diamond's vision of a tool: the government threw cash at the Indians and the money immediately bounced back into the mainstream Canadian economy. A dollar that might trade over a dozen times in Montreal had a total value of one in James Bay: in and out, and gone forever.

"We figure 80 percent of revenues leave the community within twenty-four hours," says Diamond. "Our aim is to keep the money in the villages, to build an economic base. You can have all the constitutional conferences about self-government that you want, but unless you have economic self-sufficiency, it doesn't matter."

It was this message Billy Diamond, president of the Waskaganish Enterprise Development Corporation, brought to the Native Economic Summit that was held in Toronto during the first summer of Cree–Yamaha production. The canoe the Crees brought with them to the trade show managed even to catch the eye of Princess Anne when she came to the official opening. Much to the discomfort of those attempting to usher her on to the scheduled events, the princess stayed for fifteen minutes listening to the tale of the joint-venture from Billy Diamond, and left joking that she must look into getting one for the Royal Yacht *Britannia*.

That special order never came through, but others did. Cree–Yamaha made seventy-five of the smaller boats in their first year, phased in the larger boat in the second, and by the third were beginning to sense that a profit was not far off. "The company is very small," says Mark Aoba, "but it will be expanded in the future. This is just a beginning."

In the summer of that third year, 1988, Billy Diamond negotiated a deal with the managers' cooperative that had taken over the Hudson's Bay Company stores throughout the Canadian North. The Bay stores purchased two of the boats outright, and negotiations were undertaken to have the Bay take on regular shipments of the boats on consignment. It had taken 320 years, but the Hudson's Bay Company posts were finally starting to work for the Crees. A dealer from Nova Scotia took two boats. More were shipped to British Columbia, Maryland, Florida. Thanks to the longtime papal connection, a dealer from Italy was scheduled to travel to Waskaganish and see if the Cree boats might find a market among Mediterranean fishermen.

The Crees have always tried to fight for commercial developments to parallel their political achievements. With self-government, came the Cree–Yamaha boats, and beyond the highly visible canoe scheme there were as many hopes for economic development as there were political ambitions. Stanley Diamond, the younger brother of Billy and Albert, had always dreamed of owning his own store, and a small family corporation was established to help him rent out the basement of a building constructed for the school board. With the Bay selling eggs for $3.50 a dozen, Stanley slashed his price to $2.00—and sales in his first full year of running the basement grocery store surpassed $1 million. Then, in December 1987, Stanley Diamond opened the first Cree-owned grocery store as the centrepiece of the new $1.65 million Waskaganish mini-mall. Joining the Épicerie Diamond—a concession to the Quebec language law that permits no English signs—were a new hardware store, a bakery, a women's clothing outlet and a video rental store, all owned and run by Waskaganish Crees. The Cree minority, just like the far-larger French minority twenty years earlier, are determined to become "masters in their own home" themselves.

There are successes and there will be disappointments, such as the women's clothing store that soon failed in the Waskaganish mini-mall. But there are other schemes to replace those that fail. Billy Diamond has plans for milking the caviar from the huge sturgeon that twist along the bottoms of the rivers leading into James Bay. He has looked into the possibilities aquaculture might offer the Crees in trade with their new friends the Japanese. He has investigated the setting up of portable radio stations so each village could broadcast whatever it wished to the hunters and trappers that vanish in winter. He dreams of a Cree tourist trade—American and Canadian families flying in to James Bay for a week of "Cree experience"—and a burgeoning craft business that would move beyond tamarack decoys into traditional Cree jackets and the meticulous beadwork that is still practised by an aging core of elderly women, including Hilda Diamond.

He wants to build a mini-dam across one channel of the Rupert River so the Crees can produce their own electricity. He thinks there might be a market in fibreglass igloos, in foam decoys. He wants to buy a feather separator so that the spring and fall goose hunts might result in more profit than food.

He has tried, without success, to talk the other Cree villages into going in on a barge that could deliver the freight that now comes in over the winter roads at enormous expense. He has met with an eccentric Montreal inventor who has a plan to build greenhouses in the Far North, using a foam that would coat and insulate the windows at night and then burn off in the morning sun.

"And when I am through all that," Billy Diamond jokes, "I plan to go to Parker Brothers with a new game: *The James Bay and Northern Quebec Agreement.* Everybody begins with a simple agreement, but then you have to get it signed, then you have to get it to draft legislation, then redrafted, then you have to get the votes you need. Go to Cabinet and pick up your millions. Go to the constitutional conference and get screwed. And every time you think you're just about to get ahead some card comes up that says, 'Get back to your little bit of land and stay there.'"

Always, whether in humour or anger, it comes back to the James Bay Agreement. It is as if the Cree Nation began here, no matter what the problems that followed, and it was in the drawing up of this document that Billy Diamond formed his theory that "Leadership is stretching creativity." It gave the Crees of James Bay permission to dream creatively for the first time in the three hundred years that they had merely served as bit players and servants and detriments to the fantasies of others. Dreams that, in the case of Robert Kanatewat of Fort George, would only frighten his villagers and cause dissension; dreams that, in the case of Billy Diamond, have had as great an effect outside the land of the Crees as within.

"You cannot help but be impressed with him," says Kent Minami of Yamaha. "It is as if Billy Diamond has a mission for the Cree people."

"He gives you the impression," adds John Ciaccia, who helped negotiate the crucial agreement, "that he is a descendant of kings, of great leaders."

Of despots, some Crees would add. Of power-hungry dictators, self-servers and tyrants, for Billy Diamond has been called them all. With his flair for theatrics, command of language, quotable wit and sense of occasion, Billy Diamond remained the leader that politicians and press—and later, business—turned to long after he had retired as grand chief of the James Bay Cree of Quebec and returned home to Waskaganish.

Though the younger Crees were quick to give credit for what he had done *in the past*, the bitter jealousy was palpable enough that no one even bothered to deny it. "It's terrible, you know," says Jim Morrison, the general manager for Air Creebec. "I've seen the Cree community turn its back on this man. When I first came here I couldn't believe it. People would come in here and tell me things about Billy Diamond that just wouldn't be possible." Ted Moses saw it, too, and saw the same thing happen to him once he had become grand chief and the jealousies had been partially shifted from Billy Diamond to the new chief who was gaining international attention in Europe. "The Crees don't know how to say 'Thank you,' " says Moses. "Basically, Crees don't appreciate leadership. They've never given recognition for what Billy has done."

"I didn't see it at the beginning," says Albert Diamond. "But I saw it later. *Jealousy*. It first started showing up among the other Indian leaders in the Indians of Quebec Association, then among the Crees. This is something with Native people, you see, this backstabbing, this incredible bitterness. Native people are so easy to criticize. They *like* to criticize."

"Internal cannibalism," Billy Diamond calls it. "You have to learn to stand alone as a leader. I stood alone. I went through tough times. But you have to set aside all your personal wants and thoughts. You have to get yourself out of your mind, and you have to think only of your people." Then he laughs, "You know, if you're going to do something, if you're going to change anything around you, you had better have fun doing it. You better laugh. You had better laugh because, if you don't, you're going to be miserable and your project is going to be a failure. So you had better pick projects you enjoy. No one is ever going to say 'Thank you,' so you'd better find your pleasure some other way."

He stops his truck outside a large, enclosed building at the edge of the village. It is near dark, the lights of the village winking through the blowing trees beyond. In the sky you can see the rich glow of light from the mini-mall. Without actually observing them, you know that the Crees of Waskaganish are moving between the mall and the arena, where the artificial ice is being flooded for a broomball game. Later, the satellite will bring in American channels. Colour televisions not tuned to the American networks or shopping channels will be used for Nintendo games. Stereos will be played. Elizabeth will warm up some beaver in the microwave.

And Billy Diamond sits in his truck, laughing—huge, rolling shots of air that steam the windshield and fill the cab with confusion, for it is impossible to see what is so funny about sitting in front of a huge, boarded-up building that hums in the night.

"Don't you know what this is?" he asks.

"No."

"*The diesel plant!*"

Billy Diamond collapses over his steering wheel, his eyes filling with tears as he roars at the lunacy.

The village of Waskaganish, in the heart of the largest hydroelectric scheme in the world, has never even been hooked up by the white men who came to build the dams and flood the land where no one lives anyway.

EPILOGUE

In the far stands of the Sarah Stephen Memorial Arena, Billy Diamond sits alone, his glasses in one hand, the other squeezing his eyes. The double vision has not returned; he is trying to push back tears. When he looks up he sees the lights and the Sunday skaters and hears the music, but when he looks along the near boards he sees two small mittens moving along the upper ledge, the mittens clutching, breaking, dropping, rising and slamming down to clutch again, and then again—grab, release, grab again, slip, grab, release, grab—until eventually the boards give way to an opening at the players' bench and Philip Winston Diamond, aged eight, comes huffing and sweating into view.

"*Daaaaa-aaad!*" he calls, his own eyes filled with tears of frustration. "*My skates!*"

But of course it is not the skates. He is perhaps the only skater on the ice—certainly the only eight-year-old—wearing $200 custom-moulded skates. And he is the only eight-year-old in the arena not playing tag with another's toque, speeding and dipping and sweetly turning on blades that whisper on the corners. Philip's expensive blades only rasp and stutter.

They have been through this before, father and son. He would never walk, but he did walk; he would never talk, but now he will not shut up; he would have severe brain damage, but now the machines in Montreal that supposedly see as deep as the soul see nothing. Philip had fulfilled Malcolm's great dream and participated in the village Walking Out ceremony—Philip in his mock hunter's outfit towering above the younger ones. But Philip is different. The epileptic seizures alone would be enough to argue that. He gets by, and all who marvel watching him grow up cringe at the same time as they cheer, for there is always something new, something new enough and different enough that it seems, each time, that this is going to be Philip's top rung: there will be no more steps.

Sometimes Billy Diamond wished he could carry Philip around from village to village, set him down in front of a class or a church gathering or even the kids hanging around the village's new mini-mall, and let them see the meaning of determination.

What Philip was up against was lowered expectations, the same fight Crees all along James Bay have been fighting since that day in 1611 when Henry Hudson told the first Cree fur trader that he was expecting more than he deserved. Failure was not a circumstance, but an indoctrination, and it did not matter whether it came from the traders, the church, or even from within. It was, and remains, as much a fact of life along the coast as the north wind that curls now around the pumping station where "I need your body tonight" is desperately scrawled on the doorway.

For the young in James Bay, tomorrow is no longer a foregone conclusion as it appeared to be in Malcolm Diamond's day, nor is it yet the endless promise that Billy Diamond believes he can deliver. The arena has been named after the young teenager with the wistful smile who now lies beside Malcolm Diamond in the Anglican Church cemetery. Sarah Stephen, fourteen years old, was with her friends in an illegal "bar" that had been set up in one of the abandoned canoe-factory buildings by the shore when a drunken man burst in, shotgun raised. He had come looking for his brother—then Chief Henry Diamond, a cousin of Billy Diamond—and in the struggle that followed the gun went off, the pellets exploding across the room and into the chest of a frightened, cringing girl, whose parents thought she was watching TV at a friend's house.

In a quiet clearing back of the mini-mall across from the arena, bottles of rye bought for sixteen dollars in the South are going for a hundred. Marijuana, LSD, speed, sometimes cocaine, and, most treasured of all, tranquillizers, can be found in any school along the bay, the same choice, if a bit more pricey, as in any school in Ottawa, Quebec City or Montreal.

Billy Diamond's own son Ian, now fourteen and a handsome, happy kid enchanted with video games, can sit at the dinner table and talk of the shacks the kids built back in the bush for glue sniffing, and tell how he himself had dramatically stopped one day when his eyes decided the face of his closest friend was taking on the qualities of a monster from outer space.

"We've got a youth crisis coming here that will be bigger than the James Bay Project," says Billy Diamond. "Our baby boom is just

EPILOGUE

coming upon us. With all the changes in health and everybody being so much better off, we're in the midst of a population explosion."

The generation of Billy Diamond and Ted Moses and Philip Awashish coincided with the North American Baby Boom, but in fact, that population surge was not nearly so dramatic as the one that began along the coast of James Bay in the mid-1970s. But there is one crucial difference, apart from timing, that separates this Cree generation from the one Billy Diamond grew up in: "When my generation was twenty years of age, we were given the power."

This has created a predictable situation: there is no transition from one generation to the next as there was centuries ago when an old hunter would deliberately wander off into the snow and freeze to death so as not to burden those who were younger and needed the scarce food more. Nor is it even as simple today as it was when Billy Diamond, Ted Moses and Philip Awashish were children and it was accepted that children watched and learned, women ran the camp, hunters hunted and families took care of the elders. Never in their past history have the Crees had to worry about what to do with their children and young men and women, and lacking experience, they have sometimes lacked insight.

"The Crees succeeded," Billy Diamond says, "when they had nothing but they could see how to put it in place. Now, because the Crees are supposed to be so successful, they've got assets and they've got tools and that's all they think about. In the past there were Crees who urged ideas, but now they just manage *things*. The unfortunate thing is that Crees have put *people* into the category of *things*. They're trying to manage people the way they control facilities. You start to control people and you destroy the initiative pretty fast.... I can't get them to talk about it. I get a meeting on the youth crisis and everybody shows up but all they want to talk about is how much money they're spending on them. Money is not the answer."

But what is the answer? There is no shortage of critics ready to testify, even if anonymously. The priest who worries that the Crees have moved from the bush directly into a *showyan*—"money"— society without first going through a proper rural transition is convinced that the satellite television transmission, the video movies, the easy charters south have given the Crees an identity crisis of disastrous proportions. For this priest, the elders are being held prisoners in their new homes, the youngsters are being turned into people who are neither bush nor city nor comfortable anywhere in between. What happened in James Bay after the 1975 agreement happened far too fast, in his opinion, so fast it could only frighten. And for him, the desire to escape to some false solution is what explains the drugs, the alcohol, the gasoline sniffing, the evangelical religion.

"He's right," says Diamond. "It did happen too quickly. But we had to strike while the iron was hot. We had Indian Affairs on the run. We had the province on the run. We had to move fast. And we had to keep going once we had the local economic development going. We couldn't slow it down for any reason—and we still can't.

"But that they can't blame the Hudson's Bay Company anymore. They can't blame Indian Affairs anymore. They can't blame the Quebec government anymore. It's up to the Crees now. It's entirely up to them."

The James Bay Agreement remains a political issue as reluctant to pass into Canadian history as language legislation. In the second decade of the James Bay and Northern Quebec Agreement it has slowly become apparent that while the birth of the Cree Nation can be traced to the signed paper, the heartbeat of the Cree Nation lies in the fight itself—the battle for recognition, the battle for legislation, the battle for economic control—and it is the continuing war of the Crees against the province of Quebec and the government of Canada that ends up sustaining the Crees and giving them direction. And when Bourassa reclaimed the premiership the fighting began again. Unlike that spring seventeen years earlier, not a single Cree was caught by surprise when, on March 9, 1988, the Bourassa government opened its new legislative session with the announcement that Phase II of the "Project of the Century" would begin.

The first stage, said Bourassa's new energy minister—John Ciaccia, the man who had negotiated the James Bay and Northern Quebec Agreement—would be completed by 1995 or 1996. It would involve three new dams, all to the north, and a new transmission line, and would cost at least $7.5 billion, creating some 40,000 jobs.

"It is one of the proudest moments of my life," a beaming Bourassa told the National Assembly. But this, he hinted, was only the beginning. He had orders for $41 billion worth of electricity from the New England States. Phase II, as he envisioned it, would be a $25-billion project before he was finished. And then there would be Phase III . . . .

EPILOGUE

Robert Bourassa did not go into some of his more outrageous plans for James Bay. He did not tell his audience of his vision of a GRAND (Great Recycling and Northern Development) Canal that would run a massive dike entirely across the top of James Bay so that the fresh waters from the rivers could gather and be stored. And how the engineers would then manoeuvre this extraordinary supply of fresh water south through a variety of diversions—including one that would turn the bucolic Ottawa River into a wash wide and deep enough for Ocean liners—until the arid American southwest could be turned into the garden of Eden.

Bourassa even had another plan, this one to turn the clear waters of James Bay into the greatest source of energy ever imagined. It was a scheme that seemed to flow from a quote Bourassa found in Jules Verne's ancient science fiction novel, *The Mysterious Island*: "I believe water will one day be employed as a fuel and its components, hydrogen and oxygen, used singly or together, will furnish an inexhaustible source of heat and light." And Bourassa predicted that the science fiction writer of the last century would one day be proved as right about plain old water as he had been about underwater warfare and air travel.

"The legal framework of the 1975 Agreement," Bourassa argued in his book, *Power from the North*, "applies to any future developments of the James Bay area, such as, for example, the harnessing of the three rivers further south: the Nottaway, Broadback, and Rupert." The Crees, however, could not agree with him. Fifteen months before it was officially announced, the Crees had struck a side deal with Hydro-Québec that would permit the provincial utility to begin working on the initial dams and transmission line of Phase II: $15 million in cash and $95 million in bonds over the next twenty years.

And next time out, if Robert Bourassa wants Phase II to continue, the Crees say they will talk only about an equity position for the Crees. And if not that, then the Crees may consider building the dams themselves, and selling the energy directly to the Americans.

Nation to nation.

Billy Diamond stands now in the basement of the Pentecostal Church, a steel guitar aching above as the Sunday morning congregation kneels and sways in prayer. Billy Diamond, the grand chief of the James Bay Crees who once said he would never in all his life set foot in this building, now spends his Sunday mornings with the likes of Randy, who sits at a rear table shaving the peach-fuzz off his arm with a hunting knife he hides behind his Bible.

The teenagers of Waskaganish stand along the wall, sit along the steps in the far hall, refuse to fill up the front seats—but they are quiet, respectful of the man whom their parents either blame for everything or thank for everything. They do not know much about this thick, serious man at the front who holds a buckskin-covered Bible. They know nothing of his demons, being more involved these days with their own.

They know that he is the head of their school board, which is large in their small world, but they do not know how in 1987 and again in 1988 he had fought off pressure from Native leaders in British Columbia and Manitoba and Ontario and Quebec to run for national chief. They have no idea that he has refused because, as he now says, the family and the village have greater need. The man who once raced to the morning papers to see where he had placed is now proudest of the fact that Elizabeth has given her first speech, and in that first speech—to a church gathering in Moosonee—she has said, "I am Elizabeth and I am more than Mrs Billy Diamond." He now believes himself that this is true.

The teenagers fill up the folding chairs and giggle into their chests. They tilt back their ball caps and snap their gum and they wait to hear what he has to say. Billy Diamond to them is a preacher now, not the chief, certainly not the grand chief.

By the time these children became teenagers, evangelical religion was part of the fabric of Waskaganish. They have seen their parents reborn, they have seen Billy Diamond fall down and begin speaking in tongues, they have heard of the flameless flame that dances on the hands of this chosen man who is said to have great healing powers. They have seen him bounce in from the satellite, talking to David Mainse of *100 Huntley Street* and they have seen the Canadian television evangelist himself here in Waskaganish, filling the school gym because the church was not large enough for the crowds, standing with his arms raised high while his people passed garbage cans around for the people to fill with their hearts. They have even seen a man named John Munro—no longer minister of Indian affairs, no longer the enemy—standing on the same altar saying that he himself had been saved and reborn and was a better man for it.

They have all heard enough testimony to understand what religion is: basically, you screw up and then you find God. They are

EPILOGUE

still in the screwing up stage, and for the most part enjoying it, though that must never be said here.

At the front of the pale basement room, Billy Diamond paces back and forth, waiting for the youngsters to settle. He sees Randy's knife but says nothing. Twenty years ago, it would have been his knife. He clears his throat and instantly the room is filled with that great voice that has stilled Canadian constitutional meetings, Japanese board meetings, United Nations committee hearings. He has decided to speak today about "avoiding foolishness."

Billy Diamond quotes from Psalm 103 and reads from Proverbs 19:5—"... he that speaketh lies shall not escape." They pay no attention at all until, without warning, Billy Diamond leaves his Bible and begins talking about Malcolm. "Did you ever have your parents say, 'What's in your head?' " he asks, and they all laugh, including Randy. "My Dad did that. I'd get into trouble and he'd yell at me, 'What kind of head do you have?' "

For twenty minutes he speaks of Malcolm Diamond. No biblical quotations, no parables, only tales of what it was like to grow up here and to enter a world that people like Malcolm Diamond knew was out there but did not know how to deal with. He tells them of Hilda and Malcolm and what it was like for these old Crees and the grandparents of the youngsters in that room, and there is not so much as a nervous cough to interrupt. When God returns to Billy Diamond's conversation it is to tell of the power of the elements and of how easily a world can be destroyed. It is a test, he tells them. "He almost did it to our parents," he says. "But now, because we had faith, we are able to leave behind a brand new world."

He stands in a pale room, a large man in a business suit with a white lick beginning to spread through the top of his black hair, twenty years and a hundred pounds removed from the skinny kid with the Elvis Presley haircut who played Nootka in *Arrow to the Moon*, the bare-chested, arrogant brave who ridiculed the old chief, Beothuk.

> "To live we must change," the young Nootka tells old Beothuk. "To change we must know the path of change. The books of the new ones show the paths of change."
>
> "I am too old to change," Chief Beothuk says. "I die as a hunter, even as I lived as one. A chief is a chief of his people forever. My son, you must go the way of your heart. If you be

wrong, and your path be wrong, our people will be no more in the time to come."

Billy Diamond speaks and the room is suddenly silent, the knife scraping gone, the giggles suppressed as they think about parents and grandparents and what, if anything, will be in this community when they are themselves elders looking back. They listen, knowing without being told that *a chief is a chief of his people forever*.

In a few months, Billy Diamond will be chief of Waskaganish again, re-elected with the same huge majority he won eighteen years earlier when he was the twenty-one-year-old kid just back from the white man's jail. He will have decided it is not enough to preach by parable; it is at least as important to show by example. Elizabeth, who for so many years fought to get him out of politics, will move through the crowd and take to the stage, and there, in a short speech that holds far more meaning than the mere words can express, she will accept the nomination for her husband.

A few nights later in the school auditorium, the newly elected chief will preside over the annual awards night ceremony. The Malcolm Diamond Memorial Award will go, much to his delight, to Ian Diamond and be presented, much to his surprise, by Hilda Diamond, who will pull her heavy woollen sweater tight, move slowly to the stage and make a speech in Cree, her voice as quiet as Malcolm's was once loud, the words and sentiment precisely the same.

At the elementary level, Philip Diamond will be named "Most Improved Student," and the shock of hearing his name will cause the second standing ovation of the evening.

And then, just before the ice is taken out of the Sarah Stephen Memorial Arena, Billy and Elizabeth Diamond will sit and wait and watch as they have been instructed. And they will watch a heavy, sweating eight-year-old swoop and turn and dip exactly as Philip said he would, his screams of "Daaadddddd! Moooommmmmm!" as loud as the rock music blasting from the ceiling speakers.

On the cold, hard seat beside Billy and Elizabeth Diamond lies a buckskin Bible. Inside the front cover, heavily pasted to the front leaf with scotch tape, is a slightly blurred, colour photograph of Malcolm Diamond sitting on a couch with his jacket on, laughing, a photo taken just before he split the wood and filled up the freezer and went to bed for the last time.

It is the only picture Billy Diamond has of his father. A picture taken by a five-year-old named Philip, the Cree Indian who would never walk alone, not ever.

ACKNOWLEDGMENTS

It goes without saying that I am forever indebted to Lawrence Katapatuk and Charlie Diamond of Waskaganish for saving my life during the James Bay storm that stranded us all on Little Obejiwan Island in the spring of 1986. But there is also other shelter to be grateful for, and it spans a decade of sporadic visits to James Bay that always included the patient hospitality of the many Diamonds of Waskaganish—but particularly from Billy and Elizabeth Diamond and their four children. I also wish to thank Lou Clancy, Doug Sprott and Brian Willer for accompanying me on several of the many trips to Northern Quebec, and the publisher and editors of *The Ottawa Citizen* for giving me time off when time became crucial. The debt owed to all who sat for interviews and responded to letters cannot be repaid except in the hope that they find themselves—where and as expected—in this book. Thanks also to Cynthia Good and Lucinda Vardey for initial encouragement and continued support, to Iris Skeoch and Kathryn Dean for inspired editing, to David Staines and Ellen MacGregor for first readings and diplomatic suggestions, to Bill Gough for computer support, and Emmylou Harris for background.

SELECTED BIBLIOGRAPHY

This listing is a selection from the varied material consulted during the writing of this book. It would be impossible to list all the newspaper and periodical sources or the vast array of academic papers, government documents, House of Commons minutes, Senate minutes, *débats a l'Assemblée nationale*, committee testimony and court transcripts, but the author does wish to express gratitude to the Library of Parliament, the Library of the National Assembly in Quebec City, the libraries of the Ottawa *Citizen* and the Toronto *Star*, the research staff of *Maclean's* magazine and the archives of both the Cree Regional Authority in Val d'Or and the Byers Casgrain law firm in Montreal. The following are specifically mentioned, in that they may be of interest to readers wanting to know more about the James Bay Crees of Quebec and the overall Native situation in North America.

Anderson, William Ashley. *Angel of Hudson Bay: The True Story of Maud Watt.* Toronto: Clarke, Irwin, 1961.

Barman, Jean, Yvonne Hebert and Don McCaskill, eds. *Indian Education in Canada.* Volume 1, *The Legacy.* Vancouver: University of British Columbia, 1986.

Berton, Pierre. "The Legend of Almighty Voice." In *The Wild Frontier: More Tales from the Remarkable Past.* Toronto: McClelland & Stewart, 1978.

Boldt, Menno, and J. Anthony Long in association with Leroy Little Bear. *The Quest for Justice: Aboriginal Peoples and Aboriginal Rights.* Toronto: University of Toronto Press, 1985.

Bourassa, Robert. *Power from the North.* Scarborough: Prentice-Hall Canada, 1985.

Brown, Dee. *Bury My Heart at Wounded Knee: An Indian History of the American West.* New York: Holt, Rinehart & Winston, 1970.

Callwood, June. *Portrait of Canada.* New York: Doubleday, 1981.

SELECTED BIBLIOGRAPHY

Chrétien, Jean. *Straight from the Heart.* Toronto: Key Porter, 1985.

Coolican, Murray, chairman. *Living Treaties: Lasting Agreements.* Report of the Task Force to Review Comprehensive Claims Policy. Ottawa: Department of Indian Affairs and Northern Development, 1985.

Corelli, Rae. "A Canadian Tragedy." *Maclean's,* July 14, 1986, 12–23.

Francis, Daniel, and Toby Morantz. *Partners in Furs: A History of the Fur Trade in Eastern James Bay, 1600–1870.* Kingston and Montreal: McGill-Queen's University Press, 1983.

Graham, Katherine. "Indian Policy and the Tories: Cleaning Up after the Buffalo Jump." In *How Ottawa Spends 1987–88: Restraining the State,* ed. Michael J. Prince. Toronto: Methuen, 1987.

Grodinsky, William S. *The Legal and Economic Aspects of the James Bay Development Projects.* Student thesis. Montreal: McGill University Faculty of Law, 1974.

Gwyn, Richard. *The Northern Magus.* Toronto: McClelland & Stewart, 1980.

Herscovici, Alan. *Second Nature: The Animal Rights Controversy.* Montreal: CBC Enterprises, 1985.

Irwin, Stephen R. *Hunters of the Northern Forest.* Surrey, B.C.: Hancock House, 1984.

James Bay and Northern Quebec Agreement Implementation Review. Ottawa: Department of Indian Affairs and Northern Development, 1982.

Jenness, Diamond. *Indians of Canada,* 7th ed. Toronto: University of Toronto Press, 1977.

Johnson, Brian D. "Fires of Thunder." *Equinox,* nd, 26–41.

Johnston, Basil. *Indian School Days.* Toronto: Key Porter, 1988.

Lacasse, Roger. *Baie James, Une Épopée.* Montreal: Éditions Libre Expression, 1983.

La Rusic, Ignatius E. et al, *Negotiating a Way of Life: Initial Cree Experience with the Administrative Structure Arising from the James Bay Agreement.* Montreal: ssDcc Inc., 1979.

_____, Clotilde Pelletier and Paul Wilkinson, *Sketches of Communities in Northern Quebec*. Montreal: Recherches Amérindiennes au Québec, 1985.

Le Nord du Québec: Profil régional. Quebec City: Bibliothèque nationale du Québec, 1983.

Little Bear, Leroy. *Pathways to Self-Determination: Canadian Indians and the Canadian State*, ed. Menno Boldt and J. Anthony Long. Toronto: University of Toronto Press, 1984.

MacDonald, L. Ian. *From Bourassa to Bourassa: A Pivotal Decade in Canadian History*. Montreal: Harvest House, 1984.

MacGregor, Roy. "This Land Is Whose Land." *Maclean's*, June 1, 1981, 49–61.

_____. "Billy Diamond: Building an Airline for Himself and a New Sense of Prosperity for His People." *Canadian Business*, August 1986, 39–40.

_____. "The Legend of Chief Billy Diamond." *The Toronto Star*, July 3, 1983, D1–2.

Maclean, John. *Native Tribes of Canada*. Toronto: William Briggs, 1896.

Marriott, Alice, and Carol K. Rachlin. *American Indian Mythology*. New York: New American Library, 1968.

Marshall, Susan. *Light on the Water: A Pictorial History of the People of Waswanipi*. Waswanipi: The Waswanipi Band in association with The Cree Regional Authority, 1987.

Merritt, John, ed. *Aboriginal Self-Government and Constitutional Reform: Setbacks, Opportunities and Arctic Experiences*. Ottawa: Canadian Arctic Resources Committee, 1988.

Meyer, Michael, and Elizabeth Jones. "Light in the Forest: Quebec's Indians Battle for a New Way of Life." *Newsweek International*, June 15, 1987.

Morrison, R. Bruce, and C. Roderick Wilson. *Native Peoples: The Canadian Experience*. Toronto: McClelland & Stewart, 1986.

Moss, Wendy. *Practically Millionaires?: A Report on the Implementation of the James Bay and Northern Quebec Agreement*. Ottawa: National Indian Brotherhood, 1971.

Mowat, Farley. *Canada North Now: The Great Betrayal*. Toronto: McClelland & Stewart, 1967.

Newman, Peter C. *Company of Adventurers*. Toronto: Viking, 1985.

_____. *Caesars of the Wilderness*. Toronto: Viking, 1987.

SELECTED BIBLIOGRAPHY

O'Hagan, Howard. *Wilderness Men*. Vancouver: Talonbooks, 1978.

"Résumés des Présentations: La Convention de la Baie James et du Nord québécois, dix ans après." Montreal: Recherches Amérindiennes au Québec, 1985.

Richardson, Boyce. *Strangers Devour the Land: The Cree Hunters of the James Bay Area versus Premier Bourassa and the James Bay Development Corporation*. Toronto: Macmillan, 1975.

―――. "The Indian Ordeal: A Century of Decline." *The Beaver*, February-March, 1987, 15–40.

Robertson, Heather. *Reservations Are for Indians*. Toronto: James Lorimer & Co., 1970.

Salisbury, Richard F. *A Homeland for the Crees: Regional Development in James Bay 1971–1981*. Kingston and Montreal: McGill-Queen's University Press, 1986.

Schiller, Bill. "Cree Money, Jobs and Self-rule: a Model for Other Indian Bands." Part two of the three-part series, "Indian Power: The Struggle for a Better Tomorrow." The Toronto *Star*, December 6, 1987.

Scott, Duncan Campbell. "The Last of the Indian Treaties." In *Tales of the Canadian North*. Compiled by Frank Oppel. Secaucus, N.J.: Castle, 1984.

Stevenson, Garth. *The Politics of Canada's Airlines from Diefenbaker to Mulroney*. Toronto: University of Toronto Press, 1987.

Weaver, Sally M. *Making Indian Policy: The Hidden Agenda 1968–1970*. Toronto: University of Toronto Press, 1981.

Wittenborn, R., and C. Biegert. *James Bay Project: A River Drowned by Water*. Montreal and Munich: R. Wittenborn and C. Biegert and the Montreal Museum of Fine Art, 1981.

INDEX

Ahenakew, David, 198-99, 200, 201, 232, 233
Air Canada, 250, 251, 252, 253
Air Creebec, 246-55
Air Ontario, 250, 254-55
Air Transport Association of Canada, 250, 254
Allmand, Warren, 97, 141, 154, 156
Almighty Voice, 29, 58
Amagoalik, John, 233
American Indian Movement (AIM), 96-97
Amherst, Jeffrey, 56-57
Amogoalik, John, 197
Aoba, Masafumi (Mark), 264-65, 268, 272
Assembly of First Nations (AFN), 194, 196, 198-200, 232-33
"B-Team" of (BFN), 199-200, 232-33
see also National Indian Brotherhood
Association of Iroquois and Allied Indians, 199
Atkinson, George, Jr., 8
Auditor General's Report, 1986 (Dye), 235
Austin Airways Ltd., 245-48
Awashish, Philip, 29, 33, 60, 62-63, 65, 66, 67, 70-71, 75, 96, 104, 120, 125, 128-29, 160
Axworthy, Lloyd, 251

Banfield, Dr. Frank, 91
Barnley, Reverend George, 21
Bear Island land claim, 257
Bearskin, Job, 91
Bearskin, Steven, 25
Beaudoin, Jacques, 66-67, 74, 85, 87, 99-100, 134
Berger, Thomas, 154

Berger Inquiry into building of Mackenzie Valley pipeline, 154
Bernier, Captain Joseph-Elzéar, 56
Bertrand, Paul, 134
Bill C-9 (1978), 50, 84, 155-56
Bill C-46 (Cree-Naskapi Act), 215-18
Bill 50 (Quebec, 1971), 68
Black, Dr. Lyall, 176
Blackned, Fred, 66
Blackned, Mark, 28
Blacksmith, Sam, 92
Bombardier Ltd., 263
Boulanger, Romeo, 177
Boundaries Extension Act (Canada, 1898, 1912), 69, 128
Bourassa, Jean, 40-41, 45
Bourassa, Robert, xviii-xxiii, 53-55, 57, 68, 77-79, 105, 108-9, 110, 112, 114, 115, 116, 130, 149-50, 215, 280-81
Boyd, Robert, 137
Brant, Dan, 181
Brant, Joseph, 29, 97-98
Bruyere, Louis "Smokey", 199, 233
Buchanan, Judd, 130, 137, 139
Burns, Robert, 68
Button, Sir Thomas, 4

Canadian Pacific, 253
Canadian Transportation Commission, 248
Cardinal, Harold, 200
Cartlidge, Reverend Harry, 9
Cheechoo, Bentley, 255
Choquette, Guy, 129
Chrétien, Jean, 38, 55, 68, 69-70, 86, 102, 104-5, 107-11, 113-14, 115-16, 121-22, 130, 136, 164, 178-79, 180, 197, 237
Christopher (son of Billy and Nellie), 45

INDEX

Ciaccia, John, 68-69, 86, 101-2, 108-10, 116, 119-20, 121-25, 126, 128, 135-36, 138, 142, 154, 176, 274, 280
Cliche, Robert, 148
Clough, Dr. Garrett, 91
Colebrook, Sergeant Colin Campbell, 58
Columbus, Christopher, 4, 110
Constitution Act, 1982, 187, 189, 192, 197-98, 201-2, 232
Coolican, Murray, 234
Coolican task force report (*Living Treaties: Lasting Agreements*), 234
Cooncome, Matthew, 113, 236, 240
Cournoyer, Jean, 139
Craik, Brian, 75, 77, 91, 162, 240, 257
Cree Board of Compensation, 253
Cree Distribution Centre, 162
Cree Health Board, 167, 168
Cree Housing Authority, 193
Cree Regional Authority, 152, 160, 213
Cree-Naskapi Act (Bill C-46, 1984), 215-18, 235-36
Cree-Naskapi Commission, 235-36
Cree-Yamaha, 268-71
Crenna, David, 201
Crete, Marcel, 121
Croll, Andrew, 236
Crombie, David, 231, 233, 268
Cudin, Monsignor Gianpietro, 194, 238-39

Daes, Dr. Erica-Irene, 238
Davey, Jim, 196-97
Delisle, Andrew, 38, 96, 102-3, 110, 111, 112, 130
Deluce, Bill, 246, 250, 254
Deluce, Stan, 210, 224, 245-46, 250, 254
Dene and Métis Mackenzie Valley land claims, 258
Department of External Affairs, 238
Department of Indian Affairs, 40-41, 44-45, 61, 70, 91, 107, 113-14, 115, 137, 152, 174, 178, 179, 235, 236, 240, 251, 280
 internal memorandum on James Bay Agreement, 177
Des Groseilliers, Médard Chouart, 5, 92
Desrochers, Paul, 110
Di Lenardo, Guido, 193
Diamond, Agnes, 11, 16-17, 18

Diamond, Albert, 14-15, 17, 18, 125, 127, 152, 160, 224, 228, 275
Diamond, Annie, 11-12, 14-15, 18, 21-22, 72, 212
Diamond, Billy
 birth of, 11-12
 early life in the bush, 14-22
 at Moose Factory residential school, 22-27
 at school in Sault Ste Marie, 28-29, 32-35
 finds hero in Robert Kanatewat, 31-32
 in *Arrow to the Moon* (play), 33-35
 attends 1968 Indians of Quebec Association (IQA) meeting, 38-39
 meets Elizabeth Hester, 39-40
 job with Rupert House Cree band, 39-41
 job with Indian Affairs, 40-41
 torn between Nellie and Elizabeth, 42-43
 arrest and jail term for common assault, 43
 elected chief of Rupert House band, 44
 births of son Christopher and daughter Lorraine, 45-46
 marries Elizabeth Hester, 46
 takes in Nemaska Cree at Rupert House, 44, 46-47
 altercation with Jean Bourassa, 44-45
 at first formal meeting of James Bay Crees (June 28, 1971), 65-68
 becomes researcher and activist for IQA, 70-76
 birth and death of daughter Joanne, 76-77
 fall 1972 meeting of Crees and Robert Bourassa, 77-79
 testimony in James Bay hearings, 87-90
 emergence as leader and spokesman, 95-96
 meetings with American Indian Movement, 96-97
 drinking, 97-99, 120, 127, 161, 207-13
 birth of son Ian, 103
 negotiations of James Bay project, 101-2, 103, 110-12, 113-14, 120-28

293

becomes Grand Chief of the Grand Council of Crees of Quebec, 125
agreement-in-principle reached on James Bay project, 129-30
negotiation and signing of James Bay and Northern Quebec Agreement, 134-39
visits dam site, 145-46
boycotts James Bay Project opening ceremonies, 150
post-agreement organizing, 152-53
birth of son Sandy, 153
appears at Berger inquiry into Mackenzie Valley pipeline, 154
fight for legislation on James Bay agreement, 153-56
birth of son Philip, 161
marital problems and reconciliation, 161-62, 168-69, 187-89, 194-95, 196, 203, 210-11, 212, 213, 226, 227
and gastro-enteritis epidemic, 165-72
fight to improve living conditions for James Bay Crees, 174-83
at UN conference on indigenous peoples and land, 180
relationship with children, 186
antagonism to Pentecostal church, 188-89
fight to get aboriginal rights into constitution, 189-202, 232-39
meeting with Pope John Paul II, 193-95
religious experiences, 212-14, 218-21, 225-30
refuses Senate appointment, 214-15
fight for passage of Cree-Naskapi Act, 215-18
fight to get aboriginal rights enshrined in the constitution, 232-33
as business leader, 243-59, 261-76
and Air Creebec, 245-54
as consultant to other Indian groups, 257-59
and Cree-Yamaha venture, 263-73
re-elected chief of Waskaganish (formerly Rupert House), 284

Diamond, Charlie, 11, 16-17, 18, 19, 20, 21, 212, 227, 262, 269-71

Diamond, Elizabeth (*née* Hester), 86-87, 111, 127, 131, 165, 167, 183, 194-95, 196, 202, 224, 225, 229, 265, 284
second pregnancy, 73, 75
birth and death of daughter Joanne, 76
third pregnancy, 96
birth of son Ian, 103
birth of son Sandy, 153
marital problems and reconciliation, 161, 168-69, 179, 187-89, 194-95, 203, 210-11, 212, 213, 226, 227
birth of son Philip, 161
Philip's illness and its aftermath, 165, 167, 168-69, 173
religion, 168-69, 187, 188, 212, 218, 219, 228
see also Hester, Elizabeth

Diamond, George, 14-15, 18

Diamond, Gerti, 11, 16-17, 22, 23, 24, 212, 224

Diamond, Henry, 278

Diamond, Hilda, 27, 47, 169, 170, 202, 284
in Quebec National Assembly, xvii-xviii, xxiii
birth of Billy, 11-12
family life in the bush, 14-16
fever after birth of Stanley, 18-20
new house, 185-86, 202
widowed, 223-25

Diamond, Ian, 153, 202, 278, 284

Diamond, Joanne, 76, 77

Diamond, Joey, 11, 18, 21

Diamond, Lorraine, 45-46, 47, 73, 77, 153, 202

Diamond, Malcolm, xvii, xviii, 3, 47, 48-49, 66, 67, 71-72, 85, 87, 132, 169, 171, 173, 174, 175, 240-41, 283, 284
as a young man, 11-12
becomes chief of Rupert House Crees, 14
family life in the bush, 14-22
as chief, 29-31, 38-39, 44, 60
humiliated by Robert Bourassa, xxi-xxiii, 77-78
new house, 185-86, 202
heart attack, death, and funeral, 223-27

INDEX

Diamond, Philip (uncle), 28, 48
Diamond, Philip Winston (son), xxiii, 161, 167, 168-72, 173, 179, 183, 185, 202-3, 211, 225, 229, 277-78, 284
Diamond, Sandy, 153, 202
Diamond, Stanely, 14-15, 18, 273
Dorion Commission, 55, 63
Dupuis, Yvon, 121
Dye, Kenneth, 235

Epstein, Robert, 152-53, 170-71, 178-79, 193, 216-17, 227, 238, 256
Erasmus, Georges, 199, 201, 233

Feit, Dr. Harvey, 75, 91
Fenton, Dr. Brock, 91
First Ministers' Conference (1987), 232-33, 238
First Ministers' Conference (spring 1983), 196, 199
Fox, Bill, 114
Fraser, Whit, 217
Frith, Doug, 217, 233, 235
Fulton, E. Davie, 258

Geoffrion, C. Antoine, 82-83, 100
George, Gary, 177, 178, 193, 194
Getty, Don, 258
Gordeau, Eric, 163, 174, 176
Gordon, Mark, 129
Gouin, Jean-Lomer, 9-10
Grand Council of the Crees of Quebec, 125-26, 152, 160, 166-67, 213
  annual general meeting (1984), 220-21
  meeting with Pope John Paul II, 194-95
GRAND (Great Recycling and Northern Development) Canal, 281
Grodinsky, Bill, 161-62, 248, 252
Gros-Louis, Max, 38, 65, 66-67, 68, 71, 74, 111, 198, 201
Gull, Peter, 66, 128-29
Gunter, Reverend Garnet, 219-20

Hannah Bay Massacre, 8-9
Hatfield, Richard, 201
Hawkins, Norman, 134, 141
Health and Welfare Canada, 176, 178
Heap, Dan, 216
Heli Voyageur Ltée, 246
Hester, Clifford, 23

Hester, Elizabeth (later Elizabeth Diamond), 42-43, 47, 48, 49
  birth of Lorraine and marriage to Billy, 45-46
  see also Diamond, Elizabeth
Hicks, Frank, 176
House of Commons Indian Affairs Committee, 121, 177-78, 182
Hudson, Henry, 4, 92, 278
Hudson's Bay Company, 6, 7, 9, 10, 14, 21, 44, 69, 133, 162, 261, 263, 272, 280
Hughboy, Walter, 25
Hydro-Quebec, 54, 63, 68, 135, 162

Indian Act (1880), 57, 137
Indian Affairs: *see* Department of Indian Affairs
Indians of Quebec Association, 38-39, 56, 65, 66, 69-70, 74, 75, 77, 96-97, 110, 113, 121, 130, 136-37, 137-38, 142
  troubled relations with James Bay Crees, 102-3, 111-12, 120, 125
Innocan Investments, 251, 252
Inuit Committee on National Issues, 232

James Bay Development Corporation, 68, 69, 71, 73-74, 76, 90, 95, 99, 100-101, 102, 104, 105, 112, 133, 135, 136-37, 145
James Bay Energy Corporation, 126, 135, 156
James Bay Hydro Project, 4, 54, 61, 62, 65-68, 70, 134
  Phase I, 74-75
  riot and close-down at LG2 dam site, 121, 148
  LG2 dam site, 145-48
  Lévesque rally at LG3 dam site, 164
James Bay and Northern Quebec Agreement (1975), 139-44, 175, 208, 235, 237, 249, 252
  implications of, 139-42
  criticisms of, 142-44
  becomes law (Bill C-9, 1978), 153-56
  becomes part of Canadian consitution, 201-2
  as beginning of Cree nation, 274, 280
James, Thomas, 4-5
Jamieson, Roberta, 200

295

John, Marilyn, 200
John Paul II (Pope), xxii, 193-94, 195, 239
Johnson, Daniel, 54-55
Jolly, Johnny, 162
Jones, Peter, 142

Kanatewat, Robert, 31-32, 39, 45, 59-60, 66, 87, 96, 98, 99, 104, 112, 113, 116, 124-25, 126, 128-29, 145-46, 150-52, 155, 159, 235, 274
Katapatuk, Lawrence, 189, 211, 212-13, 228, 262, 269-71
Katapatuk, Mary, 10
Katapatuk, Simon, 10
Kierans, Eric, 70
Kirby, Michael, 197
Kitchen, Abel, 125, 160

La Sarre Air Services, 247
Lameboy, Samson, 117
Lamoureux, Lucien, 104
LaRusic, Ignatius, 75
Le Bel, Jacques, 88-89
Lefebvre, Patricia, 203
Lemert, Arthur, 188, 213-214
Lennarson, Fred, 258
Lessard, Lucien, 248, 250
Lévesque, René, 54-55, 149-50, 163-64, 189-90, 194, 198, 201, 236, 247-48
Lewis, Stephen, 238
Living Treaties: Lasting Agreements (Coolican report), 234
Lubicon land claim, 257-58

McDermid, John, 217
Macdonald, Donald, 107
Macdonald, John A., 56
MacGuigan, Mark, 200
Mackenzie Valley pipeline, 107, 154
McKim, Dr. William, 91
McKnight, Bill, 234, 236, 239
MacLean, Charles Stewart, 30, 175
McMurtry, Roy, 197
Malouf, Albert, 81, 82, 83, 86, 87-88, 92, 101, 103-4, 133
Manuel, George, 130, 142, 143
Mark, John, 98, 248
Mazankowski, Donald, 247, 248, 249
Mianscum, François, 91
Mianscum, Henry, 29, 160
Minami, Kent, 265, 266, 274
Miskokomom, Joe, 190-92, 200

Moar, Robert, 230
Moar, Winnie, 230
Morris, Edmund, 201
Morris, Lord Michael, 190-92
Morrison, Jim, 249-50, 275
Moses, Ted, 25, 29, 60, 66, 91, 95, 104, 114, 120, 125, 126, 128-29, 141, 160, 232, 236, 238, 258, 275
Moses, Willie, 25
Mosher, Terry (Aislin), 70
Muller, Father Hugo, 92
Mulroney, Brian, 148, 215, 232, 234
Munk, Jens, 4
Munro, John, 164, 178, 179, 180-81, 183, 194, 196, 214, 250-51, 282
Murphy, Rod, 217
Murray, Sir George, 57

Nader, Ralph, 71
Nakasone, Yasuhiro, 268
National Indian Brotherhood, 130, 155
  see also Assembly of First Nations
Native Council of Canada, 233
Native Economic Development Program, 267
Native Economic Summit, 272
Nellie (mother of son Christopher), 42, 45
Nicholson, Alan, 10
Nielsen, Eric, 234
Nishga land claim, 73, 107
Nishnawbe Aski Nation, 255
Nordair, 250-51, 252
Northern Quebec Inuit Association, 61
Nungak, Zebedee, 61, 73-74, 199, 233

Oberle, Frank, 182, 234
October Crisis (1970), 53
Oji-Cree Airways, 255
Ominayak, Bernard, 258
Ontario Hydro, 72
O'Reilly, James, 70, 73, 74, 79, 83-85, 86, 87, 88, 90, 98, 101-2, 105, 110, 112, 113, 116-17, 122-23, 125, 134, 141, 154, 170, 178, 182, 200, 248, 249, 258
Ottereyes, Billy, 135
Ottreyes, Dianne, 92

Parizeau, Jacques, 70, 148-49
Paul, Réjean F., 236
Pepabano, Richard, 205
Pepin, Jean-Luc, 216, 217

INDEX

Petawabano, Smally, 65-66
Peters, Gordon, 199, 200, 232, 233
Pinard, Yvon, 216, 217
Potts, Gary, 199, 232, 233, 257
Poundmaker, 13-14, 29
Preston, Richard, 37, 75
Pricket, Abacuk, 4
Prieur, Jean, 102

Quebec Aviation, 247, 249
Quebec Court of Appeal, 105, 112, 113, 133
Quebec Referendum (1980), 163-64
Quebec Superior Court, 81-92, 104
Quebecair Ltd., 252-53

Radisson, Pierre-Esprit, 5
Richardson, Boyce, 71, 76, 114
Riel, Louis, 13-14, 58
Robertson, Gordon, 196
Robinson, Rod, 143
Romanow, Roy, 197, 198
Roy, Bernard, 247, 249
Royal Proclamation of 1763, 83-84
Ryan, John, 152

Sagamish, Billy, 138
St Lewis, Joanne, 256
Salisbury, Richard, 69, 240
Salt, Isaiah, 39
Sanderson, Sol, 198, 199
Saunders, Russell, 231, 266
Schambach, R. W., 18, 229
Schlesinger, James, xx-xxi
Scott, Duncan Campbell, 1, 9, 51, 69, 72, 141-42, 157, 205, 254
Scott, F. R., 85, 105
Secrétariat des Activités Gouvernementales en Milieu Amerindien et Inuit (SAGMAI), 163, 174, 176
Shaintoquaish, 9
Shanush, Matthew, 66, 73, 92
Simpson, Governor George, 21
Sinclair, Jim, 199
Six Nations Indians, 98
Skinnarland, Einar, 75, 90
Small Legs, Nelson, Jr., 143-44
Smoke, Marsha, 160, 198
Sounding Sky, 58
Spence, John, 76, 90
Spotted Calf, 58
Starblanket, Noel, 142, 155

Stephen, Sarah, 278
Sterritt, Neil, 199, 200
Stewart, James, 63, 114
Supreme Court of Canada, 112, 121
Sydenham, Lord, 57

Tait, John, 176, 179, 200
Tait review of James Bay agreement, 180, 181-82
Tanner, Adrian, 75
Tellier, Paul, 178, 179
Toyama, Isao, 265-66
Transport Canada, 251, 252
Treaty No. 9 (between Government of Canada and Ontario Cree), 9
Treaty of Utrecht (1713), 7
Trudeau, Pierre Elliott, 46, 53, 69, 109, 163, 189, 196-98, 200, 201, 214-15
Turgeon, Jean, 112, 133

Union of Ontario Indians, 190
United Nations, 25, 233
  Conference on Indigenous Peoples and Land, 180
  Crees gain full observer status at, 238

Van Loon, Richard, xix, 236, 239-40
Vatican, 193-95, 238-39
Visitor, Georgie, 23, 26

Wabinoo, Charles, 142
Wapachee, Bertie, 66
Wapachee, Nancy, 165-66
Wapachee, Tommy, xxiii, 165-66, 174
War Measures Act (1970), 53
Waskaganish Enterprises Development Corporation of Northern Quebec (WEDCO), 263, 266, 267, 272
Watt, Charlie, 61-62, 66, 73-74, 81-82, 104, 115, 129, 130, 138, 150, 154, 178, 179, 197, 198, 199, 215
Watt, George, 143, 200
Watt, James, 10-11, 42
Watt, Maud, 11, 21, 42
Whiskeychan, John, 127, 187-88, 189, 218, 224, 225, 229
Whiskeychan, Malcolm, 72
White Paper on Indian Affairs, 55
Whitehead, James, 28
World Council of Churches, 258
Wounded Knee siege, 96

Yamaha Motor Canada Ltd., 264-88